THE
SAS

AT CLOSE
QUARTERS

SIDGWICK & JACKSON
LONDON

THE
SAS
AT CLOSE
QUARTERS

**STEVE
CRAWFORD**

First published in Great Britain in 1993

This edition first published in Great Britain 1994
by Sidgwick & Jackson Limited

ISBN 0 283 06198 7

Printed and bound in Great Britain by
BPC Hazell Books Ltd
A member of
The British Printing Company Ltd

Sidgwick & Jackson Limited
18-21 Cavaye Place
London SW10 9PG

Editorial and Design: Brown Packaging

I would like to take the opportunity to thank the following
people, without whose help and support this book would not
have been possible:

Karen, for being my inspiration.

Kevin, my training partner, for giving me the motivation to
keep going when I was ready to give up.

Simon, for his help with the design, and for keeping calm
when the courier failed to arrive.

David, for his patience during the hours spent on the
telephone, when I was trying to understand what must have
been extremely straightforward to him.

Already published excerpts taken from:

Soldier 'I' SAS by Michael Paul Kennedy, published by
Bloomsbury Publishing Ltd (1990)

One of the Originals by Johnny Cooper, published by Pan
Books Ltd (1991)

One Man's SAS by Lofty Large, published by William
Kimber & Co. Ltd (1987)

The Quiet Soldier by Adam Ballinger, published by
Chapmans Publishers Ltd (1992)

Shoot to Kill by Michael Asher, published by Penguin
Books (1990)

David Stirling by Alan Hoe, published by Little, Brown
and Company (UK) Ltd (1992)

Picture credits
Anne Bolt: 143; **Brown Packaging:** 6, 45, 50-
51, 64-65, 66, 67, 69, 70, 74, 76-77, 78, 79, 92-
93, 112-113, 114-115, 116-117, 140, 174-175,
182, 187, 189; **IWM:** 18-19, 21, 23, 24, 25, 26,
48-49, 54-55, 62-63; **Pacemaker Press:** 132-
133, 135, 136-137, 147; **Press Association:** 72-
73; **Private Collection:** 2-3, 14, 15, 16-17, 32-
33, 37, 80-81, 83, 85, 89, 91, 97, 98-99, 100-
101, 102-103, 104-105, 107, 108-109, 110-111,
119, 121, 126, 138-139, 153, 154, 158-159, 162-
163, 164, 166-167, 168-169, 177, 178-179, 184,
185; **Tony Rogers:** 8-9, 10, 13, 53, 58, 59, 60-
61, 123, 124-125, 129, 151; **SAS Regimental
Association:** 29, 31; **Telegraph Colour
Library:** 38-39; **TRH Pictures:** 35, 43, 46,
148-149, 160-161; **US DoD:** 170-171, 172-173,
180-181

Artworks
Terry Hadler: 40-41, 56-57, 86-87, 130-131,
144-145, 156-157; **Keith Harmer:** 75

**Front cover: The SAS storms the Iranian Embassy,
May 1980.
Previous pages: A special forces sniper takes aim
with an L96A1 sniping rifle.**

CONTENTS

PREFACE

O f all the elite military units in the world, perhaps the most famous is Britain's Special Air Service. The reason for this is because it has been very successful in its operations since it was formed in the North African desert by David Stirling in 1941. Now, in this book, and for the first time, individual SAS soldiers talk frankly and openly about those operations.

This book is not a detailed history of the Special Air Service Regiment; rather, it seeks to provide the reader with an insight into what it's like to be an SAS soldier at the sharp end of war: cross-border raids in Borneo, fighting terrorists in the deadly 'bandit country' of South Armagh, or operating behind the lines in Iraq during the Gulf War. The reader will learn what it's like to be in combat: the adrenalin rush before the assault on the Iranian Embassy, firefights with Indonesian troops in Borneo, shooting up enemy aircraft on Pebble Island during the Falklands War, and the ambushing of Scud missile batteries in Iraq. What is painted is a picture of men who are elite in every way, but who are also modest and go about their tasks with a quiet confidence and a sense of humour. From the rigours of Selection, the freezing cold of the Falklands, to the scorching heat of Oman, this is their story using their words.

For reasons of security and personal safety, the names of most of the soldiers talking in this book cannot be given. This is only proper: some are still serving in the Regiment, while others, though no longer SAS soldiers, are engaged in other covert activities.

The mark of excellence: the SAS winged dagger badge.

SELECTION

'I have a mental blue-print of the ideal SAS man. No one fits it exactly but, when I look at a man and listen to him he must come close to it.'

Lieutenant-Colonel 'Paddy' Mayne, 1944

This chapter illustrates how the concepts laid down by the founders of the Regiment in the early 1940s concerning the type and calibre of recruits and the overall ethos of the SAS has remained unchanged through five decades. It reveals how the stringent selection and training routines currently operated by the SAS continue a legacy of excellence that was established during World War II and, later, in Malaya and Oman. The common denominator of the Regiment has been, and will always be, its individual soldiers. They are special, a breed apart.

Individual soldiers of the Special Air Service must possess certain qualities that will enable them to operate effectively as part of a small team behind enemy lines, often for weeks at a time, and devoid of substantial support services. What are these qualities? The guiding principles of the Regiment were laid down by its founder, Lieutenant-Colonel David Stirling, over 50 years ago: to engage in the never-ending pursuit of excellence, to maintain the highest standards of self-discipline in all aspects of daily life, to tolerate no sense of class, and all ranks to possess humility and humour.

The SAS has possibly the most arduous military selection course in the world. As well as physical stamina, all potential recruits must have high levels of personal initiative and intelligence.

SAS soldiers have always fought in small units. In this they are no different from other troops of the British Army. An infantry section, for example, usually comprises around eight men. However, the major difference between conventional and special forces such as the SAS is that the former nearly always operate within larger groups and can call upon support services: aircraft, artillery, tanks and even naval support. But there are very few instances of SAS soldiers operating together in large numbers, the exception being the closing stages of World War II. Between March and May 1945, for example, two squadrons from 1 and 2 SAS, comprising a total of 430 men and 75 jeeps, undertook short-range reconnaissance for the British 21st Army Group east of the Rhine. However, this mission, Operation 'Archway', was an exception; most of the time SAS soldiers fight in small groups, and often behind enemy lines.

Of all the qualities looked for in an aspiring SAS soldier, self-discipline is perhaps the most important, followed closely by high levels of mental and physical stamina. The desire to get

Above: The ability to keep going when others give up is one of the hallmarks of an SAS soldier.

the job done in a no-nonsense fashion, and without acclaim, has always been high on the list of SAS priorities. Soon after the establishment of the first SAS base camp at Kabrit, Egypt, in late 1941, David Stirling reminded his first batch of recruits:

'There will be no bragging or swanking in the Cairo or Alexandria bars and that goes for scrapping too. Any energy you have for fighting will be directed at the enemy. Make no mistake, anyone who doesn't fit in will leave – there will be no second chances. Captain Lewes will be in sole charge of training and that includes my own. It's going to be tough because we have to be fit for the job we're going to do. If anyone has sensible and constructive comments to make on training, or any other operational subject, then make it. We are all here to learn.'

Some 30 years later, Michael Asher encountered the same attitude when he first met the soldiers of 23 SAS, one of the part-time SAS Regiments:

'There were no loud-mouths or bar-soldiers. There was a palpable sense of quiet determination about them, a seriousness which dealt with each obstacle as an interesting problem. There was no aspect of training which was too trivial to examine in detail: nothing was waved aside in the pressure of achieving the goal. These SAS men looked very fit, but as a matter of course rather than as a means to prove themselves "tough" or superior. You could tell at a glance that they were above "beasting" for its own sake. They were not truculent or sadistic, as the Paras had been. You could see that they might kill easily, but never for the love of it.'

To prepare SAS soldiers for the type of warfare they will undertake, the Regiment operates a rigorous elimination process, one that is designed to weed out the unsuitable quickly. The principles of Selection Training were first laid down by 'Jock' Lewes during World War II, and then refined further by Lieutenant-Colonel John Woodhouse during the 1950s. Johnny Cooper, one of the first recruits to the SAS, sums up the training ethos of the Special Air Service during World War II:

'Jock instilled into us that the end product of our training was for us to become independent in every way, operating either alone or in very small groups. We would have to develop an ingrained self-confidence in our ability to navigate across featureless terrain without any back-up whatsoever and using maps that gave little or no detail. We would have to survive on minimum sustenance and to control the use of food and water during the hot periods of the day, using the cover of darkness for offensive activity.'

The current Selection Training programme of the SAS is conducted by Training Wing, 22 SAS,

and lasts for one month. It is divided between a three-week build-up period and Test Week, which is the culmination of Selection. The course, on paper at least, sounds reasonably straightforward. It begins with a set of road runs which increase in length during the first week. This is followed by a series of marches over the Black Mountains and Brecon Beacons of South Wales to test the students' proficiency in map reading and navigation: each man is given a bergen, a map and a compass, and is then given a grid reference for the first rendezvous. When he reaches the first rendezvous he is told the next one, and so on. All the time he is being watched and assessed by the training staff. The climax of Selection is Test Week, the culmination of which is the notorious 60km navigation exercise over the Brecon Beacons, nicknamed 'Long Drag' or 'Fan Dance'. This must be completed within 20 hours, regardless of the weather, for the recruit to pass Selection.

There is no doubt that Selection is extremely tough, the more so because each man is on his own. There are no mates around him to encourage him or deter him from giving up, there are no screaming NCOs issuing threats and encouragement; there is only the individual's own drive and determination to keep him going. For some this isn't enough: they drop out and are returned to their parent unit (RTU'd in British Army parlance). This doesn't necessarily mean they are bad soldiers, far from it, but only the very best get into the SAS – men who have the will to keep on going when their bodies are screaming for them to stop, and ones whose minds are still able to function in such circumstances. One SAS trooper remembers the sense of isolation:

'There is no shouting or screaming, no encouragement or excesses; you pass or fail on the merits of your own physical and mental abilities.
'We tumbled out of bed at the crack of dawn, paraded at 0630 hours in three ranks and waited for the instructor to arrive with the day's programme. Everyone wears their own beret at the start of the day, but puts it away when the

course moves onto the Brecons or other training areas in the region. The first two weeks of Selection are when the instructors pick out the "lambs": the physically weak who they feel will not make the required times. They also weed out those whose "character" doesn't fit, for example those who are noisy and are referred to as being nothing more than a "mouth on a stick". All the unsuitable ones are quickly got rid of.

'In the old days those who were fit but unsuitable found themselves facing "sickeners": a physical punishment used to break their morale and make them quit. One involved being "issued" with several large rocks by training staff at a checkpoint. The instructors would then call at the next checkpoint to make sure the recruit was still carrying them. The worst, however, was the removal of boot laces halfway through a long march. At the end of the march the recruit's feet would be swollen and blistered like you wouldn't believe. But now this has all been done away with, and today if you're not wanted you are quietly pulled into the office and given a rail warrant. Within an hour you are gone, and all the other blokes see when they get back is an empty bed.

'There were 142 hopefuls at the start of my course, but this started to drop within the first few hours as the instructors began to siphon out those who were, in their opinion, "wasters". Once the course is up and running it's all about speed. In my previous unit I had been regarded as a very good runner, and during my training for Selection had prided myself on the weights I carried and the speed I worked at. In infantry battalions the training staff often take the speed of the slowest man as a marker, provided he is running fast enough to meet the required time, the concept being to get everyone to end up as a group. In the SAS this is reversed. The Regiment uses the speed of the fastest man as a marker – it's not

interested in everyone finishing as a group – and as a result the pace of some marches is crippling.

'For me the worst was a 10km speed march with bergens, belt order and weapons. The pain in my legs and hips will always stay with me. My face was on fire, but I knew I couldn't give in. There is no point in approaching Selection with anything less than 100 per cent commitment with regard to getting through, whatever the cost. If you can do this you'll be alright, but any nagging distraction can be enough to make blokes quit, especially any problems with wives or girlfriends. Some blokes tell their partners they're going overseas for four weeks, which gives them total isolation to concentrate on the course.

'On Selection everyone is put into syndicates of four, and the instructors will usually give a few tips and make sure each man is in his best physical shape to have a "fair crack" at the course. Our instructor, a veteran who hailed from the west Midlands, waited until we all had serious blisters before paying us a visit one evening. Seeing for himself the shattered mess that our feet had become, he suggested we each buy a jar of vaseline, rub it into our feet and then put our socks back on. "That will solve it, no problem". And he was right.

'Such philanthropy tends to disappear on the hills, where the only important thing is getting to the next checkpoint on time. If you are late or your bergen looks light, an instructor will present you with a rock to add to your difficulties. The smart ones carry it until they are out of sight, then ditch it and pick up a fresh one before they get to the next checkpoint. It's all about keeping your mind working, you see. Those who don't use their initiative fall back and fail. I remember at the end of the course there were only 17 of us left, and we had only passed Selection: there was still Continuation to go.'

All SAS soldiers, regardless of the period they served in the Regiment, agree on the tough nature of Selection Training. Lofty Large passed the course in the 1950s:

> 'At the end I was fit to drop, completely smashed. Some had already dropped. We were told that was just a warm-up. Sure enough it was. My next trick, as far as I can remember, was a 35-mile hike, with 50lb on my back, all across country ("you will not use roads or bridges") which lasted nearly two days. We went from one RV (rendezvous) to another, never knowing which would be the last. I waded the River Wye twice and slept the night on the mountains, soaking wet and cold but too shattered to notice. We had to travel alone, if two men were caught walking together they risked RTU; the same if we were caught on roads or bridges.'

Above: All SAS soldiers receive intensive training in the use of weapons, such as this SA-80.

Nearly 20 years later two more aspiring SAS soldiers had to endure the rigours of Selection and Test Week. Michael Asher (23 SAS) confirms the importance of the brain still being able to function despite the body being in a state of total exhaustion:

> 'In addition to the 55-pound bergen, I now had to carry all the food and water I should consume on the way, plus an SLR rifle and 200 rounds of ammunition. The rifle had to be kept perfectly clean and operational at all times and carried at the ready no matter how exhausted I might be...In between marches we were expected to be alert enough to take in lessons. When all we wanted to do was to collapse on our beds, the RSM's dog-shark face would be thrust in front of us in some

smoky Nissen hut, explaining how to strip and assemble a Kalashnikov AK-47 assault rifle.'

In late 1941, Captain Fitzroy Maclean was having a similar experience in the Western Desert while preparing for the SAS's very first operation behind the lines:

'For days and nights on end we trudged interminably over the alternating soft sand and jagged rocks of the desert, weighed down by heavy loads of explosive, eating and drinking only what we could carry with us. In the intervals we did weapon training, physical training and training in demolitions and navigation.'

The motto of Training Wing is 'Train Hard, Fight Easy', meaning that all SAS soldiers will be as prepared for combat as possible. Those men who have passed through Selection successfully might add that SAS training is really a series of

bloodless battles, whereas actual combat is just a bloody training session. Soldier 'I' was another who went through the hell of Selection and the culminating 'Long Drag':

'I pushed across jagged stones, squelched through peat bogs, crushed through lime-green beds of young fern shoots and picked my way across stagnant pools of water by jumping from one clump of reeds to another. The olive oil on my socks didn't help this time; the friction in my boots felt like someone pushing a hot, razor-sharp file across the skin of my ankles. Backwards and forwards relentlessly with each step, sapping my will-power and determination, until it felt

Opposite: Parachuting is a major part of training. Below: When fully 'badged', SAS troopers go on to receive training in both troop and patrol skills. Being in a Boat Troop, for example, means mastering all aspects of amphibious warfare.

as if the file was sawing against raw bone. I kept repeating out aloud over and over again as the sun rose higher and hotter, "I've got this far, I'm fucked if I'm going to jack now!" I was overwhelmed by feelings of isolation and loneliness. I felt as though I was the only person for miles around. I must keep going. The sun was getting fiercely hot. It was one of those rare spring days that was a match for the best that summer could offer.

'Midday. I'd been going eight hours and I reckoned I was still less than half-way round the course. The sun was extraordinarily hot for the time of year. Just our fucking luck, I thought, on the very day we could have done with some cloud cover and a cool breeze. As I paused

momentarily to get my bearing, my legs began to give way under the load of the bergen. My lungs felt raw, as if someone had thrust their fist down my throat and ripped a layer of skin off them. My facial expression became set in a glazed stare. What the fuck am I doing this for?, I asked myself. Do I really want to suffer like this? No answer came back. I scanned my brain

but could find no logic with which to talk myself into any more pain.'

Passing Selection Training means prospective SAS soldiers go on to Continuation Training, in which each man learns basic SAS skills to enable him to become an effective member of a four-man patrol (the smallest SAS operational unit). This entails learning standard operating procedures (SOPs), signalling, medicine, combat and survival skills, as well as negotiating a resistance-to-interrogation exercise. There then follows jungle training and a static-line parachuting course, after which those who are left become fully fledged members of 22 SAS Regiment. At any time the prospective recruit can be failed and RTU'd, a particularly cruel blow when one has undertaken six months of training and is so close to winning the famed winged dagger badge.

There is no doubt that becoming an SAS soldier means that the individual has become de facto an elite operative. However, in the never-ending pursuit of excellence which is the hallmark of the SAS, individual troopers are not allowed to rest on their laurels. There is no such thing as a fully trained SAS soldier. The Regiment sets great store by all its soldiers being multi-skilled individuals. This being the case, all its soldiers spend their SAS careers continually learning new skills. This means that four-man patrols are filled with multi-skilled individuals, which allows the unit to function effectively even if it has lost 25-50 per cent casualties.

Thus today's Special Air Service is composed of highly trained, skilled individuals who can undertake a wide variety of missions, from hostage-rescue operations to intelligence gathering deep behind enemy lines. In addition, there are many specialist units that provide logistic and intelligence back-up to the Regiment: an Army Air Corps special flight, an RAF Special Forces Flight, as well as the research and intelligence units based at the SAS's UK base at Hereford (Stirling Lines).

It is the proud boast of the SAS that its men can fight in any terrain anywhere in the world. This means continuous training in hostile regions.

THE EARLY YEARS

In its first two decades of existence, the SAS fought in many types of terrain, from the North African desert to the Malayan jungle.

During its formative years, the SAS didn't have the elaborate and comprehensive resources that it currently possesses, and there was no Selection. However, it did have its recruits – men who were physically and mentally tough. Such a person was Bob Bennett, one of David Stirling's 'Originals', who attests to the demands made upon him and his comrades:

'After a while, we began our parachute course. We started with jumping from platforms 12ft from the ground but then someone had the bright idea of getting us to leap off trucks moving at 30mph. After three attempts, we were all battered and bruised, so that was stopped. Our first live jump from two Bristol Bombay aircraft was cut short after two men were killed. That night we all went to bed with as many cigarettes as possible and smoked until morning. Next day, every man jumped; no one backed out. It was then that I realised that I was with a great bunch of chaps...Just before we went on the first mission, we did a four-day route march across the desert from Kabrit to Heliopolis airfield.'

A World War II SAS jeep kitted out for operations in North Africa. Equipped with Vickers 'K' and Browning machine guns, jeeps were put to devastating use in 1942-43 against Axis airfields.

That first mission mentioned by Bob Bennett was an attack by L Detachment, SAS, on two Axis airfields scheduled for 17 November 1941. It was designed to support Operation 'Crusader', the attempt of General Claude Auchinleck, Commander-in-Chief Middle East, to throw General Rommel's *Afrika Korps* out of Cyrenaica. The 65 SAS soldiers were dropped by parachute on the night of 16/17 November. However, it was a complete disaster, with the men and their equipment being widely scattered due to high winds. Several men were badly injured when they hit the ground and, as a result, the operation had to be abandoned. Despite this initial setback, the SAS continued to train for attacks on enemy airfields and supply depots behind enemy lines. David Stirling decided that henceforth his men would no longer use parachute drops as a means of getting to the target; instead they would be transported to their objectives by the vehicles of the Long Range Desert Group (LRDG).

This slight change in operational procedure brought immediate success: in December 1941 the SAS launched attacks against the enemy airfields at Sirte, Agheila, Tamit, Nofilia and Marble Arch. These actions resulted in the destruction of around 100 enemy aircraft. The new year brought even greater success, vindicating Stirling's belief in the effectiveness of small-sized groups operating behind the lines, as Fitzroy Maclean states:

'Working on these lines, David achieved a series of successes which surpassed the wildest expectations of those who had originally supported his venture. No sooner had the enemy become aware of his presence in one part of the desert than he was attacking them somewhere else. Never has the element of surprise, the key to success in all irregular warfare, been more brilliantly exploited. Soon the number of aircraft destroyed on the ground was well into three figures.'

What was it like for individual SAS soldiers engaged on these hit-and-run missions? Inevitably, no two operations were the same, but they all shared common characteristics. First, there was the trip to the target area. Transported by the trucks of the LRDG, the journey was usually uneventful, though constant watch had to be kept for enemy aircraft. Reg Seekings, one of the 'Originals', describes a typical trip in an LRDG truck in January 1942:

'Most of the time we were loaded to do the complete journey, which was why we needed well-run-in trucks. Everything was grossly overloaded. We'd carry food, water and petrol. We also carried ammunition. We needed lots of that...And we fed well. We got on to the LRDG ration scale which was different from the rest of the army. They had tinned fruit. They were really twenty-four-hour jobs, those patrols. You were covering as many miles a day as you possibly could, depending on the going...We were continually mending punctures...It was really tough going on those jobs. Good fun.'

Whether or not these missions were actually good fun is debatable. Nevertheless, they were highly effective, proving Stirling's point that small parties could achieve a far greater degree of success than the large-scale raids previously practised by the British in North Africa. When the target was reached, the actual action was less glamorous than might be expected. The idea, then as now, was to infiltrate the target, lay the explosives and then withdraw with as little fuss as possible (the very last thing troops operating behind the lines want to do is attract unnecessary attention).

In March 1942, a party of SAS soldiers raided an enemy airfield at Berka. The story of the operation is relayed by Bob Bennett:

'We hit the perimeter at about midnight and saw German sentries strolling along the road. As usual, we waited until they had walked by our position and then shot across the road into the trees on the other side. There, we split into two groups. I was with Paddy [Mayne], and we went for the bombers lying under the cover of the trees. We just walked down the line of aircraft lobbing Lewes bombs onto their wings. When the job was finished, Paddy and I sped out of the place.

'When we halted for a break, the bombers started to go up – it must have been about two hours as we were using time pencils of that duration. The Germans didn't seem to know what had happened: they were firing into the air or out to sea. In fact, it took them a heck of a long time to get wise.'

Bob Bennett gives the impression that destroying enemy aircraft was easy. And so it may have been at first, as the Germans and Italians were caught unawares by Stirling's men. However, airfield security was soon tightened, making it a lot more difficult to get at the aircraft. In addition, there was the constant worry that, having hit an airfield, the SAS would not make the rendezvous with the LRDG. If this happened the SAS soldiers were faced with a long trek through the desert back to base. One party that made such a journey was the one led by Bill Fraser in January 1943 after successfully attacking Marble Arch airfield. Having reached the rendezvous point but unaware that an LRDG patrol had been despatched to the wrong point, the SAS team waited. When it became clear that the LRDG was not going to arrive, the men decided to walk the 320km back to base. The training instigated by Jock Lewes came into its own. One of the group, Private Byrne, describes the journey:

'We took turns to lead, every one of us setting a cracking pace, determined to match each other's resolution. Weary beyond belief, we kept tramping on, stamping our feet into the soft desert sand and lifting them up again like automata, every step an effort...The sun burned into eyes from high overhead and was reflected up again from the sand. There was no escape from it and we longed for the luxury of sun glasses or a peaked cap. At dusk we dug holes in the sand, curled up in our blankets and tried to sleep.'

Above: Recruits undergoing parachute training at the SAS's first base at Kabrit, Egypt, in 1942.

The fact they made it back to base is testimony to the legendary stamina of SAS soldiers.

Mid-1942 witnessed a change in SAS battle tactics when Stirling's men used the US Willys jeep for the first time. The vehicles were heavily armed – twin Vickers 'K' machine guns mounted front and rear, and often supplemented with a .50in Browning heavy machine gun – and equipped for long-range desert operations: water condensers, sand mats, radios, metal wheel channels and spare ammunition. The jeeps were first used at Bagoush airfield in July 1942 to devastating effect. Johnny Cooper was one of those who took part in the raid:

'With all guns cocked we approached the silhouetted aircraft, and as we came alongside the first one, the Vickers 'K's opened up with a mixture of tracer, armour-piercing and explosive bullets. I was manning the forward single Vickers and our rear gunner had the twins. David [Stirling] was encouraging us from the driving seat and we could tell from his voice that he was delighted with the new technique. We progressed at about 15 mph and soon had two CR42s [Italian biplane fighter aircraft] on fire. As the third one burst into flames I saw Paddy [Mayne] jump out of the leading jeep, run across and throw a Lewes bomb into a cockpit. He just could not resist the temptation of doing things in the old way.'

The raid was a stunning success and resulted in the destruction of nearly 40 enemy aircraft. The SAS's long association with light military vehicles had begun.

As the campaign in North Africa came to an end in May 1943, the SAS (numbering two regiments and a total of around 600 men) faced an uncertain future. However, David Stirling (who had been captured in January 1943) had created an organisation that could fight in all theatres of war, not just the desert. For example, he had insisted that his men be trained to reach their targets by land, sea or air. Thus they were ideally suited to take part in the next phase of Allied strategy: the invasions of Sicily and mainland Italy.

During Operation 'Husky', the invasion of Sicily, the Special Raiding Squadron (1 SAS which had been temporarily renamed) was under the overall control of the British XIII Corps and was tasked with conducting an amphibious assault to capture the enemy gun battery on top of Capo Murro di Porco. The landing was scheduled for 10 July 1943, though the actual assault, like most amphibious operations, was more difficult than expected. Bob Bennett was one of those who took part:

'The sea was roaring away and the ship was heaving from side to side. As each man tried to get into the landing craft, the boats would swing away from the ship, leaving a yawning gap. We eventually got into the craft and headed for the shore. It was about 0200 hours...On the way in, we saw a smashed glider and bodies [Allied soldiers] bobbing up and down in the sea. We couldn't do anything about it, but the bosun returned and picked them up.'

The SAS encountered a new form of combat during this campaign: fighting in built-up areas. Once again, however, the exhaustive training paid dividends. The SAS approached the tasks with a cool professionalism. Bob Bennett describes the clearing of Augusta:

'You just went down both sides of the street with each group covering the buildings on the opposite side. Of course, you had the 'Back Charlie' of each section walking backwards to cover the rear. When we found an occupied building, grenades were the weapon. You just threw a few in and then smashed through the door, spraying the room with fire as you went. We killed quite a few this way, and there weren't many prisoners.'

It was a similar story during the bloody operation to take the Italian town of Bagnara on 3 September 1943:

'We used the local vineyards as cover. You were taught to reserve your ammunition, and we never used a grenade, or fired, unless we knew there was going to be something on the other end of it. The Brens and Vickers were the best weapons out there and did quite a lot of damage to the enemy.'

SAS weapons training, even in the early years, has always been extremely thorough. As they would have to operate behind enemy lines, David Stirling was insistent that all his men be familiar with the enemy's weapons. In fact, enemy weapons were favoured by many SAS soldiers. During the Sicilian campaign, for example, Bennett was equipped with a German submachine gun:

'I had a 9mm Schmeisser I'd picked up from a mined German armoured car in the desert. The British Tommy-guns were no use to us because of the weight of the ammo – you just couldn't carry enough. We carried all sorts of equipment. The grenade discharger cup which fitted onto our rifles was very effective.'

The Special Air Service was heavily engaged in the fight to liberate France and the Low Countries in 1944-45, and also took part in the campaign in Germany at the end of the war. The actions in France after the D-Day landings of 6 June 1944 fell into two main categories: to provide small-scale, tactical support for General Bernard Montgomery's 21st Army Group, and to operate behind enemy lines with local *Maquis*

Below: David Stirling (left) and 'Jock' Lewes talk about operational plans in North Africa, 1942.

groups to disrupt enemy logistics. In the four months after D-Day, some 2000 SAS men were dropped behind enemy lines in France and the Low Countries. Operating in uniform from more than 40 bases, they hit enemy vehicles, railway lines and German military personnel.

As ever, the success of individual SAS missions relied on the skills of the individual soldiers involved. One such operation was Operation 'Kipling', which took place between 13 August and 26 September 1944 in the area west of Auxerre, central France. Captain Derrick Harrison was a member of the SAS team, and he provides an interesting insight into the way SAS soldiers fought behind the lines in France. Both men and jeeps were parachuted into the area by the RAF and, once a base had been established, the jeeps ranged far and wide searching for enemy forces. In one incident on 23 August Harrison, with two jeeps, decided to investigate why smoke was rising into the air from the

village of Les Ormes. When they got nearer they were informed by a fleeing civilian that the Germans were shooting up the entire village. Harrison's subsequent actions are typical of the quick reactions possessed by SAS soldiers:

'In such situations plans are made at great speed, but they are, nonetheless, plans... Our only hope was a surprise attack: drive through the village at speed and trust to our firepower. The Union Jacks on our jeeps jerked into life as we accelerated into the village square. In the road stood a large German truck and two staff cars, blocking the way through. A crowd of SS men in front of the church dashed for cover as I opened up with my machine guns, and as the vehicles burst into flames, I saw some of the Germans fall. But now I was in trouble. My jeep had come to a sudden halt, my Vickers jammed and the Germans were firing back [the other jeep was in the square, a short distance behind Harrison's].'

Many men in such circumstances would have made a run for it or surrendered. However, Harrison, displaying that typical SAS knack for coolly assessing the situation, decided on another course:

Below: A different theatre: an SAS soldier liaises with partisans in Italy, 1943. The Regiment fought in Italy up until the end of the war.

Above: SAS paratroopers in the fuselage of a Beverley aircraft during the Malayan campaign.

'I had grabbed my carbine and was now standing in the middle of the road firing at everything that moved. Germans seemed to be firing from every doorway. I felt my reactions speed up to an incredible level. It was almost as if I could see individual bullets coming towards me as I ducked and weaved to avoid them. And all the time I was shooting from the hip, and shooting accurately.

'Suddenly, my right hand was warm, wet and with slippery blood. I had been hit. This posed another difficulty: how to change magazines. Somehow, in a fumbling manner, I managed...I moved to the left and saw some 20 men moving through the small walled orchard towards me. Fire! Change mag. Fire! Slowly they fell back, leaving some of their number dead or wounded.'

Harrison managed to reach the other jeep, which made a speedy retreat from the village, leaving some 60 Germans dead and wounded, together with one truck and the two staff cars destroyed. For his bravery that day, Harrison deservedly won the Military Cross. His actions

Above: A four-man patrol takes a breather while on a deep reconnaissance mission in Malaya.

also illustrate that other quality found in SAS soldiers: the ability to keep thinking even when the situation is desperate. This has saved the lives of many SAS men who have been in a tight spot.

The SAS crossed into Germany in the early months of 1945. They took part in many reconnaissance operations and were closely tied to regular formations. Rather than being engaged in deep-penetration hit-and-run raids, the SAS formations were for the most part employed just ahead of the advancing Allied formations. As such they were often subjected to ambushes, which made losses disproportionately high, and the general hostility of the population made operating behind the lines difficult. The jeeps being used by the SAS at this time had been further modified: the whole of the front was covered in armoured plate, there were semi-circles of bullet-proof glass to protect the driver and front gunner, and some were fitted with a wire-cutting device above the front bumper. The

SAS obsession with keeping all equipment in first-class condition was always in evidence. Bob Bennett, the veteran of North Africa, was with D Squadron, 1 SAS, at this time:

> 'The jeeps always came first. Whenever we halted for the night, each crew checked the tyres, gave the engine the once over and sorted out any faults. Everyone was mechanically minded and many men had been with jeeps since the desert days.'

The balance sheet for the SAS at the end of the campaign in northwest Europe was very favourable: nearly 8000 enemy soldiers killed or wounded, 4784 captured, over 700 vehicles destroyed, including seven trains (an additional 33 trains had been derailed) and 164 railway lines cut. However, with peace came rapid demobilisation, and the Special Air Service was officially disbanded.

It took a conflict in the Far East to provide the impetus to recreate the Regiment. The

Malayan 'Emergency', which began in June 1948, was to result in the reformation of the Special Air Service and the further refinement of its wartime role. The conflict between the British administration in Malaya and the mainly Chinese Malayan Races Liberation Army (MRLA) was to last 12 years, but ultimately the British defeated the Communist Terrorists (CTs), not least due to the efforts of one man and his unit.

Lieutenant-Colonel 'Mad' Mike Calvert was, in many ways, cast in the same mould as David Stirling: he was a man of vision who looked to unconventional ways to solve problems. He was a veteran of the Chindit campaigns in Burma during World War II and had ended the war in Europe as commander of the SAS Brigade. After the initial successes against the CTs in Malaya, the latter had withdrawn deeper into the jungle, from where they launched attacks against British targets. It soon became apparent that the authorities needed a deep-penetration unit to locate and destroy the CT bases.

General Sir John Harding, Commander-in-Chief Far East Land Forces, commissioned Calvert to write a report on all aspects of the war in Malaya. Following six months of research, which involved working with police and Army units and conducting lone reconnaissances in the jungle, he submitted his report. In it he described how he would set up a specialist counter-insurgency force which could live, move and fight the guerrillas in the jungle.

In 1950, in response to the report, Harding authorised Calvert to form the Malayan Scouts. His three- and four-man patrols began to operate effectively against the CTs, laying ambushes, gathering intelligence and establishing contacts with the Aborigines (the original inhabitants who had been forced into the interior by successive waves of invaders). The Scouts, after initial problems, became very successful and this led to the reformation of 22 SAS in 1952. In addition, Calvert believed one of the keys to victory lay in winning over the indigenous Aborigines. This was the beginning of the famous 'hearts and minds' policy that was used in subsequent campaigns.

What was it like fighting in the Malayan jungle? Johnny Cooper, an SAS veteran of World War II, gives a vivid account:

'In areas of dense bamboo we had to do a lot of cutting with our machetes and didn't move very quickly. Worse, the noise we made carried for miles if it wasn't masked by the screams of monkeys. When we moved through swamps, the noise was terrible and, covered in leeches, we were lucky to cover 200yds in an hour.

'Moving through primary jungle was much easier as there was little ground vegetation, but we had to watch out for snakes. We tried to avoid well-used tracks as the CTs often set up ambushes or pig traps of sharpened bamboo along the way.'

Jungle fighting required nerves of steel, endless patience and great reserves of physical stamina. Life on operations was invariably grim: clothes could be soaked with rain or sweat, the environment was mostly dark and damp below the jungle canopy, and there was the ever-present threat of booby traps or an enemy ambush. In addition, there was always the possibility of stumbling on the local wildlife: elephants, tigers, snakes, water buffalo (which could be very hostile), hornets and mosquitoes. Despite this, Cooper for one did not find the jungle itself intimidating:

'I never had a feeling of claustrophobia in the jungle. It was intensely quiet and very cool, and in the more mountainous states in Malaya we would come across many rivers and fast-flowing streams. Carrying up to 60lbs in a bergen plus personal weapons limited the length of time between halts on a patrol. The only Malayan landscape which was a real nightmare were the swampy areas, notably in Selangor. Before my initiation there, I found it hard to believe that it could take up to one hour to cover five hundred yards. The mangrove trees were not particularly tall, so the sun did penetrate, and the water level could be anything up to three feet in depth. The idea was to go from tree to tree stepping on the roots, but every so often you would find yourself up to the waist in gooey black mud. Pulling oneself out with a heavy rucksack on the back was no easy task. In the swamps we also made the acquaintance of the tiger leech which not only sucked blood but hurt as well.'

As the men of the SAS gained skill in the methods of jungle warfare, new tactics were tried in an effort to trap the elusive foe. One of these innovations was 'tree jumping', a parachute technique pioneered by the SAS. As CT camps were located deep in the jungle, it took foot patrols a long time to reach them, giving the enemy the opportunity of escaping. Therefore, the decision was taken to drop men by parachute onto the thick jungle canopy and from there they would use ropes to descend to the ground. The first operational jump was carried out by 54 men in February 1952 near the Thai border. Their role was to act as a blocking force in an operation involving Gurkhas, Royal Marines, Malay Police and more SAS soldiers on the ground. None of the men deployed by parachute were hurt and so the tactic was judged a great success. In fact parachuting into thick trees was a highly dangerous tactic, which was confirmed during subsequent operations when there were many injuries. During Operation 'Sword' in January 1954, for example, three SAS soldiers died when they crashed into the jungle canopy.

By 1958 the conflict in Malaya had almost been won, and the SAS had played a significant part in the victory. In the jungle it had won the hearts and minds of the Aborigines and had made the jungle an unsafe place for the enemy. Both the Malayan Scouts and the SAS proved that British soldiers, so long as they possessed the right qualities and were adequately trained, could operate in the jungle for long periods and take the fight to the opposition. Indeed, many SAS troopers became legendary jungle fighters. And Sergeant Bob Turnbull, a Yorkshireman, became an expert linguist and tracker.

It has always been the proud boast of the SAS that its men, because of their exhaustive training, can fight in any terrain at a moment's notice. In 1958 the SAS was mostly a collection of jungle warriors, but an incident in the Middle East led to the Regiment once again fighting in the searing heat of the desert. The British government, because it had treaty obligations to the Sultan of Muscat and Oman, found itself being dragged into a counter-insurgency campaign there in the 1950s.

The autocratic rule of the Sultan was being challenged by rebels led by Sulaiman bin Himyar, Ghalib bin Ali and Ghalib's brother, Talib. Armed insurgents had occupied the Jebel Akhdar (meaning 'Green Mountain') in the north of the country in 1957 and declared it independent of the Sultan. The latter called on the British for help, and they despatched an infantry brigade, which restored the Sultan's authority around the Jebel. However, the rebels were still secure on the mountain plateau itself, which covered an area of 350 square kilometres and was surrounded by high peaks. Access to their positions was via narrow passes which could be easily defended. Sooner or later, the British and royalist forces would have to storm the position, a formidable, and potentially bloody, proposition to say the least.

It was inevitable, perhaps, that the Special Air Service should be selected to act as the vanguard. The 70 men of D Squadron arrived in Oman in November 1958 and began operations straight away, establishing positions on the northern side of the Jebel. Several weeks before they had left Malaya, the SAS soldiers undertook training exercises for the new type of terrain they would be operating in, as a corporal of the squadron relates:

'Everything was done in the heat of the day. We set up a series of hard marches with bergens, weapons and ammunition, and at the end of each march there was more and more range work, more and more open work, as opposed to work which we'd always done in jungle, and longer range marksmanship, well over the 25 or 30yds which we had previously engaged in.'

The terrain was extremely inhospitable, and was entirely different from that encountered in Malaya. In addition, the rebels were excellent shots and this, combined with the lack of cover,

Above: A motley crew: 16 Troop, D Squadron, 22 SAS, just before the Jebel Akhdar operation.

made movement during daylight difficult. An indication of the type of conditions and enemy the SAS was up against is given by a trooper from D Squadron:

'We got to the top and we found positions that the enemy had obviously occupied, so we decided to get into their positions rather than make new ones of our own, because we knew enough about them to realise that they would spot a new position on the skyline the same as we would if it was our area. At about 0630 the sun came up and we fried and fried and fried. We had two extremes. At night it was cold enough on top of the mountain to freeze the water bottle, and we weren't as well equipped then as we are today. All we had were OG [olive-green] trousers and jackets and a very thin standard issue pullover. We didn't take sleeping-bags on a 24-hour recce since all they did was slow you down, and anyway, we didn't intend to sleep, not knowing whether they had established night piquets.

'Around about 1400 hours I had another three men with me in my patrol and we were looking down and covering an area when, lo and behold, I saw this Arab start making his way up. He got up to within 300yds of us when he must have spotted some sort of movement because he shouted up at me, obviously thinking I was one of them. So we shouted down, but then he decided, having had his rifle on his shoulder in the sling position, that something wasn't quite right here, so he took it off, whereupon I shot him. My mate alongside me shot him as well and we just blew him away. Within 30 seconds we were under fire from numerous places. They were hyperactive and their reaction was perfect. They started shooting from all areas and concentrating fire on us. Further along the ridge, the other half of our troop was trapped and one of them, Corporal 'Duke' Swindells, was shot.'

Aggressive and bold leadership has always been the hallmark of SAS soldiers, and it was no exception on the Jebel Akhdar. One such officer, who would later achieve fame as the commander of British forces during the 1991 Gulf War against Iraq, was Captain Peter de la Billière. A machine gunner from D Squadron remembers one particular action that de la Billière was involved in:

'As de la Billière's troop had done the recce, they would do the nearest bit and would put a 66mm rocket or Carl Gustav rocket into the [rebel] cave – several in fact. Our troop was designed to cover them and we were on a slightly higher ridge about two or three hundred yards above them. We climbed up that night, early morning came and I was behind the Browning. I had persuaded John Watts that the ideal weapon for Oman was the .30 Browning where you had the range you didn't have with the LMG [light machine gun], but, like all machine guns, it attracts a lot of attention. We set the gun up overlooking the cave and then, first thing in the morning, several men came to the entrance of the cave and were about to start leading the donkeys out. Whereupon, three rounds rapid from the Carl Gustav went straight in the middle and whoof, they blew the cave in and a fair number of them to pieces. Once again, within a minute and a half, we were all under attack. They were amazing in their reactions plus their knowledge of the ground. They were born for it and their reactions were fast. We were under attack from their mortars. We were under attack from their LMGs and from individual tribesmen who were all spoiling for a fight. But, with the help of my machine gun and the RAF who arrived, we extracted ourselves without loss.'

In January 1959 the decision was taken to make a determined push against the rebels. The newly arrived A Squadron under Major Johnny Cooper was tasked with assaulting the enemy from the north while D Squadron attacked from the south. The attack went in at 0300 hours on 26 January. The key to the assault was a strenuous climb running from the village of Kamah up between the Wadi Kamah and the Wadi Suwaiq. A lie had been spread among the Arab donkey handlers that the main attack would come from the direction of Tanuf. This information quickly reached the rebels, who prepared to meet the SAS in the heights above Tanuf. The first attack, however, came from the north, led by Major Cooper:

'I attacked Aquabat al Dhafar with three troops while one, with all the machine guns from the others, laid a barrage on Sabrina [the top of the mountain]. Tony Jeapes' troop was the one that scaled the pinnacle on the high side and got over the top and killed three or four. When Tony got on the top and scarpered these boys, he poured fire down on the other side and won the firefight...By morning my three troops had Sabrina, and the enemy retreated.'

The attack on Sabrina persuaded the rebels to send reinforcements from the village of Saiq to blunt Cooper's attack. Meanwhile, A Squadron left Sabrina and headed down to Tanuf to join D Squadron for the final push.

By 1800 hours on 26 January, A Squadron was in Tanuf and resting, and then both squadrons were loaded into trucks and transported to the assembly area at Kamah. At the same time, a diversionary attack was launched by the SAS up the Wadi Tanuf by a single troop. From Kamah the two squadrons, heavily loaded down with kit, began their ascent. The ruse had been so successful that the men encountered little opposition, though as Cooper remarked of the climb, 'it was bloody difficult and we were carrying a hell of a lot of weight.' Following the SAS were more British troops and contingents of the Sultan's Armed Forces.

Taken by surprise, rebel resistance soon crumbled. The SAS had reached the plateau and were mopping up all opposition. The enemy leaders fled to Saudi Arabia and their men were disarmed. It was a classic SAS operation, and is neatly summed up by Johnny Cooper himself:

'It had to be done quickly. If you'd sent in a battalion of infantry it would have cost a lot of money. Here you were sending only a small gang. It was an SAS job because we had the ability to carry pack-mule loads and we were all very fit.'

In fact, the Jebel Akhdar operation was a supreme example of how a small, specialist force, if led correctly, can achieve results out of all proportion to its size. The SAS mission did not end with the assault on the Jebel. The men then began an immediate 'hearts and minds' campaign to turn the local inhabitants into supporters of the Sultan.

The next SAS operation was to see the Regiment return to the jungles of the Far East, specifically Borneo. By this time SAS drills and procedures had been amended and refined since the days in North Africa during World War II. For example, the Regiment's soldiers were learning how to operate with helicopters, and jungle warfare techniques had been perfected in the jungles of Malaya. However, one thing that hadn't changed was the calibre of recruits accepted into the Regiment. If anything, the entry requirements were higher than ever. By 1960 the Regiment had its own base in the UK and, thanks to the earlier efforts of Lieutenant-Colonel John Woodhouse, it had an excellent Selection Training programme that quickly weeded out those who were unsuitable material. The British Special Air Service was now truly one of the world's elite units.

Below: A photograph that conveys the conditions encountered by SAS soldiers on the Jebel Akhdar.

BORNEO

Militarily, the jungle can be a potential disaster area, but in the early 1960s the SAS fought a highly effective jungle campaign in Borneo, and, in a series of top-secret cross-border raids, struck a number of decisive blows against the Indonesian Army.

The jungle in Borneo is of two main types: primary jungle and secondary jungle. The former contains trees that can grow up to a height of over 60m, forming a thick canopy of leaves that ensures very little light reaches the jungle floor. This means visibility can be reduced to 50m or less, though a bonus is that there is little undergrowth to hinder movement. Secondary jungle occurs where sunlight reaches the jungle floor, such as around river banks and where primary jungle has been cleared. In this type of terrain the ground is covered by grasses, ferns and shrubs. Movement is slow and can be very tiring, with many hours spent hacking a path with machetes (this is invariably very noisy and will therefore alert an enemy of a patrol's presence – something an SAS unit will wish to avoid).

Everyone sweats in the jungle (Borneo was unlike the cool, mountainous regions encountered by Johnny Cooper in Malaya), but soldiers carrying heavy loads will perspire a lot more. In addition, disease and parasites thrive in a jungle environment, thus soldiers need to be on their guard against infection. What qualities are needed to fight in the jungle?

A patrol moves along a river in Borneo. Fighting in such terrain can be an absolute nightmare, as the humidity is oppressive, and soldiers have to be on constant guard against ambush.

First and foremost is physical fitness. Wading through a swamp for hours on end, for example, carrying a weapon over your head, is a severe test of fitness. To achieve the required level of fitness the Americans believe a soldier should go into the jungle 'lean and mean' to fight. But the SAS takes a different view: it encourages its soldiers to go into the jungle overweight because they will invariably lose a lot of weight and come out 'lean and mean'. Mental preparedness is also important. The jungle is dark, dank and can be claustrophobic. Soldiers need to be 'switched on' to operate effectively, otherwise lethargy and apathy can quickly set in. A veteran of A Squadron describes his first contact with the jungle:

'The humidity of the jungle is not immediately obvious because the canopy of trees casts a psychological shadow of coolness. So you think, well, this isn't so bad after all. But then the humidity hits you, and within an hour both your trousers and shirt are saturated with sweat as the body soaks up the rising warmth. The best way I can describe it is being inside a greenhouse which has no lights. The sun can be scorching the tops of the trees, but on the ground the atmosphere is constantly damp.'

Wearing the right gear is also very important: one of the most important items of clothing is footwear. The feet and legs must be protected at all times. Contrary to popular opinion, most animals – snakes, wild pigs and large mammals – will move away from people who are moving through the jungle. However, there is still a risk of walking into a scorpion or spider's nest, and if this happens and you're not wearing tough boots, the consequences can be dire. However, the standard British Army issue items were not always up to the required standard:

'Canvas boots to allow the feet to sweat were issued, but early designs suffered due to the poor quality of the material. Some blokes used their initiative and got cobblers in Singapore, who could make you a pair of shoes in an hour, to stitch a piece of soft leather to their DMS (Direct Moulded Sole) boots. Others had bartered to acquire the more professional-looking US and Australian jungle boots, which had a hard rubber sole with breathable strong uppers.'

The head was also protected, though the SAS had to tailor the issue item to its own needs:

'Whoever designed the standard British Army "bush" hat had obviously never been in the jungle. It was probably great for keeping the sun off on Brighton beach, but it was useless in the *ulu* (jungle). The brim was so big that it actually blocked out what little light the jungle offered, and when moving through dense areas of jungle it often caught on branches. To solve the problem we employed the standard regimental answer to problems: cut it off.'

Likewise with the legs and arms: they must be protected at all times from bites and scratches:

'Anyone who went into the jungle with a short-sleeved shirt was asking for trouble. Shirt sleeves were always rolled down to stop insects from clinging to you and to prevent your arms coming into contact with foliage, the sap of which could give you a nasty rash.'

Ironically, animals could also pose a danger to the patrol as they ran away from the troops who were moving through the jungle:

'The *ulu*, the name we called the jungle, is alive with a background noise of wildlife, which increases to a thunderous roar at dawn and last light. However, great care is needed when moving because the animals can sense your approach and disappear, leaving a silence which can compromise your position to an alert enemy.'

This, then, was the type of terrain and the conditions SAS soldiers found themselves

Above: Royal Marines move along a river in the Sabah region of Borneo, 1965. Boats were a quick way to travel, but were vulnerable to ambushes.

campaigning in during the 1960s in Borneo. What was the background to the conflict? Malaya, the former British colony, was pushing hard in the early 1960s for the formation of a new political entity in the region, to comprise Sabah, Sarawak, Brunei, Malaya and Singapore (on the Malay Peninsula), and which would be called the Federation of Malaysia. The general idea was supported by Britain but was violently opposed by President Sukarno of Indonesia, who saw the scheme as a hindrance to Indonesia's expansionist aims. The bulk of the island of Borneo was actually part of Indonesia, and was known as Kalimantan.

In early 1963 Sukarno began the infiltration of insurgents from Kalimantan into Sarawak and Sabah, a process that was speeded up when Sabah and Sarawak were officially incorporated into Malaysia in September 1963. The British responded to this action, forming a force of Malaysian, British and Commonwealth troops to fight the insurgents. Part of this effort was the Special Air Service. Not that the British had an easy task: Major-General Walter Walker, the Director of Operations Borneo, had only five battalions to cover some 1500km of jungle-covered, often unexplored, border. He also had to contend with an internal threat in the shape of the Clandestine Communist Organisation (CCO), whose recruits came predominantly from the Chinese settlers in Sarawak.

The first SAS unit to arrive in Borneo, in early 1963, was A Squadron, 22 SAS, and the Regiment's commander, Lieutenant-Colonel John Woodhouse. Walker originally wanted to use the SAS as a kind of mobile reserve, dropped by parachute onto the jungle canopy in order to recapture areas captured by the Indonesians. Woodhouse, convinced this tactic would result in high casualties, persuaded him that the SAS would be better suited to operating in small patrols along the border, where they could gather timely intelligence concerning enemy incursions. Though it numbered only 70 men, by operating in two- or three-man patrols the squadron was able to field 21 patrols along the entire length of the border. They also stayed in the jungle for long periods: one patrol stayed in the Long Jawi area for six months.

Contact with the local inhabitants formed an important part of SAS operations and a 'hearts and minds' policy (see Chapter 2) was quickly implemented. The procedure was for the patrol to establish contact with the local inhabitants and gain their trust. Often the SAS soldiers would live with the locals, sharing their longhouses and helping with the planting and harvesting of crops. In this way, over time, trust was built up between the natives and the SAS soldiers. The man most responsible for winning over these people, however, was the patrol medic. The work he did in curing their ills reaped substantial rewards when it came to gathering intelligence concerning enemy strengths and dispositions. But that was later in the campaign. The first SAS deployment, at the end of 1962, was to Brunei:

'The Regiment had served in the Malayan conflict, so we were fairly well qualified for jungle operations. President Sukarno, nicknamed "the mad doctor", was doing everything in his power to unite the whole area under his leadership. Some rebels tried to foment trouble in Brunei, but this was quickly suppressed by British forces (though not SAS). We flew into Singapore, where we were briefed by a Gurkha major concerning the situation in Borneo. Several battalions, which had been serving in Singapore, were subsequently deployed to Sarawak, including 650 Gurkhas.'

Once in Borneo the SAS was tasked with gathering intelligence. The Regiment also trained a number of irregular forces, known as Border Scouts, as aids to intelligence gathering. They were created by Major-General Walker as part of an effort to establish a defensive intelligence network along the border with Kalimantan. The Scouts were recruited from the indigenous tribes of the region and were trained by SAS soldiers in a number of camps. Armed and trained as paramilitaries, the Border Scouts were not combat troops. Their task was to move

through the jungle unseen and gather valuable information. When they did engage Indonesian forces the consequences were often dire: in September 1963, for example, a Border Scout post at Long Jawi, 45km from the border, was wiped out by a large party of Indonesian troops. But in the intelligence-gathering role the Scouts could be invaluable for acting as the 'eyes and ears' along the border, and individual Scouts were often attached to SAS patrols to aid communications with the indigenous tribes in the area where the soldiers were operating. During the initial stages of the campaign the SAS's role was straightforward:

'Our role was very simple, ie to go into the jungle and gather information about the Indos and their tactics. We did this by befriending the local tribes and lying up in a deep-camouflaged "hide" [covert position] on the border to monitor activity. We didn't initially mount fighting patrols, whose sole purpose was to go and engage the enemy, but in the course of this intelligence work we did occasionally get bumped by an Indo ambush. We also sprang one ourselves from time to time.'

The SAS patrols also established ambush sites for other units and potential helicopter landing zones. Any intelligence that was collected was relayed back to SAS headquarters by high-frequency radio, where it could be acted upon immediately. The Indonesian incursions into Sarawak began in April 1963, by which time A Squadron had an effective 'hearts and minds' policy up and running. The unit was relieved by D Squadron in May 1963, and the SAS began to pay attention to likely Indonesian infiltration points: the tracks leading through Stass at Long Jawi, the plains along parts of Sarawak's western frontier, the valleys south of Pensiangan, and the estuaries of eastern Sabah and Kalabakan. During this time the squadron also undertook a reconnaissance of the previously unexplored area in southern Sabah known as 'The Gap'.

Despite the British effort, Indonesian incursions increased steadily during the winter of 1963-64, especially along the borders of Sabah and Sarawak. SAS personnel, because of their knowledge of the terrain and the relationships they had established with the indigenous tribes, began to assist regular infantrymen in stopping infiltrations by escorting them to ambush sites. The increasing number of Indonesian incursions meant SAS patrols encountered the enemy more often. A trooper from D Squadron relates of one such contact:

'In late 1964 our four-man patrol was heading back to base camp after six days in the *ulu*. The plan was to get back before last light, but the mountainous countryside and the Indos had other ideas. A rope toggle is standard equipment in the jungle. It is about 5m long and is used for crossing fast-flowing rivers or streams by hooking the toggles together. This simple system allows the team to hook up to each other and cross dangerous water with some degree of safety.

'Anyway we reached a section of the river that was narrow but deep. We were armed with Armalites [M16s]. When the Regiment first arrived in Borneo the SLR was standard issue, but within a short space of time the American Armalite was introduced. Though it doesn't have long range, it is light and compact, and is ideally suited to jungle warfare. We scanned the opposite bank for any signs of an enemy presence. So far, so good. Then, as I prepared to cross over, I saw a black flash on the other side. Before I could react the river bank was being riddled with machine-gun fire, quickly followed by frenzied bursts from the Armalites. Our

Below: Effecting a river crossing in Borneo, which invariably results in being covered in leeches.

Iban scout [native inhabitant of Sarawak] had earlier warned us that something was wrong. They were amazing those little guys, they could see and hear things that we would never perceive. I was bloody glad we had them, I can tell you. Anyway, our scout had dived behind this boulder as the GPMG and Armalites put a hail of shot into the space where we had seen the

hostile. The Indo didn't have a chance, he went down in an instant.

'The contact was over in seconds and the jungle fell silent. We had killed one Indonesian but there might be more nearby. By this time I had taken cover and, like everyone else, scanned the area for signs of any more of the opposition. Then we quickly bugged out and moved

the Indo's head and stuffed it into his bag! "Good money, good money," he kept repeating, referring to the bounty he would receive from the Brunei government.

'Ibans were natural trackers and several patrols developed a strong rapport with their own man. Ours would always carry an old pack he had acquired from an infantry battalion. It was full of what appeared to be tree bark and animal skin, which he often chewed on, giving his teeth a tobacco-stained look. They were great blokes, though their headhunting habits were a little disconcerting. We had to continually remind ourselves that it was part of their culture and had been going on for years. It was naturally encouraged by the Brunei government, who wanted as many Indonesian soldiers dead as possible, hence the bounty. The Ibans then suddenly stopped acquiring heads and started to collect ears (the heads were taking up too much space in their bergens!). Mind you, their habits stopped anyone going into their backpacks!'

SAS soldiers received thorough training before being sent to fight in the jungle. All the Regiment's men were taught the basics of jungle survival skills, such as finding food and water, constructing shelters, working with primitive medicines and jungle navigation:

'Specialist training for this type of warfare is essential. Without good jungle knowledge you can easily fall victim to the terrain and its hostile environment. If you don't know how to operate in the tropics you can end up being killed.'

Specialised training and state-of-the-art equipment often go hand in hand, and the popular image of the Special Air Service is of a body of men kitted out with the very best that money can buy. Though this might be true now,

downstream, taking up defensive positions and waiting for the Indos to mount a follow-up ambush. However, they didn't bother and we speedily crossed the river. There is one interesting postscript to the story. Our tracker, who spoke English, said he would check the body. Before we knew what he was up to, he came running back with a big smile on his face. He had cut off

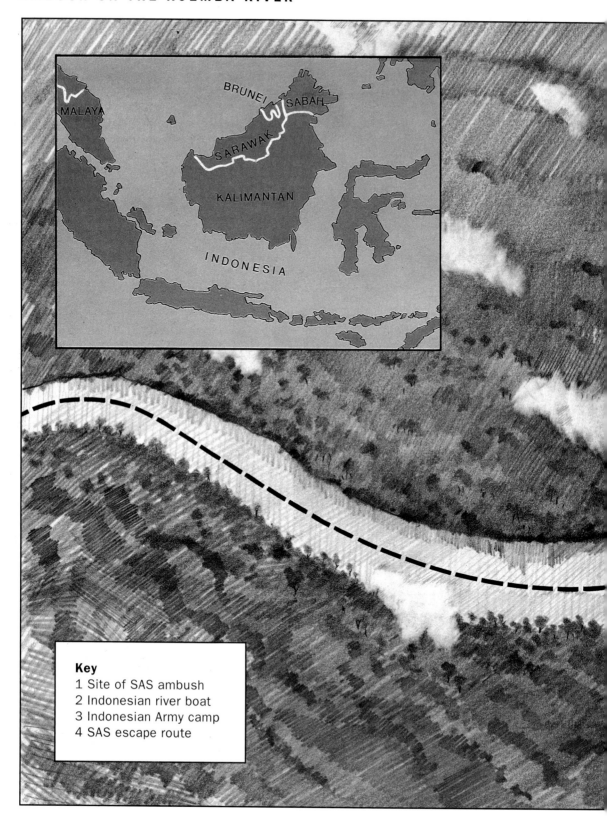

Key
1 Site of SAS ambush
2 Indonesian river boat
3 Indonesian Army camp
4 SAS escape route

in Borneo this certainly wasn't the case, as this ex-trooper from A Squadron relates:

'At that time we carried 'A-frame' bergens – so called because of the arrangement of the metal bars that held the bergen – and a motley collection of webbing pouches that were hijacked from various sources. The pouches always held our top priorities: ammunition and survival kits. In the main we used the '44-pattern webbing which has top fasteners to allow easy access to the water pouch. We usually combined these with bits of Aussie kit. A '58-pattern yoke was added to this customised system to take the weight from the hips to the shoulders. The webbing was held together by a quick-release belt which had been adapted from RAF heavy-load straps, thus we could jettison the kit quickly if we had to run like fuck after being bumped. However, the overriding factor was that every piece of kit could be easily fitted onto any set of webbing carried by other members of the team if the need arose. The thing was, in the early 1960s the Regiment was reduced in strength and we didn't have the priority for equipment that other units had. As a result, we sometimes looked like a bunch of military misfits, having begged, borrowed and stolen a lot of our personal equipment.'

At the beginning of the Borneo campaign the Regiment had only two squadrons, but this soon changed when it became clear the SAS was achieving excellent results. B Squadron was reformed in January 1964, and in 1966 a fourth squadron, G Squadron, was formed from guardsmen who had been conducting SAS-type operations with the Guards Independent Parachute Company in Sarawak.

Despite the increase in numbers, the SAS role remained the same: intelligence gathering. This was made more difficult by the fact that the enemy was not a bunch of ill-armed bandits:

'Of course we got involved in ambushes and firefights, but the image of the SAS charging through the *ulu* with guns blazing at ill-equipped Indos couldn't be further from the truth. The Indos were well armed and organised. It wasn't a situation where you could launch a battalion offensive to crush the guerrillas in one clean swoop. The terrain didn't allow it and neither did the enemy. They had a big advantage in that they knew the terrain, its dangers and, like us, had recruited tribesmen as informants to supply their chain of intelligence with hard-core information. The only way forward for us was to play the same game.'

Though the idea of administering medical aid to native men and women is perhaps contrary to the media image of the SAS, the 'hearts and minds' policy was the key to winning the intelligence war. The concept had been devised by the Military Commissioner in Malaya, General Sir Gerald Templar, to defeat communist insurgents there in the 1950s. It concentrated on gaining the trust of the local inhabitants by learning their language, customs and sharing their lifestyle, and thus winning them over. An SAS trooper describes the standard procedure:

'The four-man patrol would first monitor the village – it wasn't a case of just walking in and saying hello. A lot of these people were very nervous about meeting whites, especially if the Indos had stirred them up. In any case, we always remembered that headhunting was one of their pastimes. When it was deemed safe to enter we did so and attempted to strike up a conversation with the headman. We also offered minor gifts, mainly from our ration packs, to the children. Usually the meeting would go fairly well. If it did we would then leave the village, to return a few days later. You've got to be patient with these people.

'The make-up of an SAS four-man patrol is a medic, a signaller, an explosives expert and a linguist. In Borneo our medics soon became expert "bush doctors", setting up surgery amidst

villagers whose ailments would shock the most hardened NHS doctors. These one-man field hospitals were a great success. The improvement in health of those treated boosted confidence and resulted in many patrols being invited to eat with the local community. It was invaluable in winning over the locals, and allowed us to collate vital intelligence about the Indos which we could use to break their supply routes. The locals also gave us bits of information, which were useful in building up an overall picture in the area we were operating in.'

Life on operations didn't just involve living with the natives. Many SAS patrols established observation posts deep in the jungle. Working in covert 'hides' is never easy, but in the jungle SAS soldiers encountered fresh difficulties:

'All year round the dense undergrowth of the jungle hides a host of potential hazards that can drive you mad if you are sat rigid

Above: An SAS team is evacuated by a Wessex helicopter after an operation. SAS patrols also guided heliborne troops to ambush locations.

in a jungle "hide" trying desperately not to make any noise as you monitor the enemy. Red ants, scorpions, leeches, snakes, huge flying beetles and wild pigs head the list. The important thing to remember about all these creatures is that the jungle is their home, and if you leave your kit on the deck they will set up camp inside it. Leaving your boots open to the elements outside your basha is to invite scorpions and small snakes to crawl inside.'

Moving through the jungle, straining to see and hear the slightest sounds that may indicate an enemy presence, soldiers sometimes forget that there are animals around them. A former member of B Squadron tells of a particularly painful experience he had when on patrol near the Indonesian border in late 1964:

'As point man, the leading member of the patrol, I signalled for the team to stop and listen, a common military practice carried out to hear for any sounds of an enemy you can't see because of the undergrowth. As I stood up I was hit several times in the face by what felt like tiny darts. I fell to the ground and quickly discovered I had been stung by a number of hornets. The pain was excruciating and my face quickly swelled to the size of a melon, forcing the patrol to abandon the whole operation. Other teams ran into similar problems with snakes and scorpions.

'In the sticky climate the body is forced to work overtime, and the risk of infection is ever-present. A simple sweat rash caused by not washing, for example, can turn into a health hazard within days, a fact discovered by many of the battalions who served in Borneo. Water is crucial to survival in the jungle. The huge amount of fluid loss meant that each man had to drink at least six bottles of water a day when he first went into the jungle, though this would drop as he became acclimatised to the conditions. As a consequence, each man carried the standard three water bottles and more in his bergen. Essential items of kit were water sterilisation tablets. These killed the tiny water worm that was known to live in the rivers and streams and which could cause a serious stomach upset that could put a trooper out of action for days, even weeks.

'A millbag, used to drain moss, flies and insect debris from still water in areas of deep primary jungle where running water was difficult to find, reduced the risk of contracting leptospirosis, a disease spread via the urine of infected animals, which could be fatal. Malaria was kept at bay by taking paludrine.'

By the winter of 1963-64, because of the substantial rise in enemy activity, it became clear that the British would have to go on to the offensive in order to contain the situation. Therefore, in June 1964 the government authorised Walker to launch the first top-secret 'Claret' raids across the border to pre-empt the build-up of enemy forces in Kalimantan by striking at the opposition's forward bases. The first was launched in June against an Indonesian camp at Nantakor and was entirely successful. The SAS soldiers were usually lightly armed and carried a minimum amount of supplies. They called themselves the 'Tip Toe Boys' because they hit the opposition and then vanished. The Regiment also trained 40 specially selected Border Scouts, known as Cross-Border Scouts, to support its clandestine raids. The Scouts' initial training was supervised by Major John Edwardes of A Squadron, 22 SAS, and their first mission took place in August 1964. Thereafter, they were active along the border, especially in western Sarawak and around Bemban.

An SAS trooper who took part in the 'Claret' operations remembers the procedures for cross-border missions:

'It was impressed upon us that there was to be no evidence left in Kalimantan that British troops had been operating there. Thus casualties, no matter how serious, were always taken back with us, though we could not call in helicopter casualty evacuation. These raids were never officially recorded, but they did give the Regiment the free rein it had been seeking with regard to crossing the border and attacking Indo military targets, which had been identified by our scouts and our own men. A dangerous, though effective, method to hit the enemy's camps was to track an Indo patrol across the border, identify its position, and then call up a "killer" group from an infantry battalion to mount a first-light raid.

'Every SAS patrol was preceded by personal and team checks. We all carried morphine in a metal ampoule around our necks, along with identification disks and a watch. Items of kit such as watch straps were an open invitation to a leech to make itself at home. They always positioned themselves between the strap and your skin, which was extremely irritating. In addition, little things like making sure the buttons on your shirt sleeves had not come off were seemingly unimportant, but they were a barrier to leeches and made the difference between being comfortable and having a thoroughly miserable time. If any man was killed on a "Claret" job he was immediately stripped of any identification and the body buried. We couldn't afford to take any chances.'

Both A and B Squadrons conducted a number of cross-border raids in the second half of 1964. B Squadron was concentrated in the Pueh range of hills in western Sarawak, which was a favourite route for Clandestine Communist Organisation (CCO) agents making their way to Lundu on the coast to foment trouble (the CCO had many cells operating in Sarawak, and the organisation was provided with arms and training bases by President Sukarno). D Squadron replaced A in early 1965 and it also carried out a number of cross-border recce missions. One such operation,

in the Sentimo swamp, resulted in the sinking of an Indonesian river boat by a four-man patrol (see diagram on pages 140-141).

In late May 1965, D Squadron was replaced by A, the latter being commanded by Major Peter de la Billière. In August he launched a series of cross-border raids which kept the pressure on the Indonesians. The standard formation for SAS 'Claret' missions was the four-man patrol:

'Usually the lead man would be armed with a shotgun, the second and third men with Armalites, with the rear man carrying a general purpose machine gun. We experimented with a number of formations, including putting the machine gunner at the front. To make it easier for him we took the butt off and used the gun's sustained fire back plate instead. We also got an armourer to remove the flash

Below: An SAS trooper with captured Indonesians. Captives could be a good source of intelligence.

eliminator. The idea was that if we were bumped the point man could open up and spray a burst of wild fire into the bush, which would keep the Indos' heads down and give the rest of the team vital seconds in which to locate the source of the ambush and direct controllable fire at it. Well, that was the theory.

'At first we had a host of problems with the shotgun cartridges. They were paper and they swelled up in the humidity of the jungle. Even carrying them in a plastic bag didn't solve the problem because the bag just filled with condensation. In the end they were replaced by plastic cartridges, which pleased everyone no end.'

Stealth is a major part of SAS operations, but during the cross-border raids the soldiers of the Regiment had to maintain extra vigilance. Even simple procedures presented problems:

'Our bashas, or jungle beds, had to be off the ground to avoid the legions of ants and wild animals that passed by. You can make them easily enough by cutting some wood and building a stretcher and perching it on an A-frame of branches, or constructing a box-type arrangement between a number of trees. However, the

Below: SAS-trained Iban tribesmen bring in Indonesian prisoners following a cross-border raid.

noise created when cutting the wood could be a problem and so we often used a hammock strung between two trees, with a poncho tied overhead to keep the dew and the early morning rain off. After last light we usually got out of our OGs (olive-greens) and put a zoot suit on (a one-piece item of clothing made out of parachute silk which was light and comfortable to sleep in and gave us a chance to dry out our kit).

'Our ration packs, or rat-packs as they were known, consisted of the standard A-, B- and C-type menus and, if you were unlucky, a Gurkha menu, full of curried this and that. Other nutritional delights included meat blocks coated with a disgusting taste of salt.'

Crossing the border was fraught with danger, as the Indonesians were excellent jungle warfare soldiers and they knew their own territory very well. A member of A Squadron describes a cross-border raid into Kalimantan in August 1965:

'When we were across the border we always dismantled our bashas before first light and then moved to a higher position, where we would stop for food and make a call to base camp. At first we made good progress and the journey was uneventful, but then we reached a clearing and we sensed something was wrong. So we sat still for several minutes just listening. Nothing happened. Ten minutes later we got up and moved off, only to walk straight into an Indo ambush. A split second after they opened up we were pouring fire into them. I fired my Armalite from the hip, though in truth it was impossible to see the target and we could only fire at the general area we believed the attack was coming from. In what seemed like a long time, though no doubt it was only a few seconds, we had pulled back and were in cover. We stopped firing, none of the lads had been killed but one had been wounded.

'Next thing I heard what appeared to be a herd of elephants thundering through the bush towards us. It was the Indos coming straight for us to finish the job. Their superior knowledge of the jungle gave them an overwhelming self-confidence. Our Armalites had a hand grip fitted to the stock to give us a better hold, and I tightened my grip as the opposition got nearer. My heart was pounding and I could feel droplets of sweat running down the sides of my face. The first Indo appeared, to be literally cut to pieces by a fusillade of 5.56mm rounds. The look on his face was one of surprise as the bullets tore through his uniform and into his body. He went down. We then hurled grenades into the path of the other Indos, and the whole area was suddenly filled with the choking smell of cordite.

'Then everything was still, with only the lingering smoke from the grenades being a reminder of the act of carnage that had just taken place. I clipped a fresh magazine into my weapon and gingerly edged forward. The other lads did the same. We found the Indos, or what was left of them, a few metres in front of our position. Their eyes were open and a look of pain was etched in their faces. One looked like he was only about 18 years old, which was sad. Then again, he was prepared to kill so it was him or us. After taking details of their unit markings and anything they were carrying that might be useful to the intelligence boys, we legged it. Turned out that the Indos were the remains of a patrol that had been chewed up by a group of Gurkhas on our side of the border. They were heading back to their camp when they came across our patrol.'

The SAS raids continued into 1966, by which time it had become apparent to the Indonesians that Britain would continue to support Malaysia and that the war would not be over quickly. The Indonesian military overthrew President Sukarno in March 1966 and hostilities ceased five months later. The victory was mainly due to the SAS, which had demonstrated what a small number of properly trained and motivated soldiers could do.

THE BATTLE OF MIRBAT

Of all the actions that the SAS has taken part in since its creation, the one that occurred at the small Omani port of Mirbat in July 1972 is perhaps the most famous. It remains an outstanding example of the martial skills of individual SAS soldiers.

What took place at Mirbat is a fine illustration of the weapons skills and overall calibre of SAS soldiers. In addition, it came at a crucial time in the war between the Sultan of Muscat and Oman and the forces of the communist People's Front for the Liberation of the Occupied Arabian Gulf (PFLOAG), and was probably the one event that eventually ensured that the British-backed Sultan achieved victory. But why were British soldiers fighting in Oman in the first place?

Oman as a country has very little going for it, being poor, barren and having an inhospitable climate. This has produced a population which is hardy and extremely poor, whose main support in their lives is an unshakeable belief in Islam. Typically ruled over by autocratic despots, the country resembles a medieval kingdom with twentieth-century trappings. Britain had signed a treaty of friendship with the

SAS troops and *firqat* in Oman during the war against the PFLOAG. Ex-communist guerrillas trained by the SAS, the *firqats* were hardy, if at times infuriating, fighters.

Sultan of Muscat in 1789, giving the East India Company commercial rights in exchange for the protection of the Royal Navy. The treaty was mutually beneficial: Oman was a sea-going nation that had interests in East Africa, Zanzibar, Socotra and Baluchistan, but its interests were threatened by the many pirates who infested the Gulf. The presence of the Royal Navy did much to make the seas a safe place for trade. By the twentieth century the pirates had disappeared, but the British were happy to maintain the ties that had been built up with the various rulers of Oman. And then came along a new factor: oil. Oman is situated on the southeast corner of the Arabian peninsula. This means that it is strategically vital as far as the West's oil supplies are concerned, as a hostile regime could technically halt those supplies.

In the late 1950s the British were called on to support the Sultan, Said bin Taimur, in his efforts to defeat the rebels in the north of his country. Fortunately, the British government had the SAS at its disposal, and two squadrons, supported by some conventional units, did the work of two battalions and defeated the rebels in the famous Jebel Akhdar operation. The country seemingly settled down. However, the policies of Said bin Taimur were repressive to say the least, and in the province of Dhofar, in the southwest of his country, they resulted in the people taking up arms against him in 1962. The Dhofaris formed the Dhofar Liberation Front (DLF), which had as its aims the modernisation of the province and the rather nebulous policy of 'Dhofar for the Dhofaris'. Essentially traditionalist and emphasising the Moslem religion, the DLF's fighters were poorly equipped and trained. In response, the sultan deployed around 1000 men of the Sultan's Armed Forces (SAF) to the area to contain the rebellion. Initially this worked, but to the west, in the Marxist People's Democratic Republic of Yemen (PDRY), storm clouds were gathering.

In the PDRY there was another group, the PFLOAG, which entered the war in Dhofar. The DLF was quickly subsumed into the larger,

more radical group, and soon the scales were tipped against the sultan's forces. In fact, the SAF didn't have the manpower or training to conduct an effective counter-insurgency war. By 1970 the communist PFLOAG, backed by both the Soviet Union and China, had control of the whole of the Jebel Dhofar. Said bin Taimur was staring defeat in the face and the PFLOAG

Right: Soldiers of the Sultan's Armed Forces (SAF). The SAF worked closely with the SAS in Oman.

sensed victory. However, as so often happens in war, events were to take a strange turn.

In July 1970 Said bin Taimur was deposed in a bloodless palace coup by his son, Qaboos, who immediately announced a general amnesty and plans for civil development in Oman. That same month, the first SAS detachments arrived in the country to support the new sultan. They were called British Army Training Teams (shortened to BAT Teams) so the British government, ever the pragmatists, could deny that any of their combat troops were present in Oman. The SAS set about implementing a 'hearts and minds' policy (see Chapter 2), which was aided by the new sultan's measures, and the situation stabilised. But victory was another matter. The SAS

received an unexpected boost in its efforts when a number of rebel fighters, alienated by the anti-moslem and hard-line communist ideology of the PFLOAG, surrendered to the Omani government. The leader of the men, Salim Mubarak, advocated turning his men into an anti-rebel group, called a *firqat*. The SAS began training Salim's men, and very soon the first of many *firqats*, the *Firqat Salahadin*, was formed.

By the end of 1971 the Omani government had made substantial gains in Dhofar, with a number of *firqat* groups up and running and the SAS 'hearts and minds' programme working well. The rebels, in response, decided that a victory was needed to persuade the people that their cause would eventually triumph. They decided to mount an attack against the coastal town of Mirbat, some 65km east of Salalah. The following account of the battle is told by a current member of the Regiment, using first-hand accounts told to him by SAS soldiers who fought in Oman in the early 1970s:

'Mirbat. What a god-forsaken place it is. A few mud-built houses clustered around the bay, with some strongpoints located to the north. It was July 1972, the monsoon season was under way and the whole team felt cheesed off. There were nine SAS soldiers in total, including the boss, Captain Mike Kealy. He was only 23 years old and was regarded as being "green". Although most guys in the Regiment have respect for their officers, Kealy was still called a "baby Rupert" by his men. Nevertheless, he was to prove shit-hot when it came to the crunch.

'For three months the SAS soldiers had been at Mirbat as the resident BAT Team, training the *firqats*, or "firqs" as they were called, in the use of infantry weapons. The enemy, the *adoo*, were always in the surrounding hills, but the SAS didn't bother about them too much. They would launch the odd artillery attack on Mirbat which usually fell well short, but apart from that it was pretty quiet. The soldiers had more trouble with the "firqs", who could be real pains in the arse if they

wanted to be. Once they got something into their heads that was it. They called the SAS soldiers "batmen" and believed they came from a special bat regiment, and nothing could alter their opinion.

'Anyway, the training went on and the days ticked by. The weather was miserable (it was the monsoon season): depressing drizzle always hanging over the town and a blanket of low cloud hiding the hills and mountains that surrounded the town.'

The fact that the SAS soldiers could not observe the surrounding hills was a disaster, for in those hills the rebels were assembling a large amount of firepower and men to ensure they would achieve victory. The balance sheet of the opposing forces made grim reading for the SAS men. The rebels numbered around 250 men, all of them seasoned fighters who believed in, and were prepared to die for, their cause. They were armed with a variety of weapons, including Kalashnikov automatic rifles, 75mm recoilless rifles, mortars and Carl Gustav rocket launchers. The SAS soldiers had no idea of what was about to hit them:

'For the most part the SAS men wore cut-down jungle hats, and some of the lads stitched a neck flap to the rear to avoid getting too much sun on the back of their necks, which can cause sunstroke and sickness. Light olive-green trousers and green fatigue shirts were supported by plain green windproof jackets to combat the cold nights. On their feet they wore soft pigskin boots, nicknamed "desert wellies". As always they never went anywhere without their "belt order", which included water, ammunition, survival and escape-and-evasion kits. For weapons they had the SLR and American M16 rifles, plus L42 sniper rifles.

'The men's tour had been uneventful and they were more than ready to be

Right: Have M16, will travel. A member of D Squadron, 22 SAS, in Oman, 1971. The casual appearance belies a trained medic and linguist.

relieved by the next team. The day of departure came through – 19 July – the same day the *adoo* intended to take the town. When people see pictures of the *adoo* they think they were a bunch of ill-armed bandits. Nothing could be further from the truth. Their attack on Mirbat, for example, was well planned. They knew the bad weather would prevent any air cover from the Omani Air Force based at nearby Salalah, and it would also stop any SAS reinforcements being flown in by helicopter. Like all guerrilla groups, the *adoo* had a pretty good intelligence network operating, and they knew when SAS teams were being rotated. The Omanis are notorious gossipers, and although the SAS men used the grapevine for their own use, there was nothing they could do to stop the reverse happening.'

The SAS team at Mirbat was not entirely alone. Other forces defending Mirbat included 30 *askars* (tribesmen) holding the Wali's Fort and 25 gendarmes occupying the Dhofar Gendarmerie Fort. These units were armed for the most part with aged bolt-action Lee-Enfield rifles, but worse was the fact that some of the *adoo* had allowed themselves to be spotted by the defenders, who had despatched a 60-strong *firqat* to investigate, further weakening the garrison. Among the heavier weapons possessed by the defenders was an old 25-pounder field gun in a sandbagged pit beside the Gendarmerie Fort, and an 81mm mortar in a sandbagged pit beside the Batthouse, the BAT Team's HQ. On the roof of the Batthouse was a GPMG and a 0.5in Browning heavy machine gun:

'Just before dawn on 19 July, the team's relief day, the day when they would be out of Mirbat for good, the *adoo* began their attack. It was just before 0530 hours, the time when they could make the maximum use of the uncertain light which, combined with the poor weather, meant it was almost

Right: SAS men unload a Beverley transport aircraft in Oman under the watchful eye of a comrade.

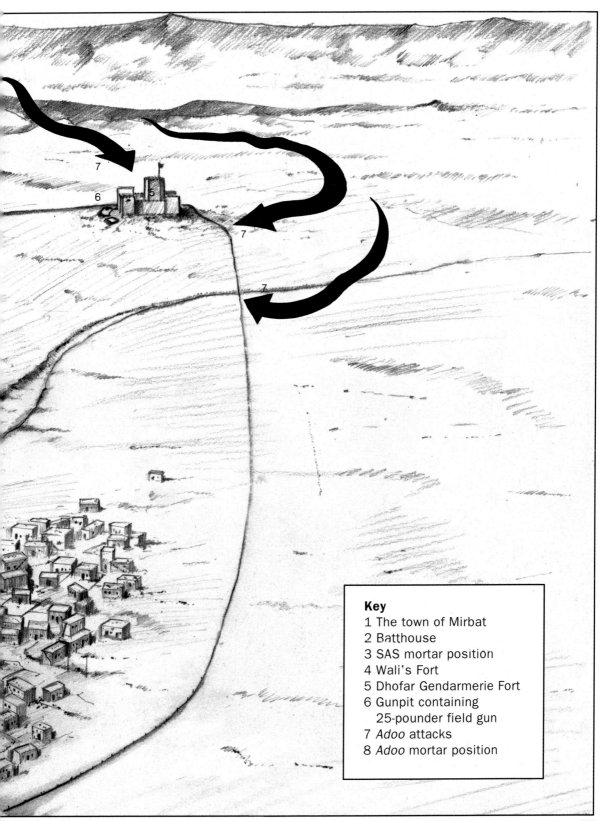

Key
1 The town of Mirbat
2 Batthouse
3 SAS mortar position
4 Wali's Fort
5 Dhofar Gendarmerie Fort
6 Gunpit containing
   25-pounder field gun
7 *Adoo* attacks
8 *Adoo* mortar position

Above: An SAS 81mm mortar, similar to the one used at Mirbat, pounds *adoo* positions in Oman.

impossible for the sentries to spot their stealthy advance.

'Some 1000m north of the perimeter wire which protected the team's area (a sort of barbed wire cattle fence), the *adoo* cut down eight Dhofar gendarmes who were patrolling on the Jebel Ali. Poor bastards never had a chance, they only had old Lee-Enfields and they wouldn't have even seen the enemy coming for them. The distinctive noise of AK-47s echoed across the valley, alerting the SAS men to the enemy's presence. At first they didn't realise the extent of the attack, but Kealy rushed to the roof of the Batthouse to see what was happening.

'The SAS soldiers scanned the scene. The Wali's Fort was near the shoreline of Mirbat Bay and contained the *askars*. To the northeast lay the Gendarmerie Fort, which held around 25 men, though they were only armed with Lee-Enfields. Suddenly the *adoo* appeared, ghost-like, out of the early morning haze: lines of men

armed with automatic rifles advancing steadily towards Mirbat. Moments later there was a deafening roar of gun and mortar fire as the *adoo* opened up. The battle had begun.

'The odds were not very good. On the roof were Captain Kealy, Corporal Pete Wignall, Trooper Tobin, Trooper Savesaki and Corporal Roger Chapman. They had two machine guns on the roof: a GPMG and a Browning .5in, and they were to play a crucial part in the battle. Beside the Batthouse, in a sandbagged pit, Lance-Corporal Harris manned the 81mm mortar. As soon as the fighting had started, Corporal Labalaba, a huge Fijian, had sprinted over to the 25-pounder beside the Dhofar Gendarmerie (DG) Fort to help the Omani gunner load the beast, as well as give the terrified man some moral support.

Above: An SAS Land Rover on the Jebel Dhofar. Because of mines, road travel was often difficult.

'Thump, thump. As the light began to improve the SAS men could make out well-spaced groups of guerrillas firing their rifles in a controlled manner. Hand-held RPG-7s were aimed and fired, their rockets slamming into the DG Fort. Then there was the sound of mortar bombs hitting the earth as the enemy gunners endeavoured to find their range. It soon became obvious that the *adoo* were directing their efforts against the DG Fort. They weren't stupid: if that fell they could systematically eliminate the BAT Team and their allies no matter where they tried to hide, as it overshadowed the town and everything else.

'By now the SAS had opened fire: the ripping sound of the GPMG, the deeper throb of the Browning, and the clatter of automatic rifles. The controlled fire from the Batthouse began to take affect: *adoo* fighters started to go down as they were hit by double taps and short machine-gun bursts, but still the enemy kept coming. All the SAS positions were under heavy fire now, and the forts were taking hits from rockets and mortar bombs. The lone SAS mortar was replying, and in the distance the 25-pounder was frantically firing into the ranks of the enemy.

'On the roof of the Batthouse, enemy rounds were whizzing through the air and slamming into the sandbags as the *adoo* pressed home their attack. The SAS soldiers were drenched in sweat as the adrenalin raced through their bodies. Each man's mind focused on his training: stay alert, search for a target, think, think, only fire controlled bursts. The machine guns were exacting a fearful toll on the *adoo*, but still the enemy kept coming.'

The situation was not good. The *adoo* were hitting the SAS with all their firepower: automatic weapons, medium and heavy machine guns, mortars, 75mm recoilless rifles and a Carl Gustav rocket launcher. Kealy must have realised that this was no probing attack, the numbers of guerrillas involved convinced him of that. At the radio Kealy informed provincial headquarters at Salalah what was going on. The Wali's Fort, DG Fort, Batthouse and Mirbat itself were now all under fire from the enemy. Kealy was in effect surrounded on three sides. Undeterred, the SAS soldiers and local levies were fighting back, but for how long?

'Kealy requested an air strike, but he knew that it was a forlorn hope because of the weather – the *adoo* had played their trump card and it was working. Rockets slammed into the DG Fort, sending masonry into the air and leaving gaping holes in its wall. Then its tower disappeared in a pall of smoke and dust. By this time the walls were riddled with hundreds of bullets. How much more could it take?

'Over the radio came the message that Laba had been hit. The 25-pounder had gone quiet. Laba had been hit in the chin, but with remarkable composure all he would say was, "enemy are getting a bit close". Savesaki volunteered to get some medical aid to his compatriot. Kealy agreed. Savesaki raced off towards the gunpit. Bullets whistled around him as he dodged and weaved his way forward. The SAS men covered him as best they could, but he was really in the lap of the gods. And then he had made it and dived into the gunpit to relieve Laba.

'Kealy called Salalah again to request casualty evacuation. Then sudden quiet descended over the battlefield as both sides drew breath. The fight had been raging for about an hour, and each side needed time to reorganise and bring up fresh ammunition. On the Batthouse roof empty cartridge cases and spare magazines littered the floor. The soldiers were

drained and grimy. But there was no time for lounging about. Fresh ammunition was brought up and prepared for the second round. The sound of sporadic gunfire echoed around them as they waited for the next *adoo* attack.'

In the gunpit Savesaki had fixed a shell dressing to Labalaba's face to stop the flow of blood. The Omani gunner had been shot and seriously

Right: Sultan Qaboos inspects SAS and *firqat* fortified positions on the Jebel Dhofar. After Mirbat the *adoo* were forced onto the defensive in Dhofar.

wounded, and the 25-pounder's gun shield had been riddled with bullets. But then Savesaki was hit himself in the shoulder and head, and he fell back against the sandbags that protected the position. He was still able to fire his weapon, however, and as he did so the wounded Labalaba continued to load the gun on his own.

Kealy couldn't get in contact with the gunpit or the DG Fort, and so he decided to go to the fort himself, taking only one other man, Trooper Tobin, with him. The requested helicopter then appeared out of the cloud, but as it tried to swoop in to land it was fired upon by the enemy and forced to retire. This signalled the renewal of the battle as the *adoo*, convinced that victory was within their grasp, made their final push. Reaching the gunpit, Kealy and Tobin relieved the wounded Fijians. From the 25-pounder's ammunition bunker Kealy sent a radio message to the Batthouse requesting an immediate air

strike. At that moment Labalaba was killed by a bullet and the rebels began to close in on the gunpit. Then Trooper Tobin was shot, and both the gunpit and DG Fort were being hammered by rockets and gunfire. Savesaki and Kealy calmly picked off enemy guerrillas, but then a grenade was lobbed into the pit and Kealy prepared to die. However, miraculously, it failed to go off. But Kealy still needed a miracle to save both him and his command. He got it:

'After Kealy and Tobin had reached the gunpit the *adoo* had attacked with even greater ferocity. Their dead littered the ground but still they kept coming. The SAS mortar was firing so quickly it appeared to be on automatic, and the barrels of the machine guns were getting hot. Then, from nowhere, two Omani Strikemaster jets appeared, streaking their way overhead and heading for the enemy.

being. The fact was that there were still loads of enemy guerrillas out there who would soon re-group and launch another attack. The SAS needed help, and quick.'

At Salalah there were 24 members of G Squadron, who were speedily loaded into helicopters and flown to Mirbat. A second attack by Strikemasters inflicted further casualties on the *adoo*, as the men from G Squadron, fresh and heavily armed with GPMGs, launched a ferocious attack on the enemy after they had been landed. The reinforcements were landed in two lifts, the first advancing inland and clearing enemy positions around the DG Fort, while the second group cleared areas near the shore.

By lunchtime the battle was over and the SAS had achieved a great victory. It had lost two men dead, Corporal Labalaba and Trooper Tobin, and two seriously wounded, but the cost to the enemy had been far greater: over 30 dead on the battlefield and many more dying of their wounds later.

Far more important than the physical losses, however, was the loss in prestige that the rebels had suffered as a result of Mirbat. They had lost many of their best men, and the fact that they had heavily outnumbered their opponents added insult to injury. Far from convincing the Dhofaris that the sultan and his British advisors were finished, the battle reinforced the credibility of Sultan Qaboos. The civil aid programme designed to improve the living standards of the Dhofaris was stepped up. There were more defections from the *adoo* and the SAS continued to take the war to the enemy. By 1974 the enemy was cleared from all the valleys in central Dhofar, and a year later the *adoo* were being pushed back to the Yemeni border. The Yemenis themselves, seeing that the PFLOAG was going to lose, began to withdraw their support. In September 1976, the SAS squadrons were withdrawn from Oman as the war had been won, but victory had been achieved not so much by force of arms; rather, the SAS's 'hearts and minds' policy had been the key to success.

They began to pour cannon fire into the *adoo*, cutting down some and sending others darting for cover. The enemy attack had been halted. Kealy radioed for Harris to hit targets near him, but they were so close that he had to haul the barrel up to his chest and grip the weapon with his legs before he could fire it.

'Then the aircraft were gone, but they had saved the day, at least for the time

PRINCES GATE

When a group of terrorists seized hostages at the Iranian Embassy in London in 1980, the SAS carried out a stunning rescue that confirmed it as a crack hostage-rescue unit.

The year 1972 was a turning point for Britain's SAS, although at the time neither the Regiment nor its political masters realised it. In West Germany the Munich Olympics were taking place. Security at the games was low-key, and it was thus relatively easy for a number of terrorists from the Palestinian group 'Black September' to take hostage and then murder 11 Israeli athletes. The outrage was all the more tragic because it was played out before the full glare of the world's media. For the West Germans the whole episode was a nightmare: once again Jews were being murdered on German soil. As a result of this disaster, the Federal Republic established what was to become one of the most expert counter-terrorist units in the world: GSG 9.

Many other Western governments, including the UK's, realised they were also very vulnerable to these types of terrorist outrages. Their capacity to respond effectively when a terrorist incident occurred on their soil was limited. Thus they too took the decision to establish dedicated counter-terrorist units. In 1973, a Counter Revolutionary Warfare Wing was established at Stirling Lines, the UK headquarters

The lull before the storm: 'Red Team' members photographed minutes before their assault on the Iranian Embassy. Note the sledgehammer carried by the man on the left.

Above: Stun grenades, similar to the type used by the SAS at the Iranian Embassy.

of 22 SAS – the Regiment had been given the responsibility of being Britain's hostage-rescue unit. This was not really surprising. After all, the Regiment had always had a wartime Counter Revolutionary Warfare (CRW) brief. As applied to the SAS, CRW operations involve infiltrating areas by sea, land or air; gathering intelligence about the location and movement of enemy guerrilla forces; ambushing and harassing insurgents; undertaking assassination and demolition operations; border surveillance; implementing a 'hearts and minds' policy; and training and liaising with friendly guerrilla forces. Now, hostage-rescue was added to the list.

At Hereford every member of the Regiment's Sabre Squadrons was, and is, put through a close quarter battle (CQB) course, and a special building, known as the 'Killing House', was constructed to refine hostage-rescue skills. A member of the Regiment describes the sort of drills currently carried out in the 'House':

'Inside the "Killing House" live ball ammunition is used all the time, though the walls have a special rubber coating which absorbs the impact of rounds as they hit. Before going into any hostage scene or other scenario, the team always goes through the potential risks they may face. The priority is always to eliminate the immediate threat. If you burst into a room and there are three terrorists – one with a knife, one holding a grenade and one pointing a machine gun – you always shoot the one with the gun, as he or she is the immediate threat.

'The aim is to double tap [two shots fired in quick succession] the target until he drops. Only head shots count – in a room that can sometimes be filled with smoke there is no room for mistakes. Hits to the arms, legs and body will be discounted, and constant drills are required to ensure shooting standards are high. If the front man of the team has a problem with his primary weapon, which is usually a Heckler & Koch MP5 submachine gun, he will hold it to his left, drop down on one knee and draw his handgun. The man behind him will then stand over him until the problem with the defective weapon has been rectified. Then the point man will tap his mate's weapon or shout "close", indicating that he is ready to continue with the assault. Two magazines are usually carried on the weapon, but magnetic clips are used as opposed to tape. Though most of the time only one mag is required, having two together is useful because the additional weight can stop the weapon pulling into the air when firing.

'The aim is to slowly polish your skills as a team so that everyone is trained up to the same level, thinking on the same wave length and aware of each other's actions. The "House" is full of corridors, small

Below: The Heckler & Koch MP5K submachine gun, as used by SAS hostage-rescue teams.

rooms and obstacles, and often the scenario demands that the rescue be carried out in darkness (a basic SOP on a live mission is for the power to be cut before the team goes into a building). The rooms are pretty barren, but they can be laid out to resemble the size and layout of a potential target, and the hostages will often be mixed in among the gunmen. Confidence in using live ammunition is developed by using "live" hostages, who are drawn from the teams (the men wear body armour but no helmets). They usually sit at a table or stand on a marked spot, waiting to be "rescued". The CQB range also includes electronically operated figures that can be controlled by the training staff. At a basic level, for example, three figures will have their backs to you as you enter the room. Suddenly, all three will turn and one will be armed. In that split second you must make the right assessment and target the correct "body" – if you don't you will "kill" a hostage and the gunman will "kill" you.

'A variety of situations can be developed by the instructors. For example, they may tell the team leaders to stand down minutes before a rescue drill starts, forcing the team members to go through on their own. Other "funnies" include smoke, gas, obstacles to separate team members from their colleagues, as well as loudspeakers to simulate crowd noises and shouting.

'New weapons and ammunition are continually being tested in the "House", and among the latest introductions is a new fragmentation round. It explodes on impact, so if a team has to storm a boat it will hit the bulkheads and burst without ricocheting, unlike ball rounds.

'Speed, fast reactions and slick drills are the key during CQB drills. Four-man assault groups are normally split into two teams of two, and each man is given specific areas inside each room to clear.'

By the late 1970s the SAS was fully trained in hostage-rescue tactics. As usual, the Regiment

had approached its new role with determination and thoroughness. Two of its men, Major Alastair Morrison and Sergeant Barry Davies, had taken part in the dramatic rescue of German hostages by GSG 9 at Mogadishu, Somalia, in 1977, and numerous cross-training exercises had been undertaken with the American Delta Force and France's GIGN. The Regiment felt confident that it could tackle a hostage-rescue scenario, but of course there was a nagging doubt about how the training would stand up in a real incident. There was only one way to tell if the SAS was fully prepared: if a hostage situation occurred somewhere in the United Kingdom. In May 1980, one did.

On the morning of 30 April 1980, six armed terrorists of the Democratic Revolutionary Front for the Liberation of Arabistan (a region of Iran not peopled by Iranians but by ethnic Arabs) burst into the Iranian Embassy at No 16 Princes Gate, London, and seized 22 hostages. The terrorists were armed with Skorpion submachine guns, Browning automatic handguns and Soviet-made grenades. The Iraqi-backed terrorists then issued their demands: the release of 92 Arabs being held in Iranian jails and a safe passage for themselves once this had been achieved. If the authorities didn't obey these demands, hostages would start dying.

As police negotiators began the tortuous task of calming the situation and wearing down the terrorists over the telephone, specialist units began to arrive at the scene to seal off the immediate area: D11 police marksmen, C13 anti-terrorist officers, the Special Patrol Group, and members of C7, Scotland Yard's Technical Support Branch. However, these were only supporting actors in the drama: the central players had yet to arrive.

A Special Projects Team was immediately despatched from Hereford (all Sabre Squadrons are rotated through counter-terrorist training at Stirling Lines, and at any one time there is a squadron, divided into Special Projects Teams, on 24-hour stand-by for anti-terrorist and hostage-rescue operations). Codenamed 'Red

Practising hostage-rescue drills: clearing rooms with handguns and submachine guns.

Team', it consisted of a captain and 24 troopers from B Squadron. Also at the scene was the commander of the Regiment, Lieutenant-Colonel Mike Rose, who implemented an 'immediate action plan'. When it became clear that a rescue attempt would not have to be mounted immediately, a 'deliberate assault plan' was formulated, which would be put into effect at the time and choosing of the SAS. 'Red Team' was continually put on alert for an assault due to the terrorists' threats against the hostages. However, though nerve-racking, they turned out to be false alarms. Reinforcements in the shape of 'Blue Team' (another 25 men) arrived during the afternoon of 2 May. Meanwhile, the negotiations went on.

As they were doing so, both SAS assault teams studied every scrap of intelligence that could be gathered concerning the building. Microphones were installed by MI5 in the walls and down the chimneys (see diagram No 1), allowing the police and the SAS to determine the whereabouts of the terrorists and the hostages. A full-scale model of the embassy was constructed by Army engineers at Regent's Park Barracks. At government level, Prime Minister Margaret Thatcher consulted with senior members of the Ministry of Defence, MI5, MI6 and the SAS. These meetings, known as the Cabinet Office Briefing Room (COBRA), came to the conclusion that caution and patience was the best policy. Nevertheless, time was running out.

The government's refusal to make concessions, combined with the non-appearance of the Arab mediators demanded by the terrorists, made the atmosphere inside the embassy tense. The leader of the terrorists, Awn Ali Mohammed, codenamed Salim, sounded edgy and volatile as he spoke to police negotiators on 5 May. By early evening things were going seriously wrong, and several shots were heard from inside the embassy. Then the dead body of the embassy's chief press officer, Abbas Lavasani, was dumped on the pavement outside the building. Sir David McNee, the Police Commissioner, telephoned COBRA and

Shotguns, such as this Remington 870 pump-action model, are used to blow off door hinges.

reported that he was handing over control to the SAS. At 1907 hours, Lieutenant-Colonel Rose formerly took control and implemented the rescue plan. Operation 'Nimrod', the codename for the SAS rescue, was under way.

The story of the assault on the embassy and the subsequent rescue of the hostages is told by the men who took part:

'When we had arrived at the start of the siege, we had been told to be ready to storm the building within 15 minutes. This would mean going in using firearms, stun grenades and CS gas and trying to reach the hostages before they were killed. At that stage we had no idea of the hostages' whereabouts. I looked at the embassy and thought of clearing 50 rooms one by one, while all the time looking out for the terrorists and their prisoners. Fucking nightmare.

'However, because the negotiators did their stuff, we were given a few days in which to prepare a more comprehensive plan, and we spent the time familiarising ourselves with every part of the building. The plan, like most good ones, was fairly simple: "Red Team" would enter and tackle the top half of the building, while "Blue Team" would clear the lower half of the embassy. We would also have the support of a multitude of snipers, which gave me, for one, a reassuring feeling.'

On the roof 'Red Team' waited like a coiled spring. The plan was for two teams of four men to abseil down to the second floor balcony at the back of the building, another group to assault the third floor, while more men would blow in the skylight on the fourth floor to enter the building that way. 'Blue Team' was tasked with clearing the basement, ground and first floors. 'Red Team' began the operation, but then almost wrecked it:

'We were on the roof waiting for the order to go. We had all made our last-minute checks – respirators, weapons, assault suits and stun grenades – and now we wanted to be off. The adrenalin rush was unbelievable. The word was given and we started to descend from the roof. I fed the rope through my descender as we moved quickly and silently down the side of the rear of the building. Then, disaster. The boss got snagged in his harness. Some of the lads tried to help him, but then one of them accidentally broke a window with his foot. Shit!

'All hell broke loose as orders were screamed over the command net to storm the building. Snipers started firing CS gas into the embassy. We couldn't get the boss free. Looking down I saw the lads from "Blue Team" using sledgehammers to break the glass and get in. The sound of gunfire filled the air as black-suited individuals started disappearing into the embassy. Jesus, what chaos!'

At the front of the building, on the first-floor balcony, a four-man SAS team placed a special frame charge against the windows. But before it could be detonated the men had to yell at one of the hostages, BBC man Sim Harris, to back away from the window inside the embassy. After a few seconds there was a terrific explosion as the frame charge was detonated:

'Then we were in. We threw in stun grenades and then quickly followed. There was a thundering bang and a blinding flash as the stun grenades went off. Designed to disorientate any hostiles who were in the room, they were a godsend. No one in here, good. I looked round, the stun grenades had set light to the curtains, not so good. No time to stop and put out the fire. Keep moving. We swept the room, then heard shouts coming from another office. We hurried towards the noise, and burst in to see one of the terrorists struggling with the copper who had been on duty when the embassy had been seized: PC Lock. One of the lads rushed forward

A brief glimpse of one of the terrorists at the front door of the embassy as he picks up some food.

Above: SAS soldiers on the roof of the embassy conduct their final checks before the assault.

and got Lock away, then pumped a long burst from his MP5 into the terrorist. The bullets hit his head and chest, sending his lifeless body sprawling against the wall. One down, five to go.

'Lock was bundled out and we continued our search. The building was filling with CS gas and smoke. We had to free the hostages and get out as quickly as possible. Where the fuck were they?'

Originally it was thought the hostages were being held in an office at the rear of the building, and 'Red Team' expected to find them there as the troopers smashed the glass and then hurled in stun grenades. But the rooms were empty. The SAS team leader was still caught up in his rope, and flames started to lick round his legs as the inflammable material inside the rooms was set alight by the grenades. Fortunately, one of

the second wave of abseilers cut him loose and he crashed down onto the balcony. One of the SAS soldiers smashed a window and hurled a stun grenade into a room containing a terrorist (see diagram No 2). The latter ran from the room, but the SAS man raised his MP5 and pulled the trigger. It jammed. The soldier then drew his handgun and chased after him. The terrorist ran to the telex room, where three of his companions had started firing on the hostages. The SAS soldiers had to act quickly:

'We heard the screams of the hostages coming from the telex room. "Shit, they're killing them all," I heard my mate shout. We raced into the room [see diagram No 3]. Fucking pandemonium.

There was a figure on the left with a grenade in his hand. One of the lads shot him with his Browning, a well-aimed shot to the head which killed him instantly and blew his brains all over the place. We ordered everyone onto the floor. The terrorists had mixed themselves in with the hostages, and the latter were now going out of their heads. The women were screaming as we started to bundle them out of the room. One terrorist was identified, pulled out of the line and made to lie on the floor. Then he moved suspiciously and was shot – can't take any

chances. His body was turned over; there was a Soviet hand grenade in his hand.

'Another terrorist was shot trying to make his way down the stairs with the hostages. Keep moving. We forced our way into other rooms and began clearing them. Shoot off the lock, kick in the door,

Above: As the assault went in, other SAS soldiers deployed around the embassy to provide fire support. The weapon on the left is a silenced MP5.

stun grenade, wait for the bang, then in and clear it. Empty. Keep going, and so it went on. By this time it was getting

Above: Chaos at the back of the building. A tangled SAS soldier is helped by his comrades as the embassy burns. But the attack goes on.

difficult to see, as the building was filling with smoke and the CS gas was working itself into every nook and cranny. I changed my magazine for a full one. Then we received the order across the command net – building clear, hostages safe. Time to leave. I was caked in sweat and my mouth was parched, but I felt elated because the operation had clearly been a success.'

The hostages and the one surviving terrorist were bound and secured on the embassy lawn until each one could be identified. Five of the terrorists had been killed inside the embassy: Salim on the first-floor balcony, two in the telex room, one in the hallway near the front door and one in an office at the back of the building. Only

one hostage had been killed by the terrorists in the assault, and another had been injured. For the Regiment it had been a vindication of all the years of training for hostage-rescue operations, but the aftermath was both good and bad for the SAS. One of those who took part, known as 'J', who now works with a personal protection firm in London, describes the result of the siege:

'Princes Gate was a turning point. It demonstrated to the powers that be what the Regiment could do and just what an asset the country had, but it also brought a problem we wished to avoid: the media spotlight. In addition, for the first few years after the siege Selection courses were packed with what seemed like every man in the British Army wanting to join the SAS. We just couldn't cope with the numbers who were applying, and so we had to introduce extra physicals on the

Above: It's all over. All those evacuated by the SAS were bound and checked on the embassy lawn. One of them turned out to be a terrorist.

first day just to get rid of the wasters. The same problem affected R Squadron, the reserve, and the sergeant in charge was overwhelmed with recruits.

'Another problem was that everyone wanted to be associated with the embassy siege. So now, many years later, there are loads of blokes going around saying they were at Princes Gate. The security industry attracts them like flies. At the last count I had interviewed some 700 blokes who took part at the Iranian Embassy!'

THE PEBBLE ISLAND RAID

The Argentinian aircraft stationed on Pebble Island during the Falklands War posed a potential threat to the British landings at San Carlos. The SAS was therefore sent in to deal with them – the scene was set for a classic raid.

During the Falklands War, the airstrip on Pebble Island was used by the Argentinians as a base for several of their ground-attack aircraft.

The island itself, a small stretch of land some 35km long, is a desolate, windswept place. At the time of the Falklands conflict it was home to only five families, who all happened to live near the airstrip. As the island is situated to the northwest of West Falkland, the Argentinian aircraft would pose a major threat to any British forces that were put ashore on East Falkland. They therefore had to be destroyed before the landings could take place. The Special Air Service was given this mission. The raid against the airstrip took place on the night of 14/15 May 1982, but beforehand intelligence had to be gathered. Timely and accurate intelligence is crucial to the success of any special forces mission, and the one against Pebble Island was no exception. The following account is from a member of D Squadron who took part in the action:

A wrecked Pucara ground-attack aircraft lies on Pebble Island airstrip after the SAS raid. The loss of the 11 aircraft was a grave material blow to the Argentinians.

'At our initial briefings we were told that Argie engineers had landed on Pebble Island and were preparing the airstrip as a maintenance base for their aircraft, which had been flown in from the mainland to support the garrison at Stanley. This was confirmed when an RAF Harrier pilot, returning to *Invincible* after a bombing raid, had observed a Pucara taking off from the airstrip. The Pucara is piss-poor in any air-to-air encounter so our Harrier pilots weren't too bothered about them, but in the ground-attack role it's another matter. Designed from the start as a counter-insurgency aircraft, the Pucara is armed with two 20mm cannon and four 7.62mm machine guns. In addition, it can carry an external payload of 1500kg, including bombs, napalm and rockets. Against lightly armed troops who have just conducted an amphibious landing a small number of Pucaras could inflict a great deal of damage, so they had to be taken out.

'On 10 May, eight of the blokes from the squadron's Boat Troop had gone ashore in kleppers [two-man canoes used by the Regiment and the Special Boat Squadron] to assess the level of enemy activity, while on board the carrier *Hermes* a plan to launch a strike against the airstrip was put into effect. Some of the lads, ever the pragmatists, suggested bombing it, but this was discounted for two reasons. First, the civilians lived too near the airstrip. Second, the Harriers wouldn't have enough time over the target area [the two carriers *Hermes* and *Invincible* were situated well out to sea before the landings to protect them from any airborne attack] to guarantee all the aircraft would be destroyed.'

With all the problems inherent in an air assault, the decision was therefore taken to use D Squadron in a classic hit-and-run raid. To the public imagination and the media, this is what the SAS is all about, but to the men who have to carry out the mission it is an operation that is fraught with dangers and pitfalls.

'People just don't realise what's involved with these types of missions, and that goes for some of the top brass too. I talked to the guys who did the recce after it was all over and they were well pissed off. They were dropped on a remote headland several kilometres from Pebble and had to paddle across the open sea before they could set up an OP [observation post] on the island. However, the high winds made the sea journey a nightmare; you just don't realise how windy it is in the Falklands, even the gorse bushes are bent double by the non-stop wind.

'Once they eventually got on to the island they had another problem: establishing a "hide". In the open terrain this was extremely difficult, as the ground provided very little cover either from the enemy or the elements. It looks a lot like Brecon, ie very few trees and loads of gorse bushes. Mind you, at least on Brecon you don't have that bastard wind, well, not all the time.'

The observation party had three main tasks: to confirm the presence and number of Argentinian aircraft on Pebble, to assess the strength of the enemy in and around the airstrip, and to work out routes into and out of the area for the raiding party. Once in place, the OP reported back to *Hermes*. The news was not good:

'Our shore-based team confirmed there were several Pucaras operating from the airstrip, but the number of Argentinian personnel on the ground was difficult for them to assess in the limited time available. In addition, the routes to and from the objective were reported to be like the rest of the Falklands: bare and easily monitored by the Argentinians. Fucking great!'

The temporary home for D Squadron during this time was the carrier *Hermes*. When the ship left Portsmouth on 5 April 1982, there was a small party of SAS soldiers on board, along with a company of Royal Marines and some Special

Boat Squadron (SBS) personnel. More SAS soldiers joined the vessel at Ascension Island. When in British service (she is now with the Indian Navy and called *Viraat*), *Hermes* was essentially an anti-submarine carrier, being kitted out with Sea King helicopters and a small number of V/STOL (Vertical/Short Take-Off and Landing) aircraft. In the Falklands conflict she could also have fulfilled another capacity: transporting the whole of 3 Commando to the war zone. In the event, it was decided that *Hermes* would carry the helicopters and Sea Harriers and not Royal Marines.

Life on board was cramped to say the least (the ship was the headquarters for Rear-Admiral John Woodward, the commander of the main group of surface warships during Operation 'Corporate'), but the SAS soldiers struck up a good rapport with the aircrews of 846 Naval Air Squadron, who had three Sea King helicopters with which to support special forces operations. These would be the aircraft that would transport the men to Pebble Island:

'The aircraft had no special equipment in those days, although the crews did have considerably more flying hours and experience than other pilots. A big bonus, which we were all pleased about, was the sudden issue of passive night vision goggles to Navy pilots. This piece of kit, in its most basic form, looks like a pair of hi-tech binoculars, but it enhances any night situation into a green image of daylight to assist the aircrew's view. Ironically, this treasured bit of equipment, which was already widely in use with the Americans, was issued to the Somerset-based Naval Air Squadron by the Royal Aircraft Establishment just days before they flew aboard *Hermes*, leaving very little time for training.'

With all the available intelligence gathered, the raid was scheduled for the night of 14/15 May. Originally, the SAS had been given the task of destroying the Argentinian aircraft, their ground crews and the island's garrison. However, because of strong headwinds *Hermes* took longer

Above: Two-man klepper canoes, the type used by the reconnaissance team from D Squadron's Boat Troop during the Pebble Island operation.

to reach the flying-off point than expected. This meant that the SAS soldiers would have only a short time on the ground to carry out their tasks. The aircraft thus became the priority target. The Sea Kings would have to be back on *Hermes* before daylight, as she and her escorts (the frigate *Broadsword* and the destroyer *Glamorgan*) had to be well east of the island to minimise the threat posed by the Argentinian Air Force. The source continues:

'As we prepared our equipment and attended the first flight briefing with the boss of 846 Naval Air Squadron, this guy appears, he was a stores officer I think, and told us that we would never get off the deck until the weather improved. He had a point. The wind had been blowing throughout the day, which prevented the helicopter blades being spread on the flightdeck (below deck they were stowed with their blades folded). However, late in the evening there was a "weather window" which allowed the helicopter handlers, or "chocheads" as they were known, due to their habit of crawling under the helicopters and placing wheel chocks on the aircraft, to prepare the three Sea Kings for the mission.'

The Sea Kings of 846 Squadron are optimised as assault transports and are designated Sea King HC MK 4. Designed to fly in all weathers, they are fitted with a complete avionics suite which includes doppler navigation radar, auto-pilot and an auto-hover system. The fuselage can hold up to 19 fully equipped troops, and the aircraft can also be fitted with machine guns, rockets and rocket pods if required.

As the helicopters were prepared for the mission, the 45 men of D Squadron who would carry out the attack were given a final briefing:

'At the int briefing we were told that there had been more confirmed sightings of enemy aircraft operating from the airstrip. Additional information collated from some Royal Marines who had served in the Falklands several years before the invasion revealed that the airstrip was less than 100m from the nearest house, and that the whole area was flat and open, confirming our own information from the lads in Boat Troop. This made us a bit nervous, because if we were bumped we would have bugger all cover from enemy fire.

'The raid was given the codename Operation "Prelim". The plan was to use two groups to provide fire support for the raiding party, while another would seal off the approaches to the airfield. An additional fire group would escort the raiding party to the airfield and wait in reserve to react to any Argentinian anti-ambush party that had been prepared as a result of their watching us. The raiding party, or killer group, would hit the aircraft and plant explosive charges on them, or would use LAWs if an enemy presence prevented the charges being placed.'

The LAW is the M72 Light Anti-tank Weapon, an American throw-away rocket launcher. It is useful for SAS-type operations because it is light, which means several can be carried by one man. It is also accurate and can penetrate armour up to 335mm thick (though the version used in the Falklands by the SAS was only effective against light armour). Because it fires a high explosive warhead, the M72 is potent against targets such as stationary aircraft.

The SAS also had heavier support in the shape of an 81mm mortar and naval gunfire support from HMS *Glamorgan*, an air-defence ship for *Hermes*. The mortar had gone ashore with Boat Troop, though the actual bombs were carried by the men of the raiding party, who dropped them at the base plate before moving to their starting positions. Also put ashore was a forward observation unit from 148 Battery, whose job was to give exact coordinates to *Glamorgan* and then observe and correct the shelling as it came in. Following the final briefing, the men were issued with their personal equipment:

'Every one of us carried M16s with three spare mags each and an additional 200 rounds of 5.56mm. We don't usually tape a spare magazine to the one already in the weapon. For one thing, you can change a mag for one in a pouch just as fast as two that are taped together. And anyway, when you're in the field crawling through all the shit to get to the objective, such as mud and water, it all gets into the mag taped to your weapon. When you change mags and insert the spare one, all the shit gets pushed into the receiver. You then get a jam just when you don't want one, ie in the middle of a firefight.

'The M16 is a good weapon for short-range work because it's short, light and has a high lethality close in. It's not so good for long-range work, though, and it certainly doesn't have the stopping power of the good old SLR [Self-Loading Rifle].

Right: The briefings are over, all that remains is the long journey to the target in the Sea Kings.

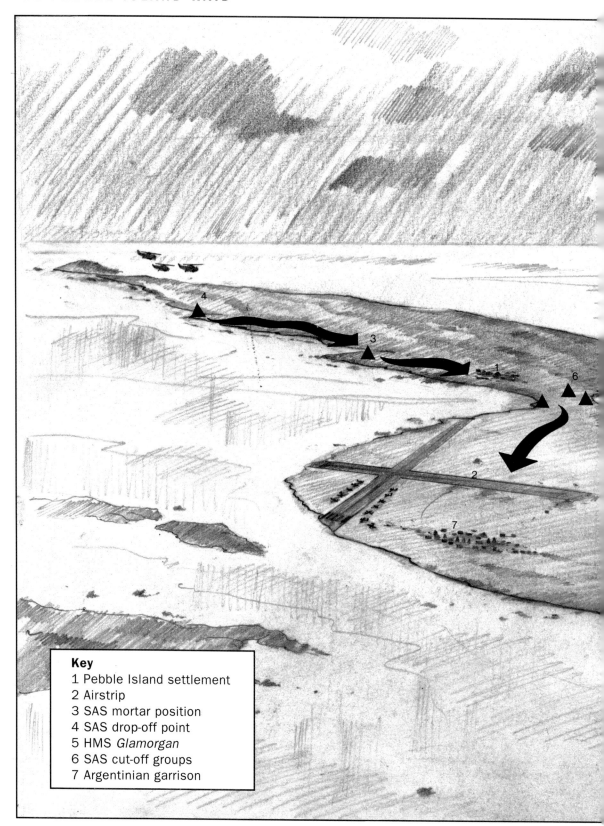

Key
1 Pebble Island settlement
2 Airstrip
3 SAS mortar position
4 SAS drop-off point
5 HMS *Glamorgan*
6 SAS cut-off groups
7 Argentinian garrison

Still, the weight saving over the SLR is worth it, and that goes for the ammo too, and anyway, for the raid we only needed a weapon for close work. We all took great care of our M16s as the weapon doesn't really like rough handling, which can be a bit of problem, especially in terrain like the Falklands where it's continually damp and windy. The Americans first touted the M16 as a self-cleaning weapon, and didn't even bother to issue cleaning kits. Naturally, there were a host of jammed guns when it entered service. They then issued cleaning kits very quickly, but not before several of their guys had been killed because of jams.

'Some of the weapons were fitted with M203 grenade launchers firing high explosive grenades. People get excited about grenade launchers but I don't see the point a lot of the time. OK, you've got a weapon that can throw a grenade over a distance of around 300m, which is a greater distance than a man can throw (even in the Regiment!), but the grenade only goes in a straight line. It can't go around cover, unlike a hand-thrown grenade. In addition, and this is something a lot of people don't realise, two-thirds of actual grenade tends to be the fuse, which means you don't get as big a bang as you expect. Add to this the M203's general inaccuracy, and you get the general idea. Still, for hitting a stationary aircraft at short range they are effective enough, and that's why we took them.'

Webbing and clothing are also important on special forces operations, and this was no different for the Pebble Island mission:

'The contents of our webbing is always a high priority. In addition to carrying rifle magazines and grenades, Falklands webbing included a survival pack, water bottles, a bivvy bag [a Goretex sleeping bag cover] and food. Each one of us customised our webbing according to taste. For example, a lot of the lads carried two '44 pattern water bottles with metal mugs, which are ideal for making a brew and

saving space. Waterproof matches are always a priority and are usually carried in small plastic containers, which are themselves waterproof. Each man will also have his own medical kit, though one person in the section will always carry a specialist medical bag. Syrettes of morphine are always carried around the neck for easy access, and two field dressings are usually taped to the webbing.

'Woolly hats are always worn, as a lot of body heat can be lost if the head isn't covered. In any environment, but especially the Falklands, you have to guard against hypothermia. We all wore climbing gloves, with the fingers cut out to make handling things easier, as a reserve. We all had white phosphorus grenades, with a good old nine milly pistol tucked under the arm in a holster. To stop us freezing our bollocks off we wore either green Goretex jackets or windproof arctic smocks, a lot of the blokes choosing the latter because they have huge pockets which can hold little extras, such as food.'

Though protection against the cold is very important, the Pebble Island raiders weren't over dressed. They still had to perform their task, and they were carrying a lot of equipment. If they were wearing too many clothes they would sweat heavily. This isn't a problem if you are moving, but if you stop then the sweat will cool, resulting in loss of body heat.

'We wore DPM [Disruptive Pattern Material] lightweight trousers. They are thin but they dry out very quickly after getting wet. Norwegian Army shirts have been a favourite with the Regiment for many years, and I wore one with a headover: a woollen tube that slips over your head and can be worn around the neck depending on the weather.

'Against the bitter wind a Norwegian Army shirt and a smock doesn't feel that warm, but as soon as you start to tab the body heats up and you're not so cold. Any spare clothing is stashed in the bergen. It's

Above: A Sea King helicopter, as used by the SAS.

always better to wear fewer clothes when moving and to save warm, dry clothes for an emergency. Our bergens also contained binoculars, a tripod-mounted scope and night sights, the latter being a variant of the Individual Weapon Sight used in Northern Ireland. We each carried enough rations to last us three days, just in case we were trapped by the weather. Another very popular item of clothing was a set of quilted green trousers, which were ideal for zipping over your lightweights when lying up in a "hide" during the day.'

As *Hermes*, *Broadsword* and *Glamorgan* sailed towards the island, the men readied their equipment. Buffeted by heavy seas, the three ships made slow progress. *Broadsword*'s Sea Wolf short-range surface-to-air missile system became defective and she began to slip behind. *Glamorgan* sailed to within 10km of the shore to give gunfire support and to be on hand should the helicopters have to ditch. The carrier sailed to within 60km of the island, much closer than

was originally planned, to give the Sea Kings a shorter flight in the strong winds. As the hour approached for them to board the aircraft, the SAS men completed their last-minute checks:

'At around 2200 hours we made our way to the hangar. It was a hive of activity, as an army of engineers carried out maintenance on the tightly packed Harriers and Sea Kings to ensure there were enough aircraft for round-the-clock missions. We settled in a corner near the lift well, the huge mechanical ramp, with all our gear. A Navy mechanic asked me if I wanted a "wet", the maritime slang for a cup of tea, and I readily accepted his offer. Some of the lads drank, others smoked. It's funny, none of us discussed the job we were about to do, or the fact that some of us might not be coming back. We talked about home, football, the weather, our rations, anything but the mission.

'We made our way to the flightdeck. The Sea Kings were revved up, their blades spinning, as their aircrews went through their final checks. We sat crouched near the first aircraft, the South Atlantic wind combining with the draught from the rotors to lash us. My eyes narrowed to slits as I tried to stop thinking about the cold. If only the wind would fuck off! *Hermes* pitched and rolled in the heavy seas, her 28,000 tons battling with the ocean. Just as I thought I would be frozen to the deck, salvation. A "chochead" called forward the first stick. I heard someone shout "Thank Christ for that" as we rushed forward and entered the Sea King.

'Now the textbook says that the Sea King has a voluminous fuselage, and so it does if the team is wearing just T-shirts and shorts. But here we were, tooled up for the raid with bergens, webbing and weapons, which meant there was fuck all room for any of us. Thank Christ we didn't have any GPMGs or Milans. I wedged myself in a corner and waited for what seemed like an eternity before we lifted off. Then I began to sweat, shit!

'The noise inside the fuselage was deafening as the helicopter flew low over the pitching ocean towards land, skimming the waves to avoid detection by enemy radar. We didn't know if they had any on Pebble Island, but better to be safe than sorry. It wasn't long before we touched down on the island, and once we did we moved like fuck to reach the objective. We couldn't afford to waste any time, the old rust bucket *Hermes* wouldn't be hanging around, and anyway our colleagues already on the ground had established safe routes for us.'

The movement to the objective turned out to be uneventful. The Argentinian garrison on the island maintained a poor state of vigilance, which is surprising considering that they must have known that the aircraft would be a target. Nevertheless, the SAS soldiers were in a heightened state of alert as they advanced:

'I'll never forget the amount of sheep on Pebble. In Ulster, sheep and cattle are a major problem when moving about in the early hours. If you disturb them they will run wild, which will alert the locals to your activity. So here we were, moving towards the target with thousands of sheep all around us. Fortunately the guys from Boat Troop knew exactly where we could tab fast and where to move with caution. I had this vision of the Argies bumping us and a fucking great big fire-fight erupting with all these sheep being caught in the middle and blown to pieces.

'The mortar rounds we were carrying were dropped off at the base plate, and within an hour of being landed the cut-off group peeled away to take up position and secure the two routes heading towards the airstrip. By this time the cold was beginning to get to everyone. That's the one thing about the high command, they always find the most inhospitable places for us to fight a war in! I remember thinking how it was like being on top of Pen-y-Fan in winter, only in Brecon it is possible to move off the mountain and take shelter from the wind.'

There were six Pucaras on the airstrip, along with four Turbo-Mentor light aircraft and a Skyvan transport. There were a total of 12 Argentinian Pucaras in the Falklands, and if the SAS could destroy half of them it would be a big bonus for the Task Force. Both sides expected the Pucaras to take a heavy toll of the British after they had landed. However, the soldiers of the SAS had other ideas:

'The terrain was open and bare, just as we had been told. We approached the airstrip. I could see a large house to my left, which had a line of wind-battered trees to one side. I also made out some outbuildings and what appeared to be a windbreak for the house's garden. The area was riddled with fences and gates which were clearly part of a scheme to herd sheep into the pens around the house.

'I waited with the cut-off group before joining the killer group. Mountain Troop went forward, but then we spotted an enemy sentry and everyone froze. My heart started pounding and I tightened the grip on my M16. Instinctively, I slipped off the safety catch. We thought we had been spotted, but our luck was in, he didn't see us. We crept onto the airfield and laid charges on seven of the aircraft. Moments later the place erupted as we opened up with our small arms and LAWs. Using three-round bursts, I emptied a magazine into a Pucara, the bullets ripping into the nose and cockpit, sending shards of perspex into the air. Overhead para-flares from *Glamorgan* lit up the night sky. Where the fuck were the Argies?

'To my left a 66mm rocket slammed into the side of another Pucara, engulfing it in a fireball. The crackle of small-arms fire filled the air as the explosive charges started to detonate. I clipped a fresh mag into my M16 and looked around for fresh targets. By this time all the aircraft were either burning or had been riddled with bullets, their undercarriages shot away and their fuselages full of holes. In the background I heard the crump of artillery shells exploding as *Glamorgan* fired high explosive rounds into the enemy's ammunition dump and fuel stores. The opposition was nowhere to be seen. This is too good to be true, I thought.

'The forward observers had done a champion job. Now they were directing the gunfire to cover our retreat. We did a quick check on the aircraft, trying to identify them all and making sure they were disabled. When you're on a raid you don't fuck around. Time is precious. If you've achieved the element of surprise things go your way for a while. But in fact you're very vulnerable, and for all you know there might be an enemy battalion behind the nearest hill waiting to fall on you like a ton of shit.

'Then the raiding party and the cut-off team re-grouped and prepared to move

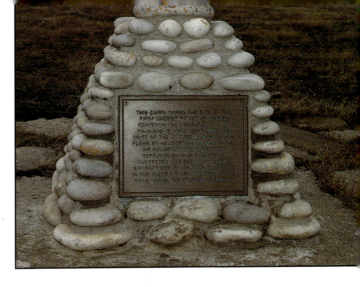

Above: The cairn commemorating the raid.

out. Just before we did, we received enemy small-arms fire. One of our boys went down. Instinctively we returned a hail of fire, each man firing controlled bursts from his weapon. Those that had M203s fired grenades at the Argies. It did the trick because we received no more hostile fire. We continued to fall back, more quickly now lest the enemy were re-grouping for another go. The wounded man was grabbed and hauled along (we never leave our wounded behind, it's an unwritten law in the Regiment).

'We bugged out at speed, reaching the landing site to await our lift back to *Hermes*. Bang on time the choppers came in, and a happy D Squadron was lifted out. I for one had expected a heavy firefight when we got to the airfield, but it never materialised. We could have hit the garrison if we had had more time, but as it was we all felt pleased with ourselves.'

The raid had been a total success. For the loss of only one man wounded, the SAS had destroyed six Pucaras, four Turbo-Mentors and a Skyvan. In addition, a large amount of Argentinian ammunition had been destroyed and the commander of the garrison had been killed. Far more important, though, was the fact that there were no Argentinian aircraft on Pebble Island to interfere with the landings at San Carlos Water, and the enemy's morale had been dented.

FALKLANDS: BEHIND THE LINES

Lying in 'hides' under the eyes of the enemy for weeks at a time, acting as a spearhead for conventional units, and shooting up enemy units – the men of the Regiment tell of their part in the Falklands War.

The British Falkland Islands are not a good place to fight. Logistically, for example, they are a nightmare, situated as they are some 13,000km from Great Britain. Thus when Argentinian forces invaded the islands in April 1982, the British Ministry of Defence was faced with organising a task force that would have to conduct an amphibious operation thousands of kilometres from home without the support of big carriers and a large surface fleet. In addition, there were no contingency plans. Military thinking at the time was dominated by potential confrontations that might take place on the central European plain between the forces of NATO and the Warsaw Pact.

A picture that amply conveys the type of terrain and weather conditions encountered by the SAS in the Falklands: cold and wet. Warm clothing, as worn by this team, is therefore essential.

There is also the climate of the islands to consider: they are for the most part cool, damp and windy, with a terrain that consists of treeless moorland and rocky hills; like Dartmoor, only worse. For special forces units such as the SAS, the geography of the area is a nightmare. Nevertheless, as soon as he heard about the Argentinian landings, Lieutenant-Colonel Mike Rose, the CO of 22 SAS, offered the Regiment's services to Brigadier Julian Thompson, the commander of 3 Commando Brigade, which would be the spearhead of any British offensive action to retake the islands. Rose had full confidence in his men's abilities, terrain notwithstanding, and in fact the Special Air Service was ideally suited to operate in the

Falklands because of its long experience against the IRA in Northern Ireland, as a member of the Regiment states:

'Our experience in the "bandit country" of South Armagh, Northern Ireland, served us well in the Falklands. However, there was one major difference: whereas the role of intelligence gathering was similar to that carried out around Crossmaglen and Forkhill, the terrain offered little concealment from enemy observation. Our "hides" were in reality scrapes dug into the peat and covered over. They were, needles to say, fucking miserable.'

The first operation the Regiment was involved in did not occur on the Falkland Islands themselves. Operation 'Paraquet' was the codename for the retaking of the island of South Georgia, which is located some 1400km southeast of the Falklands. This is even more inhospitable, with arctic weather conditions and a completely mountainous terrain covered by glaciers. The British government had decided that taking the island would be an excellent way of demonstrating to the Argentinians that Britain would use force to regain all her occupied possessions. This was excellent on paper, but to the men who had to carry out the plan it nearly turned into a major disaster.

The small task force earmarked to take South Georgia comprised the destroyer *Antrim*, the frigate *Plymouth*, the ice patrol ship *Endurance* and the tanker *Tidespring*. Designated Task Force 319.9, the flotilla was led by *Antrim*'s commander, Captain B C Young. At Ascension Island the group was joined by the fleet auxiliary *Fort Austin*, which was carrying D Squadron, 22 SAS (the men themselves had been earlier flown to the island). Other forces included Special Boat Squadron (SBS) personnel and M Company, 42 Commando, Royal Marines.

An operations room was established in *Antrim* which quickly became the focus for a number of hot debates concerning the best way of retaking South Georgia. Major Cedric Delves, the commander of D Squadron, was particularly keen for his men to have the first crack. Some of his proposals underestimated the ferocity of the weather conditions on South Georgia, but eventually it was agreed that the squadron's Mountain Troop would be landed by

Left: A wrecked Wessex helicopter on Fortuna Glacier. The SAS's first operation in the South Atlantic, on South Georgia, was nearly a disaster.

helicopter on Fortuna Glacier and then move on foot to establish a number of OPs around the main Argentinian positions at Leith and Grytviken. On 21 April the men were landed on the glacier by Wessex helicopter.

However, it soon became apparent to the troop commander, Captain John Hamilton, that the mission would have to be abandoned. His men had made only slow progress before they had been forced to stop and camp for the night. They spent a thoroughly uncomfortable night on the glacier: the wind continually blew and the snow lashed their bodies and equipment (ice got into the feed trays of the GPMGs which made them inoperable). The next day three Wessex helicopters (one from *Antrim*, two from *Tidespring*) flew up the glacier to extract the men. However, one hit a 'whiteout' (where visibility is suddenly reduced to zero by the weather) and crashed. Fortunately the crew escaped serious injury, but this meant there were only two aircraft to extract the team. They landed and picked up the SAS soldiers and the aircrew, but as they took off one also encountered severe weather and crashed.

Despite this ill luck, all the men were eventually lifted off the glacier by the surviving helicopter, the one flown by Lieutenant-Commander Ian Stanley. His bravery and tenacity won him the Distinguished Service Order and averted a major disaster which would have been a grave blow to the morale of the Task Force and the British government.

Delves, however, was undeterred, and decided that the seaborne approach would stand a better chance of success. Therefore, on 23 April the squadron's Boat Troop, using Gemini inflatables, tried to establish positions on Grass Island. However, the bad luck continued: two of the craft broke down and were swept away by heavy winds (though the crews of both were later saved). All thoughts of taking the island were temporarily put aside as news reached the British flotilla that an enemy submarine was nearing their position. The ships scattered, bringing to an end the SAS's so far unsuccessful attempt to recapture South Georgia.

On 25 April, *Antrim*, *Plymouth* and the frigate *Brilliant* (which had reached the area the day before) combined for a daring attack on Grytviken. Three troops were assembled for a heliborne assault on the settlement: one of Royal Marines, one of SBS men and another made up of SAS troopers. While *Antrim* and *Plymouth* pounded the shore (though they were under strict orders from London not to damage any of the buildings), the men were put ashore and moved forward towards the enemy. The latter was totally bemused by the sequence of events. The Argentinians were called upon to surrender, and while they deliberated *Antrim* was brought into the bay with orders to level the buildings if the enemy decided to fight it out. However, this was unnecessary: the Argentinians quickly raised a white flag and surrendered. The British soldiers who had been landed had won a victory without firing a shot. The men of D Squadron did not forget the contribution of the Royal Navy during Operation 'Paraquet':

'We were really pleased to have naval gunfire support when we were ashore, and when we returned to *Plymouth* to pick up some extra gear, we couldn't thank the crew enough for their help. They were the difference between strolling into Grytviken and having to fight our way in.'

The retaking of the Falklands themselves would not be so bloodless, but it gave the Regiment more opportunities to display its wide range of skills. Before any British landing could take place, the size, dispositions and morale of all the enemy garrisons had to be ascertained. This would mean inserting small teams of men onto the islands to watch the movements of the Argentinians. The first to go ashore were the men of G Squadron:

'We had been initially flown out to Ascension Island, and we soon got down to enjoying the sunshine and the beer. I think the high command must have been a bit worried that we were going soft because after no time at all we were heading south to the war zone. We travelled down to the Falklands in the

Above: HMS *Hermes*. Her Sea King helicopters supported many SAS operations in the Falklands.

fleet auxiliary *Resource*. As she wasn't a warship her crew enjoyed rather less cramped conditions than their Royal Naval counterparts, and we certainly appreciated our "spacious" surroundings.

'During the journey there was quite a debate about how we were going to be inserted onto the Falklands. Then this really harebrained scheme comes up whereby the whole squadron would make a HALO [high altitude, low opening] jump onto the southern tip of West Falkland from a Hercules transport. Stunned silence – we couldn't fucking believe it. OK we had steerable 'chutes, but in the South Atlantic wind there is no way you can make an accurate drop onto a relatively small bit of land after leaving an aircraft at an altitude of 10,000m. The whole squadron would have been scattered all over the South Atlantic!

'Anyway, common sense prevailed and this idea was shelved. Instead, it was decided to insert both SAS and SBS teams by Sea King helicopters flown from the carrier *Hermes*. The Sea Kings were operated by air crews from 846 Squadron, who turned out to be fucking good blokes.'

As ever with SAS operations, the men were loaded down with equipment and weapons:

'Our bergens were packed to the brim with everything from waterproofs to quilted over-trousers, rations, communications equipment and ammunition. Everyone carried a LAW [the US-made 66mm Light Anti-tank Weapon], they were flavour of the month,

being light but packing a powerful punch, and once you'd used it you could throw it away. Other kit included mini-torches, a change of clothing, gloves, woolly hat, sleeping bag and a bivi-bag which completely protected your "slug" (sleeping bag) from rain and sleet.

'As ever our belts never left our sides. They contained our emergency rations, water and personal medical pack, which

contained everything from "anti-shit" tablets, which controlled severe diarrhoea, to strong pain killers that would numb anything from a mild tooth ache to a flesh wound.

Above: Typical terrain near the capital Stanley. One SAS team, led by Captain Aldwin Wight, established a 'hide' overlooking the town and was responsible for reporting a night dispersal site for enemy helicopters, which was then bombed.

'We had a briefing that lasted three hours, during which time we were informed of the weather conditions, our drop-off point and the known dispersions of enemy forces. Afterwards we carried out our final checks and then ordered our evening meal. The crew of *Resource* did us proud and we ate like kings.'

One of Rear-Admiral John Woodward's primary tasks was to 'soften up' Argentinian positions on the islands through aerial attack,

'The insertion was to be carried out under the overall direction of the carrier *Hermes*. We were the first wave and would be landed on East Falkland under the cover of darkness (fortunately the pilots had night vision goggles to aid their approach). I remember the helicopter crewman looking at me with a look of total disbelief on his face as we loaded the bergens, he thought they were too heavy to lift, let alone carry across the island.

'Our hands and faces were heavily cammed up as we sped across the water in the Sea King towards our drop-off point. Inside the fuselage it was totally dark, apart from the reflection of the navigation lights on the pilots' control panel. The plan was for us to leave the aircraft as quickly as possible when it touched down, both to give us more chance of remaining undetected and to make the helicopter's journey back safer. The one thing you don't do when you're in "bandit country" is fuck around. To this end the bergens had been stashed in such a way that they could be pulled out by the last two who left the aircraft.

'Then we were over land and the signal was given to prepare for landing. The helicopter touched down and we were out into the cold night. We moved like lightning and the gear was off in no time. The crewman patted my arm and I saw him give me the thumbs up to wish me good luck, then he and the aircraft were gone. Then we were off, heading at speed away from the landing site (LS) in case the Argies had a fix on us and sprung an ambush. The rain started to lash down as we began our journey. We must have looked like a bunch of trolls, what with our heavy bergens, windproof smocks, webbing and waterproof gaiters to keep the wet off our ankles. After a while we made a quick stop to check our position before moving off again.

shore bombardment and reconnaissance of possible landing sites. He achieved the latter by using both the SAS and SBS, whose missions began in early May. The member of G Squadron continues with his description of the very first Special Air Service operation:

'During the march my mate whispered "what a god-forsaken hole this is". He was right. As the wind and rain buffeted us with an unending fury, my thoughts began to turn to Dartmoor and all the marches I had carried out across its miserable landscape. Yes, it was a lot like Dartmoor, except that the wind was stronger. My thoughts snapped back to the task in hand. We had four hours to reach the objective, which was 25km away. After two hours of marching we stopped and found a lying up position (LUP). We couldn't go any further because dawn was approaching

and we risked being caught if we didn't go to ground. So we had to waste a day lying around doing nothing.

'The next night we set off again and quickly reached our target area and established a LUP and a forward OP, which was manned by two men during the day, while the other two would man the main "hide", ready to give covering fire if the OP was compromised. It was bloody freezing all the time, but especially at night, and the ground was so wet that it managed to soak everything through. As a result, it was impossible to be comfortable and so the whole time was spent operating in an unending gloom.'

There were many SAS observation missions conducted during the Falklands War, but a few will suffice to illustrate the kind of work carried out. One four-man patrol was led by G Squadron's Captain Aldwin Wight. His team was landed on East Falkland at the end of April and tasked with observing enemy movements in and around Stanley. He and his men established a covert 'hide' on Beaver Ridge overlooking Stanley and began their reports on Argentinian activity. They observed that the enemy had a night dispersal area for their helicopters which was located between Mount Kent and Mount Estancia. This intelligence was relayed back to the fleet, which despatched two Harrier aircraft to find and destroy it. The attack resulted in three enemy helicopters being destroyed. Wight and his men endured their conditions for 26 days before being relieved on 25 May.

Another OP was established in a wooden hulk in Darwin harbour, which was damp to say the least. Such daring could not always go unnoticed. One SAS 'hide' near Port Howard, West Falkland, was discovered by a party of Argentinians on 10 June. The men inside, Captain Hamilton, D Squadron, and his signaller, were quickly surrounded by enemy soldiers and called upon to surrender. Disdaining to do so, they decided to fight their way out. In the firefight that followed Hamilton was killed trying to cover the escape of his comrade, who was unfortunately captured shortly after. For his bravery Hamilton was awarded a posthumous Military Cross.

Life inside a 'hide' was invariably grim, and it is a testament to the mental fortitude of

Left: Captured Argentinians. The enemy proved incapable of stopping clandestine SAS operations.

individual SAS soldiers that they could endure such conditions for so long. In addition, the sheer monotony of each day was a great challenge to staying sharp. The soldier from G Squadron describes the daily routine involved in manning an OP:

'If we had a chance for re-supply one of the first things we would request would be thick plastic to line the shallow "hides" we dug. Anything to keep out the bloody wet. A four-man team would always establish a forward OP and an LUP some distance

Left: A Wessex helicopter near San Carlos. After the British landings the SAS operated as a spearhead to support conventional units.

forward OP. The procedure in each team was the same: one man would get his head down while the other kept watch. There would be no movement or talking during the day. At night we would walk to the rear of the position and carefully cut a hole in the peat bog using a foldaway US-issue shovel – this was our latrine.

'It was impossible to cook during the day because the smell might alert a passing Argentinian, if one strayed that close, and so we only had a brew at first light. We would fish out a couple of tins of bacon burgers, or whatever came to hand, and put them in the water we were heating. When they were heated up we took them out and had the food, leaving plenty of water for a brew of tea or coffee.

'The weather was fucking awful, it was either raining, drizzling or blowing a gale, or a combination of all three. It was a real problem getting and staying warm. The wet was the real killer for me, I don't like being wet. We couldn't carry enough food to keep warm. During observation at night I would break open a bar of chocolate and eat it. It was like someone turning on the central heating, then, the next instant, you would be cold again. Bit like pissing yourself, really.

'Our first position was near Darwin, East Falkland, and the forward OP was situated near the edge of an inlet. Little happened at first, but after a few days had passed we logged enemy helicopters buzzing the ground immediately to our front. We stayed there 10 days before we received our first re-supply and fresh orders. The targets were really tasty, and it would have been very easy to take a pot at them, but our role was to sit and watch and that's what we did. Later it emerged that the aircraft we had reported were bringing in troops from Stanley to garrison the Goose Green settlement.'

behind. The LUP was nearly always situated on higher ground. This allowed it to give fire support to the forward OP if the latter was compromised and its occupants forced to bug out. There were always two men in the LUP and two in the

Something that comes across when talking to SAS men about their ops in the Falklands concerns the back-breaking loads they carried:

'In the Falklands it was a question of guys carrying vast amounts of everything. But they're was never enough room in your bergen or in your webbing and so there had to be a compromise. No one carried enough food, in the sense of keeping you well-fed, so a lot of the guys smoked because cigarettes dulled the appetite and were lighter to carry than rations.

'As far as weapons were concerned, it all depended on the task in hand. I remember one short-term job which involved observing the enemy where there was a patrol mix of M16, SLR, Colt Commando and GPMG. Each one of us also had a 9mm Browning High Power and as many Claymore mines and LAWs as could be carried. Each of us ended up humping around some 60kg of kit in total, which is bloody torture. I was carrying three types of ammunition: 9mm for the pistol, 5.56mm for my M16 (I had six fully loaded mags on me plus the one in the weapon) and around 1000 7.62mm rounds for the GPMG. In addition to clothing, rations and ammunition, every patrol also had to carry a radio and spare batteries.

'The ironic thing about the ammo is that we rarely used it, and we prayed that we wouldn't have to. The last thing we wanted was the Argies to spot us. All we wanted to do was go out, do our observing and then come back unscathed. In reality, if you had to fight your way out of a situation it meant you had let the opposition know you were there, which meant on an intelligence-gathering job you had badly fucked up. Having said that, in the back of your mind it was always satisfying to know that if you were compromised, you had enough firepower to give the enemy hell for up to three quarters of an hour.'

Despite the fact that there were some 11,000 enemy soldiers on the islands and 42 hostile aircraft and helicopters, both the SAS and SBS were able to insert teams onto the islands with impunity. Ironically, the most casualties inflicted on the Regiment during the conflict occurred during a cross-decking exercise from *Hermes* to the assault ship *Intrepid*. As the light started to fade on 19 May, one last journey was undertaken by the Sea King helicopter code-named 'Victor Tango'. Crammed into her fuselage were men from both G and D Squadrons. As the helicopter made one last circuit round *Intrepid* while its flight deck was cleared of another aircraft, something – probably a giant petrel – hit the engine and caused 'Victor Tango' to pitch into the sea. The crash resulted in 20 deaths, including 18 SAS soldiers: it was the Regiment's highest single loss since World War II.

Despite this tragedy, operations went on. In fact there were so many teams operating at this time that many of them ran into each other, with unfortunate consequences:

'Working alongside our cousins in the SBS, we were given specific areas to work in. The concept, as in other theatres of war where friendly forces work in a confined area, was to eliminate the danger of patrols running into each other. This scenario, known as "blue on blue", happened several times in the Falklands, and patrols would open up on each other until both sides realised their mistake. Fortunately there were no casualties, that is until an SAS team ran into SBS patrol. Exactly how they met each other is a mystery, but the consequence was a short, intense firefight in which one of the SBS men, Sergeant "Kiwi" Hunt, was mortally wounded. Great shame. He was one of the unsung heroes of the war, living ashore for weeks before the main landings.'

As the Task Force prepared for the main landings at San Carlos Water, the SAS and SBS were tasked with mounting diversionary attacks against the Argentinians. One of these was conducted by 40 men of D Squadron, led by Major Delves, in the Darwin/Goose Green area:

'We were still hurting from the loss of the Sea King, but we still had a job to do and just before the landings we were sent to keep the opposition's heads down at Goose Green. We knew the Argies had a sizeable

Sergeant 'Kiwi' Hunt (face uncovered), mistakenly killed by the SAS in a 'blue on blue' incident.

garrison there but we didn't know exactly how many. What we did know was that we were heavily outnumbered. Still, we were armed with GPMGs, Milans, grenade launchers, mortars and a Stinger surface-to-air missile. Our orders were to convince the Argies they were being attacked by a whole battalion. We were told to "just blast them", though any close-quarter fighting was ruled out because if we got too close they would suss us. This battle would be from a safe distance.

'We were flown in by Sea Kings, each man carrying a fucking great big load of armaments. We left the choppers and had to trudge 30km to our positions: the low hills to the north of Darwin/Goose Green.

We stopped regularly to adjust our bergens, as well as the Milans we were

Below: Poorly led, their morale low, Argentinian conscripts posed few problems for the SAS.

carrying. The weight was unbelievable. I remember thinking it was a good job we were going to fire most of the ammo because I for one didn't fancy the idea of marching back with it.

'When we reached our position we spaced ourselves out and then the boss gave the signal to open up. The next minute the night sky was illuminated with tracer rounds as the GPMGs began firing. Then the 66mm LAWs streaked across the ground and found their targets, quickly followed by the Milans. The noise was deafening. We would move from spot to spot to give the impression there was a multitude of firing positions. The Argies never knew what hit them. They did return fire, but it was wild and inaccurate and we never took any casualties. God knows how many rounds we fired that night, but the enemy never ventured from their positions and we well pleased with ourselves. By dawn we had packed up and were heading towards San Carlos water.'

The British plan was to establish a strong beachhead at San Carlos and then strike across East Falkland to Stanley, the capital. The days and weeks after the landings witnessed the SAS and SBS supporting conventional units by conducting probing missions to locate enemy forward positions. At the end of May, for example, the Regiment seized Mount Kent and held it, before being reinforced by 42 Commando, and in early June five SAS teams were landed on West Falkland. But more than anything else, it had been the intelligence that individual SAS teams had relayed back to the fleet in the weeks before the landings that had been perhaps more valuable: SAS soldiers lying for days in cramped, cold 'hides' observing the enemy and knowing that if compromised they would face certain death or capture, but still carrying out their job with the professionalism that is the hallmark of the Regiment.

Left: The debris of war. All the battles are over and all that is left for the Argentinians is defeat. It is a British victory, in no small part due to the SAS.

NORTHERN IRELAND AND LOUGHALL

In this chapter, SAS soldiers describe surveillance missions in Ulster, how they spring ambushes on IRA teams, and what it's like to work in the 'bandit country' of South Armagh.

Northern Ireland. Two words that conjure up images of civil strife, bomb-scarred towns and cities, mutilated soldiers and civilians and a hate-filled populace. For the Special Air Service, Ulster has been the location of its most long-running campaign, one which appears to have no end in sight. It is impossible in just one chapter to provide a comprehensive history of all the Regiment's actions in the Province. However, by using the words of SAS soldiers themselves, an impression can be given of the type of war being fought by the Regiment in Ulster and the kind of skills needed to fight the 'unseen enemy'. But why was the SAS there in the first place?

A British Army patrol leaves Republican 'Free Derry'. The SAS also patrols the streets of Northern Ireland, its men usually in unmarked cars and wearing civilian clothes.

British troops were first despatched to Northern Ireland in August 1969 to stop the inter-communal violence between Catholics and Protestants. This period also saw the first deployment of the SAS, when members of D Squadron, 22 SAS, were engaged in the countryside to hunt for Protestant weapons. The war in Oman (1970-76) meant the Regiment did not have the manpower to maintain a sizeable presence in the Province, though individual

officers and NCOs were posted there to carry out intelligence tasks. However, in 1976 the British government announced in the House of Commons that the Special Air Service was being deployed to the Province, specifically to South Armagh, signalling the beginning of a squadron-sized SAS presence in Ulster.

The main adversaries of the SAS in Northern Ireland were, and continue to be, the nationalist Irish Republican Army (IRA), which

IRA, was captured near Forkhill, South Armagh, though he was killed while trying to escape. However, this incident notwithstanding, the terrorist threat was not so easily dispensed with, and the SAS settled down to a long campaign against the men in black balaclavas.

What does the SAS do in Northern Ireland? In the main it carries out surveillance and intelligence-gathering missions and undertakes ambush operations throughout the Province. From the late 1970s, the SAS deployment in Ulster was as follows: one troop (usually 16 men) at Bessbrook under the command of 3 Brigade; one deployed to the Belfast area under 39 Brigade; one to 8 Brigade in Londonderry; and a fourth under the personal control of the Commander of Land Forces. However, in the 1980s there was a change in SAS deployments. The splitting up of the squadron had meant that the Regiment's effectiveness was diluted. The Army recognised this and pushed for the establishment of a single, smaller SAS unit, one that could be moved from one place to another at short notice if required. For its part, the SAS was also experiencing difficulties: each squadron tour lasted between four and six months, with a period of prior acclimatisation training and a period of leave afterwards. With only four operational squadrons, the Regiment found that its soldiers were rarely away from Ulster. For a unit that has to keep its men proficient in a wide variety of military skills, this was not desirable.

To rectify the situation, therefore, a new organisation called the Intelligence and Security Group (Northern Ireland) was set up – known as 'The Group' – which saw a reduction in the number of SAS soldiers serving in Northern Ireland from a full squadron to a troop of just over 20 men (Ulster Troop). By the mid-1980s, SAS soldiers were serving for a period of one year in Ulster Troop and were working closely within the Group with the 14th Intelligence Unit. The latter is a covert British Army intelligence-gathering organisation that was formed in the early 1970s and whose recruits are trained by the SAS. In the Group the SAS contingent and

seeks to drive the British out by force, and the smaller, Marxist Irish National Liberation Army (INLA). There is little SAS activity against Protestant terrorist organisations, mainly because these groups are not engaged in a war against the security forces. In the mid-1970s there was much IRA activity in South Armagh, but the SAS deployment there temporarily witnessed a reduction in terrorist outrages. In one incident, Peter Cleary, a senior 'player' in the

14th Intelligence Unit were commanded by a single officer. In addition, the actions of the Group and of the Royal Ulster Constabulary (RUC) special units were also integrated.

Before they go 'over the water', SAS soldiers undergo training to prepare them for the special conditions that exist in Ulster:

'The focus of training for teams heading for Ulster is rehearsing for covert ops. They will carry out procedures for getting in and out of "hides" and will practise photographing "incidents", and all the while they will be assessed and monitored by Hereford's training staff.

'I remember manning one "hide" in the Herefordshire countryside. There were two of us hidden deep inside a roadside hedge, with two more to our rear to cover us. Anyway, at 0700 hours two masked men came out of the house carrying several weapons. They then stopped in the driveway, giving us plenty of time to photograph them before they jumped in a car and left. We were well chuffed, and when we got back to base the photographs turned out to be excellent. So there we were, feeling on top of the world, when the instructors pulled out another set of photos – of us. Unknown to ourselves, another team had been stalking us and, as the pictures showed, we had failed to fully camouflage our position. We were seen. If it had been the real thing we might have been killed. It put the shits up me, I can tell you.'

The key to winning the war in Ulster is intelligence. In theory all the military and intelligence agencies in the Province work with each other to combat terrorism. However, there are suspicions that many of the different agencies are at each other's throats. MI6, for example, often prevents the RUC's Special Branch from seeing certain information, and the RUC in turn often jealously guards its intelligence. The SAS was initially given the cold shoulder by both the Army and the RUC, as the two believed that the Regiment's deployment to the Province was an indication that their efforts were judged to have failed. Despite the veneer of unity presented by all the security agencies, this rivalry, bickering and pettiness continues.

In Northern Ireland the SAS operates as covertly as possible. In 1976, for example, in the SAS's first official tour, men from D Squadron were attached to 40 Commando, Royal Marines, for their tour in South Armagh. On the ferry to Belfast they were wearing green berets and standard disruptive pattern material (DPM) smocks, and several carried L42 sniper rifles. During this tour the SAS carried out no less than 31 operations against the enemy.

But who exactly are the opposition? The original IRA was an Irish nationalist group that was formed in 1919 and which was dedicated to an armed struggle in pursuit of its aims. The

Left: A patrol waits to be extracted by helicopter after an operation in South Armagh. SAS teams make great use of helicopters in Ulster.

organisation split into two groups in December 1969: the 'Officials', the old leadership in Dublin, believed that an alliance between the Protestant and Catholic working classes would bring about a united Ireland, while the 'Provisionals', led by hardliners from Belfast, believed the only way to achieve a united Ireland was to drive out the British by force. The Provisionals soon gained the upper hand, and to this day the IRA is also known as the 'Provos'. Its list of assassinations, murders and bombings is long, but notable atrocities include the deaths of 21 people in the Birmingham pub bombings in November 1974, the bombing of the Grand Hotel in Brighton in October 1984, and killing 11 civilians at a Remembrance Day ceremony in Enniskillen in November 1987. Most of the IRA's major 'players' are known to the security forces, but catching them in the act of committing a terrorist offence, the only way they can be legally apprehended, is very difficult. Nevertheless, the skills possessed by the soldiers of the Special Air Service have proved invaluable in the Province in arresting IRA operatives and preventing terrorist outrages.

The following account concerns an SAS operation in South Armagh in the late 1970s, and is typical of the type of work the Regiment is engaged in as part of the fight against terrorism in Ulster. It is told by a member of 22 SAS:

'Orders were given in the full Ground, Situation, Mission style of all operations, with background details on the target. He was a known 'player' who had been involved in an attack on 3 Para and possibly the Kingsmills massacre [on 5 January 1976, 12 IRA terrorists had stopped a workers' minibus at Kingsmills, County Armagh, lined up the 11 Protestant passengers by the side of the road and riddled them with gunfire – only one escaped with his life]. The aim was to take him out of the circuit and crush the morale of the young "bulls" in Cross [Crossmaglen], who were waiting in the wings to follow their leaders.

'Two teams of four were tasked for the operation and rehearsals were carried out at a base in Ballykinler. The maximum range we expected to engage any terrorists was 500 metres, and so live rehearsals were essential. The brief was headed by two senior "Ruperts" [SAS slang for officers], but the most important figure was the IO [intelligence officer]. He had been in the Province for four years and was on the ball. A model of the local area was used to highlight the terrain and locate potential DLBs [dead letter boxes, points used to drop off supplies], PUPs [pick-up points, pre-arranged rendezvous in case the mission was compromised] and DOPs [drop-off points], as well as routes in and out, including an escape route and the location of the QRF [Quick Reaction Force, an Army back-up].'

The target in question was a local terrorist leader who was a major 'player'. The plan was to catch him committing a criminal act and arrest him. The SAS source continues:

'Both teams were inserted separately. It is an SOP [standard operating procedure], whether by helicopter or Q van [unmarked vehicle], that when there are two teams they will always travel apart.

'I was with the helicopter team that lifted out of Bessbrook in the early hours and landed approximately 2km from the area. Our role was to go to ground and act as the support group for the primary team, and log anything and everything that moved and which might present a threat to the primary team.'

SAS four-man patrols, because of the intensive training received by each team member in weapons handling, can lay down a devastating barrage of firepower. The teams that were on this particular mission were heavily armed. They were in 'bandit country' and were taking no risks:

'The primary team arrived on the ground by Q van and had inserted themselves into the roof of a disused barn by first light. They were heavily armed with M16s,

Above: An Army patrol at a vehicle checkpoint (VCP). VCPs are often used as cover to enable SAS patrols to secretly establish an OP.

shotguns and two M79s [grenade launchers]. In addition, each man carried a 9mm Browning High Power handgun. My team was equipped with a light machine gun, an SLR [Self-Loading Rifle] which could fire automatic and two M16s. The SLR man carried light machine gun magazines on his weapon, with his first magazine containing tracer rounds. If any fireworks broke out his job was to put down instantaneous and continuous fire so the rest of us could see the tracer and use it as a marker.

'Each team was also equipped with a Sarbe [surface-to-air rescue beacon], which had one use: emergency only. For example, if Paddy bumped us or we were heavily compromised and couldn't use the radio, then the SOP was to hit the Sarbe. Another bit of kit, the strobe, was amazing for bringing in helicopters: pilots could locate it in all weathers and use it to find the LS [landing site].'

Because SAS soldiers have to operate in all types of weather conditions, they must have the right clothing. However, the considerations of the mission in hand must come first:

'Goretex wasn't around then, but waterproofs were out. We didn't wear anything that made a noise. Boots have been a problem since the British Army was formed, and so many blokes in the Regiment buy their own, particularly US Marine jungle boots, which provide plenty of movement for the ankle but still have a strong base. But we all wore "goon boots", which were small, pullover shoe covers that had lumps of rubber on the sole. The aim was not to leave footprints as the local farmers, Fenian to a man, were quick to spot boot marks and would pass the information on to their mates in the IRA.

'Everything was camouflaged: bergens, weapons, the lot. We added a few extras to our smocks, such as a large inside pocket to carry a small radio and a few batteries. In the main, though, we wore the same uniform as other British Army units. This was because if a team decided to break cover, they would look like ordinary squaddies.'

Though the SAS engaged and killed a terrorist after three days of waiting, it turned out to be another gunman, not the major 'player'. The men were then forced to retire, having assumed they had been compromised. This is a typical example of the type of operation conducted by the SAS in Ulster which, despite the intensive preparations, can often end in frustration.

Observation Post (OP) work forms what is probably the main task of the Special Air Service in Northern Ireland. The reason is simple: SAS soldiers, because of their training and mental and physical stamina, are ideally suited to living in cramped, uncomfortable OPs for days on end. Many OP missions are conducted from Bessbrook, the headquarters for SAS operations in South Armagh. A large former cotton mill, it is now a hive of activity for the British Army. Battalions serving in the South Armagh TAOR (Tactical Area of Responsibility) base their HQ staff and support forces at Bessbrook. The support services include Q cars and Quick Reaction Forces, which can fly from the Mill's heliport to any location in the area to provide instant back-up.

The heliport, known as Bessbrook International, is roughly the size of two football pitches. The whole base is heavily guarded, having been the target of numerous IRA attacks over the years. An SAS soldier describes a typical OP mission mounted from the Mill:

'After an intelligence brief at the Mill we flew by Wessex to Crossmaglen SF (security forces) base, where we were due to meet one of our teams that had just spent several days on the ground. Once inside the base, we were briefed by the company commander of the Black Watch and an RUC officer. The aim of this was to update us on their activity in the area and the day's events at local level. Our people passed on details about known "players" seen in the TAOR, and the movements of "targets" the Provos had been monitoring, which was very relevant to the operation we were about to mount.'

'The deployment of the OP had been sanctioned after intelligence from Special Branch indicated a big hit was being planned against Cross. In the past Provo machine-gun attacks had scored massive publicity, but their favoured method was to use mortars. They weren't very accurate, but Paddy would lob a few shells in which would scare the shit out of everyone and remind the British Army that it was in enemy territory.

'We had been told by the intelligence boys that the attack would be very big, and the Provos had even been boasting in the local pubs that at least 10 British soldiers would die, so the heat was on to prevent it happening. There were only two places from where the Provos could launch such an attack, the most likely being a football field behind the base.'

Establishing a covert OP is no easy task. A position has to be found that will enable the SAS team to view the target on a 24-hour basis, but the men have to be inserted into the OP secretly. In an area like South Armagh, where most pairs of eyes are hostile, this can present problems. Therefore elaborate tactics have to be adopted:

'A disused house on the edge of Crossmaglen provided the perfect position for a long-term OP. It was detached and isolated on one side of the road, with an occupied dwelling just 100m away. The obvious dangers of inserting a team into such a position required a check by an EOD [explosive ordnance disposal] team. We left Cross late in the afternoon as part of a Black Watch patrol, also taking three Royal Engineers along with us.

Below: A Wessex helicopter brings a team into Bessbrook. Many SAS operations in South Armagh are launched from the heavily fortified base.

'Wearing standard combat gear and helmets, we were part of a 12-strong patrol which headed out of the main square towards our objective. The aim was to acquaint ourselves with the terrain around the building which we were to occupy later that evening. We patrolled up through Cross, and at a given point the soldiers from the battalion established a VCP [vehicle checkpoint] on the Cullaville Road, giving us the opportunity to check the ground and the sappers the chance to clear the building. The walk-past recce was very useful. We were equipped with bergens, Armalites and a full-automatic SLR. If we'd have carried this gear in West Belfast Paddy would probably have sussed we were SAS, but in South Armagh, or 'the cuds' as the area is known, soldiers carry bergens and Armalites all the time.'

Constant vigilance is a feature of all covert operations in Northern Ireland, as the enemy has eyes and ears everywhere. In addition, what is standard operating procedure in large urban areas such as Belfast is not always applicable to rural areas and small towns and villages. Q cars and covert vans are not easy to operate in Crossmaglen, for example, because the place is so small and the base is monitored all the time by Republican 'spotters'. Therefore, the SAS frequently employs helicopters and foot patrols as a way of getting teams into OPs without attracting attention to the initial phase of the operation. Once established in an OP, it is a question of simply waiting and watching. The SAS soldier continues his description of the mission:

'We carried everything we would need to sustain a 10-day observation: water, food, ammunition and surveillance equipment, as well as a variety of "live traps" which we planted around the building as "insurance" against any Provos who paid us an unannounced visit. We also had an escape route in case we were compromised.

'Living in a covert OP for 10 days in conditions where you could be compromised at any time by noise or smell is very stressful, especially if your "hide" is near an inhabited building. Noise is a killer, and so a variety of precautions are taken to avoid compromise, and these must be enforced at all times if success is going to be achieved.

'After entering the building the bergens are placed in ready-to-move positions and are never moved again. Soft shoes, trainers or desert boots are put on and combat boots are stowed away – they are too heavy and are difficult to sleep in. We had one collapsible camp bed, which we had "liberated" from an American para, and erected it straight away. Cameras and night scopes were set up and plastic bags for human waste were put to one side. A second bag for empty food cans was also put to one side. It is imperative to trap all smells – like noise they can literally be a killer. They can attract dogs and cats which will compromise the operation.'

Inside the OP there is little to do except to try to keep alert, for any lapses in concentration can be fatal. Though the men's lives are on the line, the temptation to take risks to relieve the boredom is great. Only through strict self-discipline can the pitfalls be avoided. This is where the SAS's training comes into its own:

'Smoking is out, and I remember the problems of trying to operate and sort out equipment in the pitch darkness inside the attic of the property. Even using a torch for a few seconds is too risky. The procedure was for one man to get his head down, one to monitor the radio, while the third carried out surveillance, this is all standard SAS SOP.

'Food is a real problem. At no time did we eat it warm, and the only time we had hot drinks was at first light when we could use a "bluey" with no fear of anyone being

Right: A plain clothes SAS soldier photographed in South Armagh. The weapon is a silenced MP5.

around to hear its gas burning. We drank tea – coffee smells – and ate a variety of cold meats and tinned food.'

Never far from the soldiers' minds are thoughts of being discovered:

'Camouflage cream is a must at all times for two reasons. First, although we could not see any broken or damaged tiles, a white face shines and might therefore be seen by a passer-by. Second, if someone accidentally entered the property and compromised our operation we needed the element of shock to surprise them.'

'Wearing desert boots, combat trousers, black roll-neck jumpers and woolly hats kept us warm, and gave us the opportunity to move about quietly. We weren't too worried about getting

it is vital, and operational details such as DLB arrangements are made by whisper, again its an SOP which is instinctive. At night a team of ours at Cross mounted DLBs in which they delivered fresh sandwiches and supplies, such as radio batteries and other items, and took away our waste. This procedure centred on pre-arranged RVs, which often gave us the chance to exchange operational details and receive additional orders. Goods were exchanged or left in a bergen, and we in turn would deliver bergens full of waste, as well as 'shot' film that had to be returned for developing as quickly as possible.'

SAS soldiers are trained to fight as well as gather intelligence, and uppermost in each man's mind was the state of his weapons:

'Magazines on our weapons were changed every day, because a sustained period in an OP can cause the mag spring to seize and result in a stoppage. If this happens and the OP is bumped, you're fucked.

'In Ulster most of the blokes like the M16 because it can deliver more rounds than the SLR or even the new SA-80. It's also fairly small, making it useful for OP work in a covert "hide". A weapon that is gaining in popularity with the Regiment in Ulster is the Heckler & Koch 53, which is basically a scaled-down version of the G3 rifle, though it also looks like the MP5.'

bumped by the opposition because we each had a 9mm Browning High Power in a shoulder holster and our main weapons were always close by.

'To give us an arc of observation for the scope and camera we removed a small part of a brick, which gave us plenty of vision to monitor the road, the houses and the potential mortar base plate on the playing fields. Nobody talks during the day unless

Relaying information back to HQ can be a real problem for SAS teams:

'Communications can be a fucking nightmare, depending on which radio band you are using. VHF, for example, often interfered with local television sets when they were switched on and basically told the locals that the military were in the area. Thus if you are operating from a

property you never transmit during daylight hours if you can help it.'

Despite the nerve-wracking nature of OP work, there are still the mundane, everyday matters to attend to. These demand proper attention or the OP can be compromised:

'Our rubbish and human waste was bagged up and sealed all the time. Our urine was bottled and food packed in plastic containers, but the rats still found us. Rats are a major problem in OP work around Cross, and their presence can cause you to make noise in an effort to stop them attacking waste and refuse. The attic where the three of us lived was crawling with the little fuckers. They were big and would stop at nothing to get at the food or rubbish we had.

'We asked Cross to supply rat poison in a future DLB, which eventually resulted in a bag of 17 rats being shipped back to base in a bergen. The boys back at Cross thought it was some sort of joke, but in fact it was a real problem because we couldn't just leave them in the OP. By the time the operation finished we had returned more than 90 dead rats.'

'After several days your beard starts to itch, your hands are black and you smell. During insertion we had sighted a room full of hay and, in an inspired moment, had spread some on the floor of the attic to dull any noise and absorb our body smells. We were quite chuffed with ourselves. When we got back to Crossmaglen, however, after stripping off for a shower we realised it wasn't such a good move: our legs were covered in ticks and it took ages to get them off.'

Procedures for re-supplying covert OPs are continually being tested and re-tested, as they are vital and must be carried out efficiently if the OP isn't to be compromised. In the 1970s the DLB system was in operation, but the risk of this being a target for an IRA ambush meant the system has now changed to the Live Letter Box (LLB) method:

'The LLB system is much better. A covert car will drive to a pre-arranged RV with its rear window down (there's always two blokes in the front of the car), with another car, a back-up, some distance behind. Anything that has to be got rid of – exposed film, waste, wet sleeping bags – will be thrown onto the back seat of the car, while the bloke in the front passenger seat will pass the stuff requested by the patrol out of his window to the patrol members. Then they will be off.'

OP work is unglamorous, dangerous and tedious, and is perhaps not everyone's idea of what the SAS does in Ulster. However, it is vital to the intelligence war that is being waged against the terrorists, and is perhaps the best weapon in the armoury of the security forces.

Ambush operations are another part of the SAS's war against terrorism. They can be spectacularly successful, but they can also be controversial and raise the spectre of the Regiment operating a shoot-to-kill policy in the Province. However, the SAS is aware that any ambush operation will be subjected to intense legal scrutiny, and therefore impresses upon its men the importance of adhering to the Army's rules of engagement. An example of the difficulties facing the Regiment when springing ambushes is provided by an incident which took place in County Tyrone in August 1988.

In June, British intelligence collected an invaluable clue concerning a forthcoming IRA operation to assassinate a former RUC officer who worked in Omagh. The SAS, working in conjunction with the Army, the intelligence agencies and the RUC, decided to set an ambush to prevent the murder attempt. The identities of the local IRA operatives were known to the security forces: Martin and Gerald Harte and Brian Mullen, who together formed the Mid-

Left: A soldier from D Squadron, 22 SAS, on active duty on the outskirts of Crossmaglen in the 1980s. His ordinary DPM dress, lack of headgear and standard M16 rifle give no clues as to his unit.

Tyrone Brigade. The intended victim was informed of the IRA's plan, and he agreed to continue driving his truck to work along his regular route to establish a movement pattern which would be observed by the terrorists.

The SAS plan was for the truck to 'break down', and then a team from the Regiment would lie in wait around it until the IRA hit squad arrived. However, the Mid-Tyrone Brigade didn't just have this operation on its books. On 20 August 1988, it blew up a coach carrying 35 members of the 1st Battalion, The Light Infantry, as it travelled along the A5 from Aldergrove Airport to the barracks in Omagh. The IRA team used nearly 100 kilos of Semtex in the attack, which hurled the coach 30m through the air. It was a devastating attack: eight men were killed, and many more were horribly injured. For the IRA it was a spectacular victory.

The SAS did not let the incident alter its plans: the operation went ahead as planned. On 29 August, the terrorists returned to their arms cache, indicating the murder attempt would take place the next day. During the early hours of 30 August an SAS soldier took the place of the target and drove the truck to the pre-arranged ambush point. At the same time, a three-man SAS team left the barracks in Omagh and walked to a derelict farmhouse near the village of Drumnakilly. They were armed with Browning High Power handguns and had 9mm Heckler & Koch MP5 submachine guns as their main weapons. When they reached the site one took cover in a barn while the other two hid in hedgerows on either side of the road.

At around 1900 hours the truck stopped outside the farmhouse. The 'driver' got out of the cab and unloaded the spare tyre to give the impression he had broken down. He knew the IRA would soon get to know of his whereabouts – the enemy had a host of eyes and ears in the area. Sure enough, later that day the terrorists hijacked a white Ford Sierra and, told of the whereabouts of the truck, made their way there. They were wearing black balaclavas, blue boiler suits and were armed with Kalashnikov AK-47 assault rifles and Webley revolvers – a heavily armed team out to kill an unarmed civilian, but that's what the IRA is all about.

The security forces had been trailing the IRA team on the day of the ambush to give the waiting SAS soldiers information concerning their whereabouts. However, the surveillance was abandoned when it was feared one of the unmarked cars had been identified by a potential hostile. The SAS team was blind. The SAS man at the truck, therefore, didn't realise who was in the white Sierra as it raced towards him, although his instincts told him something was wrong. He was right. He sprinted to a nearby wall as the IRA men opened up with a hail of automatic fire. As bullets kicked up the earth around him he made a frantic dash for cover, and made it.

The car screeched to a halt and the terrorists prepared to jump out and finish him off. At that moment a ferocious barrage of 9mm bullets hit the car as the three hidden SAS soldiers opened fire. The Harte brothers and Mullen were killed instantly, the Mid-Tyrone Brigade had ceased to exist. The SAS soldiers radioed for a Lynx helicopter to take them back to Omagh as RUC and Army units sealed off the immediate area. The operation had been a stunning success.

What was to follow was a public relations debacle, as the British government remained silent on the operation as the media and Republican commentators screamed that it was a revenge killing for the bus bombing. The SAS in particular was disturbed that no one officially contradicted these claims. Only belatedly did the Defence Secretary, Tom King, deny that the SAS was operating a shoot-to-kill policy. The operation was a brilliant military action which then turned into a propaganda victory for the IRA and its supporters.

A few months before there had been an even greater victory for the SAS, one which had gone down in the annals of the Regiment as one of its greatest successes against the IRA: the ambush at Loughall. In late 1986 and early 1987, the IRA had increased its campaign of terror in Northern Ireland with a series of bombings, beatings and murders. The Republican movement had stepped up its military activity in an attempt to make Ulster ungovernable. For their part, the security forces were on a state of high

Above: An SAS soldier practises ambush skills inside a converted aircraft hangar in Ulster.

alert. But they received a godsend when, during routine surveillance, an IRA member was overheard on the telephone talking about a planned attack on the RUC station at Loughall, County Armagh, by the East Tyrone Brigade.

The East Tyrone Brigade was known as the 'A Team' within the IRA, and for good reason. It had carried out a number of daring attacks against the RUC and the British Army. In December 1985, for example, it had assaulted Ballygawley RUC barracks with AK-47 assault rifles and Armalites. Killing the two guards on the gate, the IRA team then raked the barracks

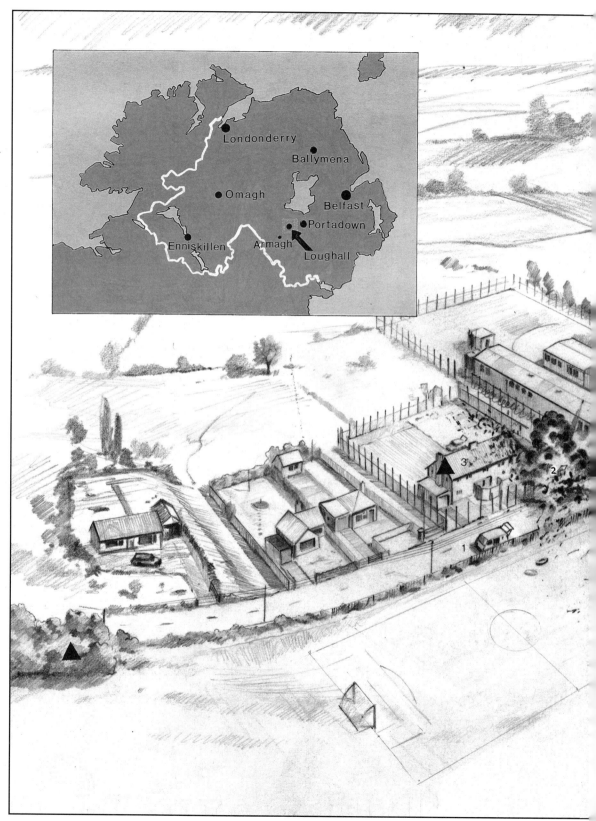

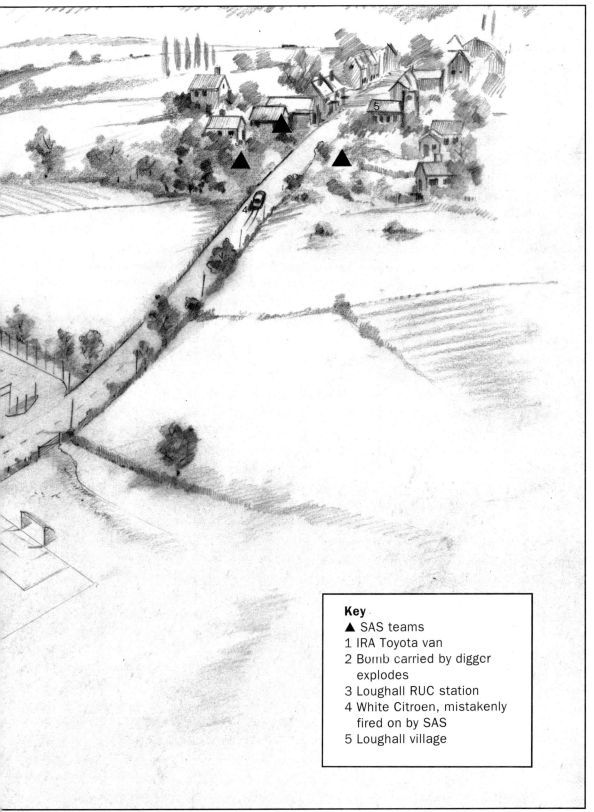

Key
▲ SAS teams
1 IRA Toyota van
2 Bomb carried by digger
  explodes
3 Loughall RUC station
4 White Citroen, mistakenly
  fired on by SAS
5 Loughall village

with gunfire before planting a large bomb inside the building. The subsequent explosion totally destroyed the barracks. The RUC station at the Birches, County Tyrone, was also attacked by the team. They loaded a large bomb in the shovel of a mechanical digger and rammed it against the wall of the building after first breaching the security fence. The explosion blew the barracks to smithereens, though the terrorists still felt the need to rake the area with gunfire after they had detonated the bomb. The attack on Loughall would be very similar, apart

Above: The aftermath of the Loughall ambush. Note the Toyota van and the remains of the digger.

from one small difference: the SAS and RUC would be ready and waiting.

Loughall is a small Protestant enclave in an overwhelmingly Catholic area. The village is a symbol of Protestant power, being the birthplace of the Orange Order. It had also been relatively untouched by the 'Troubles'; however, the IRA was determined to change that. The police station itself was a part-time, undermanned

RUC office, and the IRA planned to carry out an attack that would totally wreck the building.

The SAS was taking no chances. It was decided to reinforce Ulster Troop with more men from England. Therefore, the Regiment's headquarters at Hereford was ordered to send over more men. Soon afterwards, a 16-man troop from D Squadron was on its way to Ulster. Operation 'Judy', the codename for the ambush at Loughall, was under way. Because of the IRA's slackness, the authorities knew the date of the attack: 8 May. The SAS men and RUC snipers were infiltrated into the area many hours before the IRA terrorists were due to make an appearance. The SAS contingent was commanded by a staff sergeant from Ulster Troop, a man of great experience who would make sure the operation would be perfectly executed. At the prior briefing the men were told that the mission was an OP/React – an Observation Post able to React, a coded term for an ambush. The enemy would drive into a pre-arranged killing ground where they would be engaged and destroyed. The East Tyrone Brigade's luck was about to run out.

The SAS soldiers were heavily armed: those of Ulster Troop were carrying Heckler & Koch G3 assault rifles, those from England had M16 rifles, and there were at least two General Purpose Machine Guns (GPMGs). The men were deployed in two groups. The first, the larger one, was deployed in the copse overlooking the RUC station close to the Armagh road. In this way the soldiers, who also had the two GPMGs, could concentrate fire on the football field in front of the police station. The second group was in the station itself, with the men being at the rear and at the far end of the building in relation to where the gates were. There were also at least two cut-off groups in the village and another SAS unit close to the church.

There has been questions raised subsequently concerning the wisdom of placing men in the building, as it was known that the IRA bomb would be large and would thus damage the building and perhaps injure any occupants. Mark Urban, in his book *Big Boys' Rules*, believes the men were placed in the station because the SAS wanted to be seen acting within the guidelines of the British Army's Yellow Card rules concerning the use of force against terrorists, ie if the station was unoccupied when the IRA attacked it might be hard to justify killing the terrorists, because they did not present an immediate danger to life. However, with men in the building at the time of the attack, the IRA gunmen would be threatening the lives of security forces personnel and could therefore be fired upon legitimately.

Whatever the reasoning behind placing men in the police station, it did contain SAS soldiers as the IRA team approached its target in two vehicles:

'From my position in the copse I remember seeing the van slowly driving past the police station and then stop, followed some time later by the digger. There were three men on the digger and they all appeared to be armed [five more were in the van]. I eased the safety catch off my G3 and eased the weapon into a comfortable firing position. I could feel my heart pounding and the ardenalin flowing in my veins. Then the digger crashed into the gates of the police station and stopped, its bucket holding the bomb raised high. The terrorists then jumped from the digger and formed up in a line on the road. What the hell are they up to? They were all armed, a couple of them were carrying what looked to me to be G3s. Fucking good piece of kit the G3: compact, light and, most important, it rarely jams. That's the thing about the Provos, they always have the best that's available. Then they started shooting at the police station in an act of what could have only been bravado.

'Then our guys in the police station opened up with a hail of fire which cut down one of the terrorists. This was our cue, and the blokes all around me started to fire bursts. The amount of ammunition being expended was incredible. I began

Right: The Toyota van offered little protection to the IRA members who sheltered inside it, nor did the body armour they were wearing.

Left: The view from Loughall police station to the copse where the two SAS GPMGs were positioned.

firing my weapon. Then, Armageddon! The bomb exploded and the whole police station seemed to cave in. Everyone stopped firing momentarily, somewhat dazed, then, after what seemed like an eternity but was probably only a couple of seconds, we started up again as the dust settled. I emptied a magazine and clipped a fresh one in the receiver. The whole area was alive with the sound of gunfire. Two terrorists had tried to make a dash for the van, but were cut down before they reached it. Bullets were still hitting their lifeless bodies as they lay in the road. Another terrorist tried to escape from the Toyota by running across the football field by the side of the road, but he too was cut down.

'Bullets were spraying everywhere. By this time everyone was directing their fire at the van, and it was taking so many hits that I thought it would disintegrate (I saw it some time after the ambush, it was literally covered in blood and guts). Squeeze the trigger, squeeze the trigger, reload. I reached for a fresh mag and began firing again. Empty cartridge cases were flying all over the place, and in the background I could hear the rippling firing pattern of the GPMGs. I knew whoever was in the van would be dead for certain.'

All eight terrorists were dead. But the killing didn't stop there. Unfortunately a white Citroen car carrying two brothers, Oliver and Anthony Hughes, was fired upon by the cut-off groups in the mistaken belief that it contained IRA men. Tragically, Anthony was killed.

When the shooting died down the area was sealed off by armed police, and overhead helicopters scoured the countryside for any other terrorists who might be in the area. The SAS soldiers themselves, after ensuring there was no longer a threat, were evacuated by helicopter. The Regiment had just fought its most successful battle in Northern Ireland.

GIBRALTAR

In March 1988 the SAS shot and killed three IRA terrorists in a highly controversial incident in Gibraltar. The shootings prevented a major terrorist outrage, but why did the bombers have to die such violent deaths?

The incident in Gibraltar in March 1988 is one of the most controversial actions of the SAS in recent years. On 6 March three members of an Active Service Unit (ASU) of the Irish Republican Army (IRA) were shot and killed by four SAS soldiers on the streets of Gibraltar. The incident was the culmination of an intelligence operation conducted by British intelligence agencies, ably assisted by Spanish counter-terrorist organisations.

Following the successful Loughall ambush on 8 May 1987 (see Chapter 8), in which two ASUs – eight men – of the IRA's East Tyrone Brigade were killed by the SAS and Royal Ulster Constabulary (RUC), the British knew the IRA would mount a revenge operation. The question was, when and where? For the IRA it was, and is, much easier to hit targets in Ulster. However, greater publicity would be achieved if an outrage occurred in Britain or on the continent. There had been bombs going off and murders committed in Northern Ireland ever since the 'Troubles' began, and, to a large extent, public opinion in both Britain and Eire had become somewhat immune to the horrors there.

The Crown Colony of Gibraltar, a place that has been described as being more British than Britain, but where security is low-key. As such, it was considered an easy target by the IRA.

139

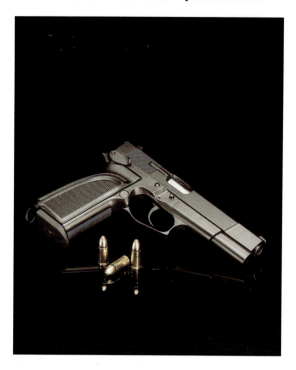

Left: The Browning High Power handgun, as used by the SAS soldiers on the streets of Gibraltar.

Gibraltar was a prize target, a location where the Union Jack flew proudly and where security wasn't as tight as in the UK or British bases on the continent. Following the SAS ambush of the IRA team at Loughall the year before, however, the British security and intelligence services were on high alert for any retaliation. MI5, the British counter-intelligence organisation, in particular, started to keep a close watch on the movements of known IRA operatives. Its diligence was soon to be rewarded.

For the Gibraltar mission the terrorist organisation assembled one of its most ruthless teams. First, there was Mairead Farrell, a middle-class, ex-convent schoolgirl who was one of the highest-ranking women in the IRA. She had served 10 years in prison in Northern Ireland for terrorist offences such as bombings and killings. Despite her angelic appearance, she was a cold-blooded operative who would go to any lengths to achieve her ends. Second, there was Danny McCann, the hard man from the Lower Falls area of Belfast. The mastermind behind a number of bombings and assassinations in Ulster, the RUC had linked him to no less than 26 murders in the Province. To the SAS he was known as 'Mad Danny'. In the IRA McCann

was known as an expert in close-quarter killing. He was, in many ways, out of control, a man totally addicted to violence whose only reason for existence was to continue the armed struggle against the British and their servants. Third, there was Sean Savage, a man who was the bomb-making expert. As such, he had the technical expertise the team needed. There seems to have been at least another team member, one whose identity has never been fully established, but who operated under the alias of Mary Parkin. Her task was to travel ahead of the team and gather intelligence concerning the target area, escape routes and when would be the best time to strike.

But to strike at what? Though there were several potential targets, such as the Governor's residence, various messes and the courts, the IRA's attention focused on a spectacular prize. Every Tuesday morning, regular as clockwork, the band of the 1st Battalion, the Royal Anglian Regiment, paraded up and down the main street at the changing of the guard ceremony. Around 70 bandsmen in full ceremonial dress performed the ceremony before marching off to a quiet square to disperse. In the square a bomb could be easily concealed in a car, for it was a peaceful spot and seemingly innocent. It was also well away from the main tourist streets, so large-scale civilian casualties would be avoided.

When considering the sequence of events that took place when the SAS soldiers engaged the IRA team in Gibraltar, it is important to bear in mind several factors before deliberating over the outcome. First, the IRA team contained dedicated, hardened operatives who were experts at their deadly trade. They were not amateurs, they would not hesitate to kill anyone who got in their way, and they would not meekly submit to being arrested. If they were carrying firearms, they would undoubtedly use them. This would be in the minds of the SAS soldiers as they moved in. Second, the actual drama was over in a matter of seconds. Events were dissected and analysed closely in the subsequent weeks and months, but it must always be borne in mind that the individuals involved had to make split-second decisions, and those decisions were taken at a time of extreme stress and fear. Third, the Special Air Service is not a civilian police force. It is a military unit whose men undertake a host of dangerous missions.

SAS soldiers leave little to chance: they cannot afford to. On operations one mistake can be fatal. In particular, all SAS men are highly trained in weapons handling. They spend hours on the range, honing and perfecting their firearms skills until they are second nature. Their reflexes become so quick that they can draw, aim and fire a full magazine of 13 rounds from a Browning High Power handgun in under three seconds. All memoirs of former SAS soldiers tell of the proficiency they attained with small arms. Michael Asher served with 23 SAS:

'We learned how to react to ambush in civilian cars, and how to take out terrorists in a crowded room, rolling and firing double-taps [two shots fired in quick succession] from our Browning pistols. We learned to shoot the terrorist and spare the hostage, to shoot in the dark and to clear stoppages.'

Adam Ballinger was succinctly informed of SAS philosophy during his Selection training for 21 SAS by one of his instructors:

' "This," said Scott [the instructor], picking up a semi-automatic, "is the fucking business. You may think you have passed your map-reading, but this is what it's all about." Scott stared passionately at the rifle: he had retrieved it from the strong-room and held it firmly. "Just as you would have failed the course," continued Scott, "if you'd failed the map-reading test, so we'll bin you if you fail your weapons test. From now until Camp, we will practise the drills over and over again. In this regiment they've got to be perfect." '

Dedicated, professional soldiers versus ruthless, veteran terrorists. When all the factors are weighed up, perhaps there could be only one outcome. But in September 1987, when British intelligence services alerted the Spanish police of the possible presence of an IRA team in southern Spain, all that lay in the future.

In mid-November 1987, three IRA members were identified in southern Spain. They were Sean Savage, Daniel McCann and a woman named Mary Parkin. The presence of the three in the area meant one of two things: the IRA was going to attack a person or persons unknown among the large number of British citizens on the Costa del Sol, or there was going to be a terrorist attack against Gibraltar. One thing was certain: the IRA team was going to commit some sort of bomb outrage. This had been confirmed when Spanish police surveying the team heard them talk about a bombing.

The IRA team then flew back to Eire. The British still had no idea of the target, but that information was not long in coming. In February 1988 the terrorists resumed their activity: 'Mary Parkin' was spotted by MI5 in Gibraltar observing the changing of the guard ceremony. As soon as she had arrived in Spain she had been placed under surveillance by the Spanish. On 1 March she again observed the ceremony, and each time had followed the route taken by the bandsmen. In London, on 2 March, the Joint Intelligence Committee, which reports to the prime minister, was of the opinion that a bombing was imminent. It then notified the Joint Operations Centre (which includes an SAS liaison officer), a body that has the power to deploy the SAS. An SAS Special Projects Team of 16 men was speedily despatched to Gibraltar.

On 4 March McCann and Savage arrived at Malaga airport under false names. They were then joined by Mairead Farrell – the team was assembled. There were also other IRA members in the area. A white Ford Fiesta was hired, stashed with explosives and placed in a car park in Marbella (it was later discovered by the Spanish police). Another white car, a Renault 5, was hired on Saturday afternoon, 5 March, driven into Gibraltar and parked to act as a blocking car for the white Ford Fiesta that contained the explosives. McCann, Savage and Farrell then drove to the colony in a red Ford Fiesta, closely followed to the border by plain clothes members of Spain's counter-terrorist unit (up to and throughout the operation there was a high level of cooperation between the various Spanish and British police forces and intelligence agencies).

In Gibraltar itself the SAS waited. The men designated to arrest the terrorists on the street were Soldiers 'A', 'B', 'C' and 'D'. Their tactical commander was Soldier 'E', who was located in the Joint Operations Room, while Soldier 'F' was the overall commanding officer and senior military advisor to the police. In addition, there was Soldier 'G', a bomb disposal expert. On the street there were several MI5 watchers and two teams of armed plain clothes Gibraltar policemen, each one designated to support an SAS two-man team.

The two SAS teams comprised Soldiers 'A' and 'B' in one team and Soldiers 'C' and 'D' in the other. Each man was armed with a High Power handgun plus spare magazines, and was equipped with a radio-microphone in his collar which provided continuous communications with the Joint Operations Room. The actual plan had been carefully prepared and each of the SAS soldiers had been thoroughly briefed. At midnight on 5 March, there had been a briefing for everyone involved in Operation 'Flavius', the codename for the apprehension of the terrorists. Present were Joseph Canepa, Gibraltar's police commissioner, Charles Colombo, Gibraltar's deputy police commissioner, and Joe Ullger, head of Gibraltar's special branch.

The rules of engagement drawn up in London for use by the SAS were later made public by Soldier 'F' at the inquest which took place regarding the terrorists' deaths. They are worth examining in full, because they belie the notion that the SAS had a licence to kill:

OBJECTIVES

1. These instructions are for your guidance, once your participation in Operation 'Flavius' has been duly authorised. You are to issue orders in compliance with these instructions to the men under your command.

2. You are to operate as directed by the Gibraltar Police Commissioner or by the officer(s) designated by him to control this operation.

Should the latter request military intervention, your objective will be to assist the civil power to arrest members of the IRA, but subject to the overriding requirement to do all in your power to protect the lives and safety of members of the public and of the security forces.

COMMAND AND CONTROL

3. You will be responsible to the Governor and Commander-in-Chief, through his Chief of Staff, for the way in which you carry out the military tasks assigned to you. You will act at all times in accordance with the lawful instructions of the senior police officer(s) designated by the Gibraltar Police Commissioner to control this operation.

USE OF FORCE

4. You and your men will not use force unless requested to do so by the senior police officer(s) designated by the Gibraltar Police Commissioner, or unless it is necessary to do so in order to protect life. You and your men are not then to use more force than is necessary in order to protect life, and you are to comply with rule 5.

OPENING FIRE

5. You and your men may only open fire against a person if you or they have reasonable grounds for believing that he/she is currently committing, or is about to commit, an action which is likely to endanger your or their lives, or the life of any person, and if there is no other way to prevent this.

FIRING WITHOUT A WARNING

6. You and your men may fire without a warning if the giving of a warning or any delay in firing could lead to death or injury to you or them or any other person, or if the giving of a warning is clearly impracticable.

WARNING BEFORE FIRING

7. If the circumstances in paragraph 6 do not apply, a warning is necessary before firing. The warning is to be as clear as possible and is to include a direction to surrender and a clear warning that fire will be opened if the direction is not obeyed.

AREA OF OPERATIONS

8. Under no circumstances are you or your men to enter Spanish territory or Spanish territorial waters for the purposes connected with Operation 'Flavius', nor are you or your men to fire at any person on Spanish territory or Spanish territorial waters.

Thus, the SAS soldiers in Gibraltar were under strict guidelines as to the course of action they could follow. They had been thoroughly briefed and knew the type of people they were up against. With all the intelligence that had been gathered on the terrorists, the authorities believed they were certain of about five things. First, there would be an IRA attack during the changing of the guard ceremony on 8 March; second, the IRA team would use a large car bomb; third, the bomb would be triggered by remote control, ie a 'button job'; fourth, the IRA team would *not use* a blocking car to reserve a parking space in readiness for the car bomb because this would mean making two trips across the border; and finally, they knew that the IRA team was ruthless and thought they were armed.

All the above points were emphasised to the arresting SAS soldiers – 'A', 'B', 'C' and 'D'. However, they were wrong on three points: the terrorists were not armed, the car driven into Gibraltar and left in the square was a blocking car and didn't contain any explosives, and the bombers had decided to use a time bomb and not a radio-controlled device. Thus the SAS teams went onto the streets of Gibraltar believing the terrorists were carrying weapons and had the means to detonate the explosives electronically. In addition, the soldiers were briefed a second time in the early hours of Sunday morning, where it was impressed upon them again of the ruthlessness of the IRA team and the fact that they would use the weapons they were assumed to be carrying without hesitation if confronted, and they would also use the remote-control devices they were carrying.

Sunday 6 March was a beautiful sunny day, and all three terrorists, looking like any other tourists, crossed the border into Gibraltar. At 1450 hours they walked along the line of parked cars in the square and paused in front of their

Above: The intended target – the resident British Army band, which would have been annihilated.

white Renault 5. They were identified positively as being the three IRA terrorists. The two SAS teams were on the streets and were near the bombers. At 1455 hours, Colombo agreed to their arrest and handed over control to Soldier 'F' and the military. At that moment the three bombers turned and headed out of the square past Soldiers 'C' and 'D'. The SAS men then reported back to the Joint Operations Room but were told to hold back. Control was then passed back to the police.

At 1525 hours, the bombers returned to the car and then headed north towards the border. Soldier 'G' then dashed from the Joint Operations Room to make a quick examination of the car. He reported back to the commissioner that he had been unable to make a detailed survey of the car, but he believed, based on what he had seen (a suspicious aerial), that it could contain a bomb. Events now moved rapidly: at 1540 hours the Commissioner of Police handed over the power of arrest to the military. The terrorists reached the junction of Winston Churchill and Smith Dorrien Avenue. All four SAS soldiers began to close in on the IRA team. Soldier 'E' passed control to the two teams on the ground. At this point Savage split from the other two and

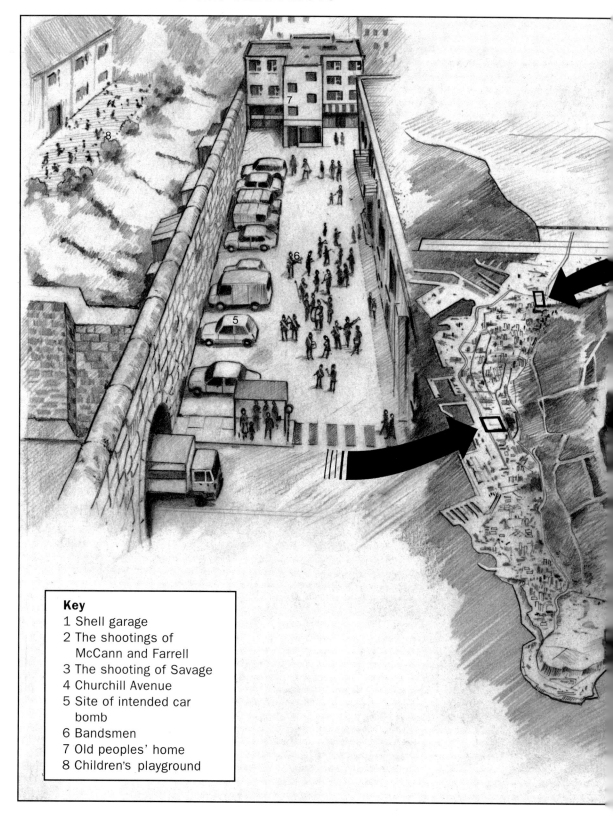

Key
1 Shell garage
2 The shootings of
  McCann and Farrell
3 The shooting of Savage
4 Churchill Avenue
5 Site of intended car
  bomb
6 Bandsmen
7 Old peoples' home
8 Children's playground

headed back towards the town centre, pursued by Soldiers 'C' and 'D'. McCann and Farrell continued walking towards the Shell garage on the right-hand side of Winston Churchill Avenue, closely followed by Soldiers 'A' and 'B'.

At 1600 hours, police headquarters radioed a police car to return to HQ at once because transport was needed to take the terrorists to jail after they had been arrested. The car switched on its siren and drove up Smith Dorrien. The siren startled the terrorists and began a sequence of events that was later described in detail by the SAS men. Soldier 'A' first engaged McCann:

'The look was alertness and very aware. At that stage, I was just about to shout a warning to stop and at the same time was drawing my pistol. I went to shout "stop" and I actually don't know if it came out. The look on McCann's face, the alertness, then all of a sudden the right elbow moving what I would call aggressively across the front of his body. I thought McCann was definitely going for a button. To me the whole worry was the bomb in the debussing area...I was drawing my weapon and fired at McCann one round into his back. I was about three metres away. We'd come up at a relatively brisk pace...Then I caught out of the corner of my eye a movement of Farrell who had a handbag under her left armpit, and grabbed at her bag. I thought she was going for the button and I shot Farrell in the back. I then engaged McCann with a further three rounds, one in the body and two in the head. He was falling all the time. His hands were away from his body...'

Soldier 'B' heard the sound of gunfire and saw Farrell draw her shoulder bag across her body. Uppermost in his mind was the remote-control device he thought she was carrying. He was also unaware if 'A' had been shot:

'So I opened fire. I drew my weapon as the shouting started and the firing began. It was all in a split second. She made a

movement to the right and I decided they were movements to detonate the device. I opened fire on Farrell and then I switched firing to McCann. I did not know if Soldier 'A' had been shot. I believed McCann to be an equal threat to myself, to the public and to my comrades.'

Savage was engaged by Soldiers 'C' and 'D', who moved in to arrest him when he turned and faced them, having been startled by the police siren. Soldier 'C' later testified at the inquest:

'Savage spun round very fast. I shouted "Stop". At the same time as I shouted, he went down to the right area of his jacket. At this stage, I had my weapon out to effect an arrest and I fired. I was about five to six feet away. I carried on firing until I was sure he'd gone down and was no longer a threat to initiate that device...I fired to the mass, to the body. He was full frontal because he had spun round. I could not take any more chances of effecting a physical arrest. I fired six rounds. Four went into the chest area, two went into the head. Savage spiralled down and then fell backwards.'

In a matter of seconds it was all over. The three terrorists lay dead, shot at close range by the SAS soldiers. Mairead Farrell was shot twice in the face and three times in the body, McCann twice in the head and twice in the body, while Savage was hit 15 times. They had all died extremely violent deaths; was it a case of overkill? Let's look at the facts.

The SAS soldiers all stated later at the inquest that the plan was for them to arrest the three suspects, and then they would disappear. At around 1530 hours they were informed by the explosives expert that the aerial on the parked car confirmed to him that the vehicle was 'suspect', which would have convinced the SAS soldiers that the terrorists were carrying remote-control devices. When they moved in for the arrest, both Soldier 'A' and 'B' said they saw Farrell and McCann make aggressive movements with their arms which made them

Above: The price of failure. The funerals of the three IRA terrorists killed by the SAS at Gibraltar.

believe they were going for the 'button' (an Army explosives expert stated at the inquest that it would have been possible for the three to detonate a bomb from the area where they were shot, testimony that was supported by an Army radio expert).

It was a similar situation for Soldiers 'C' and 'D', who were closing in on Savage. The terrorist made a sharp movement with his right arm to his jacket hip pocket, and the SAS soldiers fired because they believed he was going for the 'button'. The testimony of the soldiers reveals their SAS weapons training. Soldiers 'A' and 'D' stated that the terrorists would have to be incapacitated if they did not remain motionless after warnings had been shouted. When all three had failed to do so, they had opened fire to save lives, and, true to SAS drills, would remain firing until each target was no longer a threat. As Soldier 'E' stated: 'The intention from the moment that fire was opened was to kill him. That is standard and only by so doing could the threat be removed.'

The next day the British Foreign Secretary, Sir Geoffrey Howe, made a statement in the House of Commons concerning the incident which sought to explain the SAS's actions:

'When challenged, they [the terrorists] made movements which led the military personnel operating in support of the Gibraltar police to conclude that their own lives and the lives of others were under threat. In the light of this response, they were shot. Those killed were subsequently found not to have been carrying arms.'

The verdict of the inquest held into the shootings in September 1988 was that the three terrorists had been killed lawfully. In the final analysis, the SAS soldiers had acted according to their training and *on the information they had been supplied with at the briefing sessions*. There is little doubt that they would not have shot the three suspects if they had known that they were not armed and were not carrying detonation devices. Another of the SAS's battles was over.

THE GULF WAR

Dressed in Arab headdress, operating on foot and with Land Rovers, and armed to the teeth, SAS soldiers describe their daring Scud-busting exploits in the 1991 Gulf War.

O n 2 August 1990, around 100,000 Iraqi troops, led by six divisions of the elite Republican Guard, crossed the border into Kuwait. Within hours Kuwaiti resistance had effectively ended and Saddam Hussein, the Iraqi dictator, had achieved his goal of conquering the tiny oil-rich state. Political activity at the United Nations gave way to a military build-up in Saudi Arabia as it became clear the Iraqis could not be talked or coerced out of Kuwait. As UN troops poured into Saudi Arabia, American and British special forces units were also deployed, including elements of the Special Air Service (the story that SAS soldiers landed in Kuwait City on board a British Airways 747 jet during the Iraqi invasion is totally false).

In fact, the 1991 Gulf War was to witness the largest concentration of SAS troops on the ground since World War II. The Regiment was initially given a daunting task: the

An Iraqi tank on fire after being strafed by Allied ground-attack aircraft during Operation 'Desert Storm'. SAS teams called down many air strikes on enemy targets during the Gulf War.

rescue of British hostages. There were 800 British citizens being held in Kuwait itself, with a further 1000 in Iraq. In reality, this task would have been impossible. The hostages were dispersed to many military and strategically important locations, scattered around Saddam Hussein's domain as sacrificial lambs should Allied bombs start falling on his military installations and command centres. Though the SAS would have tried its utmost to rescue as many hostages as possible, there is no doubt that many would have been killed by Allied bombs, Iraqi guns, or even as a result of fleeing with members of the Regiment across the desert after they had been rescued, for what is possible to an SAS trooper is beyond the capabilities of an ordinary civilian. Fortunately this scenario didn't come about because the Iraqi dictator, in a rare moment of humanitarianism, let most of the hostages return to their countries of origin. This meant US and British special forces could concentrate their efforts on other tasks.

All special forces units in the Gulf were controlled by the Allied Special Operations Command of Central Command (SOCCENT). In August 1990, D and G Squadrons, 22 SAS, were in the Gulf region honing their desert warfare skills. One of those SAS soldiers remembers the rapid build-up in Saudi Arabia:

'Our Hercules touched down just before sunset, rattling past neatly parked groups of fighter aircraft which lined the apron of Riyadh air base. Compared to us they looked the "business", but from experience I knew never to judge a book by its cover. Our aged boneshaker taxied to a halt and the fuselage began to fill with engine fumes. I'm sure the RAF leak them deliberately into the cabin to send passengers to sleep. Fortunately, the load master noticed our situation and lowered the rear ramp before we chocked to death. A gush of fresh Arabian air brushed past our faces as we shuffled off the aircraft.

'We had been operating in Oman with a batch of new four-wheel drive vehicles called Light Strike Vehicles, which were designed specifically for rough terrain. We

had spent weeks putting them through a series of punishing tests. They were good, though the suspension couldn't survive a drop from a Chinook helicopter from an altitude of 100m, which we discovered when one was accidentally dropped. Still, there isn't much kit that can survive that sort of treatment. We were thoroughly acclimatised by the time we touched down in Saudi, though none of us were prepared for the piss-poor weather we would encounter later on operations.

'So there we were, a motley crew with bergens and weapons walking across the tarmac to a group of waiting trucks. Around us, an army of multinational air force personnel worked feverishly on their aircraft. We didn't know what the high command had in store for us, so all we could do was train for any likely operation that might crop up. By late December 1990, the majority of the Regiment had been deployed to the Gulf, including some blokes from R Squadron, the reserve. However, because no specific role had been assigned to us, patience began to wear a little thin.'

Ultimately, the UK special forces group in the Gulf numbered 700 men, including elements of the Special Boat Squadron (SBS) and RAF special forces aircrew. The SAS contingent comprised some 300 men: A, B and D Squadrons and 15 men from R Squadron (G Squadron was not used in the end). The RAF Special Forces Flight operated CH-47 Chinook helicopters in support of SAS operations:

'The Chinooks assigned to SF (special forces) operations were repainted in a camouflage scheme designed for night operations. The new colour was ordered after the helicopter aircrews became concerned that the original desert pink colour might be picked up by any Iraqi forces operating night vision equipment. As a result, black paint was used to tone down the Chinook's profile. Compared to the dull desert colour schemes of other

aircraft, the RAF's SF flight gave the appearance of being scruffy and dirty. Nevertheless, the colour was a success and it blended in with the local terrain. Mind you, a lot of the lads thought that it looked like a graffiti gang had gone mad with a few spray cans.'

The relationship that grew up between the soldiers of the Regiment and the the RAF's No 7 Special Forces Squadron during the Gulf conflict was a close one. The Chinooks played a major role in the behind-the-lines operations undertaken by the SAS in the war. A member of the Regiment involved in an operation in Iraq remembers the sterling work carried out by the men of No 7 Squadron:

'The throb of the twin-tandem rotors filled the fuselage as the Chinook hugged the

Above: An SAS team photographed in Oman shortly before being deployed to operate behind the lines in Iraq. Note the handles taped to the MP5s.

contours of the ground in its efforts to avoid enemy radar. Inside the aircraft the team was cramped to say the least, as the RAF boys had put in this fucking great big rubber bag full of extra aviation fuel to make sure we had the range to get to the target. We checked our weapons and kit, talk was almost impossible in the deafening noise, and anyway the cabin was in darkness. Then came the signal to ready ourselves for debussing. We arrived at the location just before midnight – we had four hours on the ground to locate and confirm that an Iraqi radar station that had been identified by aerial photographs was real and not a decoy. The Iraqis had deployed a number of German-made dummy radar stations just before hostilities started, and it was one of the jobs of the special forces to go in and confirm targets before they were subjected to Allied bombing raids.

'Once on the ground we had major problems finding the target, as we were continually lashed by freezing winds. I remember saying to myself, "I thought this was the bloody desert, not the Falklands". Anyway, our visibility was reduced to almost zero and our strength was being sapped rapidly as we tried to battle against the wind. Struggling on, we eventually found the radar station and confirmed it was for real.

'Though we were thankful the trip hadn't been wasted, I for one was very apprehensive that we wouldn't make it back to the rendezvous on time. In fact, we were an hour behind schedule when we got back. The boss radioed our position and requested evacuation. I thought we would have to spend the night on the ground because of the bad weather, but then we heard the dull throb of the Chinook as it swooped in to land. Fucking champion. However, by this time we were being lashed by both wind and sleet, and it was almost impossible for us to see each other. The boss ordered us to link arms as the RAF crewman flashed an orange light to guide us through the storm and beneath the down-draft of the rotors. It was a relieved team that sat in the comparative comfort of the Chinook as it made its way back to Allied lines.'

Several days later the same aircraft, again waiting for an SAS team, ran out of luck when it landed in a minefield behind enemy lines. It was forced to lift off immediately, having had one of its rear wheels blown off and its fuselage pitted with fragmentation holes. Despite the condition of the aircraft, though, the pilot made it back to friendly lines.

Ironically, despite the rapid build-up of British and American special forces in the Gulf,

no one knew what to do with them, apart from using them in penny-packet operations. The situation wasn't helped by the attitude of the Allied supreme commander, General Norman Schwarzkopf, who, because of his bad experiences with special forces units in Vietnam, was suspicious of elite units.

'At first Norman Schwarzkopf had opposed the idea of deploying them [special forces] behind enemy lines, on the grounds that there was no task which could not be carried out by the Allies' overwhelming air power or, later, by the conventional armoured forces. I myself was not prepared to recommend special operations unless two conditions were fulfilled: one was that there must be a real, worthwhile role for the SAS to perform, and the other that we must have some means of extricating our men in an emergency.'

The above words are those of General Peter de la Billière, the British commander in the Gulf. He had served with the SAS and had risen to eventually command the entire SAS Group. De la Billière persuaded Schwarzkopf that the special forces should be given a chance to prove themselves, but to do what? The answer came on 18 January 1991, when the first Scud surface-to-surface (SSM) missile was launched by Iraq against Israel in an attempt to bring the Jewish state into the war. The Scud is an extremely basic weapon: a solid-fuel rocket with a warhead on top, albeit one that can contain chemical or biological agents, which is pointed in the general direction of the target and is fired. It can be fired from fixed rocket sites or from mobile launchers. Ironically, the Scud could have been the most lethal weapon of the whole conflict. If Israel had been dragged into the war the coalition, containing as it did Arab nations, would have probably fallen apart, and there would have been a real possibility of Saudi Arabia expelling Western forces from its soil.

Right: A special forces Chinook helicopter, several of which supported SAS operations in the Gulf.

Above : The Longline Light Strike Vehicle, as used by the SAS for reconnaissance in the Gulf.

Therefore, special forces units were tasked with hunting down the mobile launchers and fixed sites and either destroying them themselves or calling in air strikes to do the job.

On 19 January the SAS was rushed to its Forward Operating Base (FOB), which was one day's drive away from the western Iraqi border. The SAS and American special forces, for it was very much a joint effort, had two main tasks: the tracking down of mobile and static Scuds, and

the destruction of the concealed Iraqi communications links. Saddam Hussein had built up these links over a number of years. Ironically, he had done so with the help of Western defence and intelligence agencies, who had impressed upon him the need for secure and robust communications links throughout the country. They consisted in the main of microwave links maintained by a series of communications towers, and fibre optic cables buried under the ground.

To battle the Scuds, the SAS employed two methods: the mounting of static road watch patrols, and mobile fighting columns. The road watches were in the true SAS tradition, ie they were high risk and extremely daring! Teams of eight men were inserted by helicopter up to 300km behind enemy lines, where they established covert observation posts and literally watched the road for enemy activity. If they saw any worthwhile targets, they radioed headquarters to order an air strike. The men had no transport apart from their feet, and if compromised they had only their own resources and skills to make it back to friendly lines.

The fighting columns usually consisted of around 12 heavily armed Land Rover vehicles, which formed hunter-killer groups. They operated mostly in the 'Scud Box', an area of land near the border with Jordan. Comprising some 500 square kilometres of territory, it included the Baghdad-Amman road and was usually filled with travelling Bedouins, civilian traffic and a sizeable enemy military presence. Initially, it had been anticipated that Light Strike Vehicles (LSVs) would be extensively used, though events were to prove otherwise:

'The four two-man LSVs ferried across from Oman were considered ideal for cross-border raids. They had many clever design features, including armoured seats and self-sealing fuel tanks to counter fragmentation damage. But as the Gulf situated escalated, it became clear that instead of operating on a limited scale using the two strike vehicles, the Regiment would be called upon to mount much bigger vehicle-based operations. In the event, LSVs were used by SAS patrols to monitor Iraqi movements, but they didn't cross the border into enemy territory.

'A fleet of new Land Rovers arrived for us from the UK, all stripped down for desert operations and decorated with a host of weapon mounts and additional fittings, including Southdown Protection Systems, which stopped the transmission systems from being damaged on rocks.'

The road watch patrols were conducted by B Squadron along three highways in the Euphrates Valley. There were three patrols in total, called the North, Central and South road watches. Right from the start it was apparent to the commander of the South road watch that his position was untenable and so he abandoned it and returned to base (he was lucky enough to have helicopter evacuation). The Central watch was just as precarious, so its commander also had no choice but to evacuate his team, though not before he had called down an air strike on two enemy mobile radar systems that were positioned close by. The SAS soldiers then left the area at speed, and began an epic 220km journey over four extremely cold nights before making it back to Saudi Arabia.

The story of the North watch north is one of heroism and tragedy which sums up much of what the SAS is all about. Dropped 300km from friendly lines, the men quickly settled down to a routine of keeping watch, sleeping and carrying out minor duties to keep their minds active. No one thought about their precarious position much, and if they did it was with that typical sang-froid that is the hallmark of the Regiment's soldiers. On the second day an Iraqi convoy appeared and established itself near by, though it would be more accurate to say almost on top of the SAS soldiers. When it had stopped and set itself up, the British soldiers were perturbed to discover that it was a mobile anti-aircraft battery, complete with a fearsome array of anti-aircraft guns. Very soon the inevitable happened: the SAS men were compromised, though not by Iraqi soldiers but by a group of curious civilians who were attached to the enemy convoy. The SAS men did the only sensible thing: they ran like hell. Heavily laden with bergens, they bugged out without further ado. They quickly attracted the sort of attention all soldiers wish to avoid, and very soon a hail of bullets was being directed at them. The Iraqi anti-aircraft guns were also brought to bear, and one SAS trooper had his bergen literally ripped to shreds by machine-gun fire. Ditching their backpacks, the SAS soldiers increased the speed of their flight.

Thinking quickly, they headed in the general direction of the Syrian border, eight men on a desperate venture. Behind them the countryside was alive with soldiers as the Iraqis

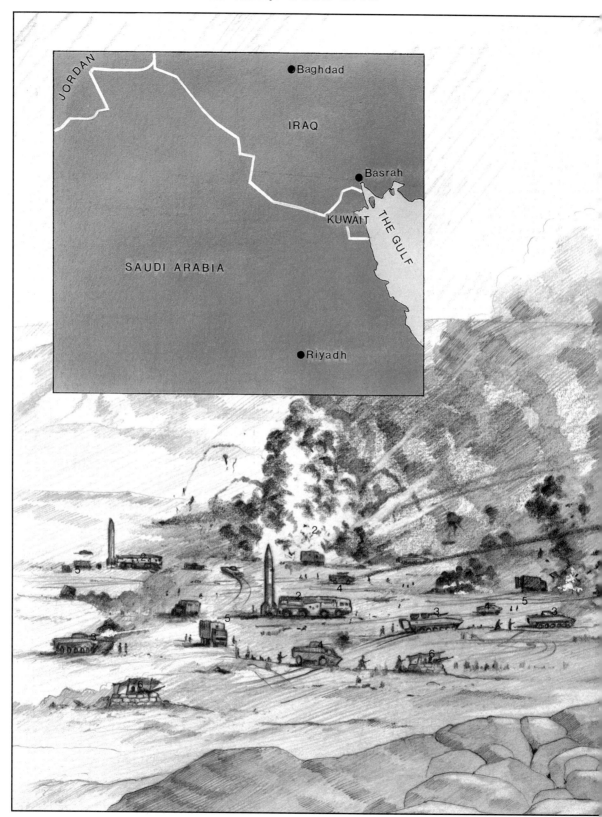

Key
1 SAS Land Rovers
2 Mobile Scud launchers
3 Iraqi BMP infantry
   fighting vehicles
4 Iraqi BRDM patrol
   vehicles
5 Iraqi trucks
6 Iraqi machine guns

desperately hunted for the unknown enemy troops who had been in their midst. The Arabian desert is an inhospitable place at the best of times, but in January 1991 the weather conditions were particularly severe. The area was being treated to a potentially lethal cocktail of rain, sleet, wind and snow, and these were the conditions the SAS soldiers had to battle against in their efforts to escape death or capture. The group split up to increase its overall chances of evasion. With few supplies and the enemy at their heels, the men were forced to maintain a

cruel pace. Inevitably, they began to falter. One, Sergeant Vince Phillips, got separated from his group in the driving sleet and died of exhaustion and hypothermia in the Iraqi hills. Another member of his three-man group was surrounded by enemy soldiers and forced to surrender. The

Above: Peter de la Billière (left), an SAS veteran who commanded British forces in the Gulf.

third, Corporal 'Z', displayed the sort of tenacity and cunning that is the stuff of screen super heroes. Walking day and night, avoiding all

contact with any other humans, taking refreshment where he found it, he covered 200km on foot and made it to the Syrian border. His achievement is all the more remarkable because for the last 48 hours of his journey he was without water. Such is the calibre of men who wear the winged dagger badge.

The other five initially had better luck. They reached the town of Al Qaim, near the Jordanian border, before being bumped by a group of Iraqi soldiers. This heralded a series of heavy gun battles as the SAS men, heavily outnumbered, held the enemy at bay with controlled, accurate fire. But they couldn't

Left: Another Iraqi target is destroyed, courtesy of Britain's Special Air Service Regiment.

had been pushed beyond their limits, but with dogged determination they had kept going. But now, beset by the enemy and the terrible weather, their systems were giving out. The last two, unbelievably, continued to head for sanctuary, but fate was to be cruel. One of them, Lance-Corporal Lane, was almost unconscious as his companion got him inside a cabin. But to no avail: Lane died of hypothermia shortly after. His companion attempted to escape but was captured. Thus ended the road watch venture, a plan that was perhaps a little too audacious. But for the Regiment the war was not over: the fighting columns were about to begin.

The first crossed the Saudi border on 20 January, a line of heavily armed vehicles from A Squadron. Though they mounted a variety of weapons, one of the most valued pieces of kit was the US-made Magellan Global Positioning System (GPS) receivers carried by the men:

> 'Before the war we had been exercising and using the GPS with great results. In the Gulf smaller sets were available, and their accuracy was astonishing. Though they were expensive, for us the GPS receivers were among the best items of kit purchased by the Ministry of Defence. They were brilliant for coordinating rendezvous sites and directing air strikes.'

Some of the dress worn by SAS soldiers in the Gulf War differed little from that worn 50 years earlier by their predecessors in the North African desert:

> '*Shemaghs*, an Arab headdress, was the order of the day. We looked a bit like a bunch of *Lawrence of Arabia* stand-ins, but they kept the sand and dust out of our faces and that was all that mattered. By mid-January 1991, we were across the border and operating in the Iraqi desert, experiencing the cold nights and savage winds. Desert combats were worn, but on their own were no match for the terrible

shake off the Iraqis, despite inflicting heavy casualties on them. Trooper Robert Consiglio, covering the withdrawal, was hit and killed (the loss of this Swiss-born soldier was keenly felt; he was reckoned to be one of the fittest members of the Regiment). Two others were captured soon after. The SAS soldiers were men whose bodies

conditions. So, Goretex jackets, climbing jumpers, gloves, arctic smocks and woolly hats were pulled out of our bergens for

warmth. Forget the idea of a smartly dressed patrol, we looked like a bunch of unshaven gypsies.

'Some teams wore chest webbing and a belt order, while others just wore a heavy belt order, which carried all the

Below: US Special Forces personnel enter Kuwait City in a Chenworth Fast Attack Vehicle.

operational equipment that had been drawn up for desert warfare: emergency food, survival kit, binoculars, compass, a GPS receiver (for the team leader), water bottles, NBC med-pack of atropine, ammunition, white phosphorus grenades,

charge packs and and as many Claymore mines as we could carry.'

The men had been thoroughly prepared for encountering Scuds:

'Our months of waiting to move into Iraq had included detailed intelligence briefings about Iraqi Scuds, how to identify them, how to spot traces of a Scud site and, most important of all, how to destroy the fucking big mobile rocket platforms.'

Another two columns, from D Squadron, also entered Iraqi territory to hunt for Scuds. They were not to be disappointed. Nine days after crossing the border, an SAS column came across a camouflaged fixed Scud site which was preparing to launch a salvo of missiles against Israel. The SAS commander quickly radioed for an air strike. Minutes later, American F-15 Eagles streaked across the sky, locked onto their target and destroyed the missile site with their ordnance. The special forces were beginning to pay back the faith that had been put in them.

It wasn't all one-way traffic, though. The SAS had to be vigilant. The vehicles were always arranged in defensive circles during rest and maintenance periods – a sort of late twentieth-century wagon train, except the Indians in this case were Iraqi soldiers. One such 'Indian' raid took place on the same day as another SAS column was ordering the strike on the fixed missile battery. A group of Iraqi vehicles stumbled across an SAS column and started to fire at it with small arms and heavy machine guns. The SAS soldiers, whose reflexes are never slow, almost instantaneously returned fire and a savage firefight ensued. As is often the case in such encounters, the side with the strongest nerves and the steadiest trigger fingers often comes out on top. And so it was. The Iraqis were beaten off, losing 10 dead and three vehicles.

The SAS's favourite hunting ground was Wadi Amij, near the town of Ar Rutbah, which was nicknamed 'Scud Alley'. On 3 February 1991, a fighting column from D Squadron was operating in the 'Alley' when it spotted an Iraqi Scud convoy of 14 vehicles. The SAS

Above: A Sea King lands SBS men on the roof of the British Embassy in Kuwait City, February 1991.

commander called up an air strike and the troopers watched as American A-10s and F-15s raked the enemy column with rockets and bombs. A trailer and its Scud took a direct hit, the vehicle being thrown into the air in a red fireball of burning explosives and petrol. A truck was flipped onto its side and an armoured personnel carrier was riddled with holes, its occupants killed as shrapnel tore through their bodies. But amidst the death and destruction it became apparent that the aircraft had not done the whole job: there were still some vehicles intact. The SAS column therefore opened up with its Milan anti-tank missiles. The rockets streaked across the flat terrain and began to find their targets. But the Iraqis spotted their adversaries and returned fire with their small arms and anti-aircraft guns. The latter's rounds kicked up sand and earth around the SAS jeeps as

the battle intensified. Rather than risk heavy casualties, the SAS commander gave the order for his vehicles to pull back, while at the same time radioing for another air strike. He knew the Iraqi column was like a beached whale – it wasn't going anywhere after the pounding it had taken. A few minutes later, as the SAS vehicles headed away, the men heard the satisfying thump and crump of aircraft bombs hitting the enemy column for a second time. Intelligence gathered later revealed that all the Iraqi vehicles had been destroyed.

Not all encounters between Iraqi Scud convoys and the SAS occurred in 'Scud Alley'. The following account is told by a member of one of the Regiment's fighting columns, who at the time was returning to the Saudi border:

'After three days we had failed to locate the site we were looking for and had problems raising our FOB. We used a burst form of transmission which basically stores your message then transmits it at speed so the enemy can't get a fix on you. Therefore, the decision was taken to leave "Scud Alley" and head back towards the Allied border. Our Land Rovers were fitted with Milans, machine guns and Mark 19 automatic grenade launchers. The Milan is a fucking good piece of kit: accurate, reliable and has excellent armour penetration capabilities. It also has an effective range of 2000m, which means you don't have to get too close to the opposition to score a direct hit. The Land Rovers didn't have Milan mounts as such. However, good old SAS ingenuity came into its own. We used a home-made bracket improvised from wood and para-cord and strapped to the roll bar.

'As we moved through the barren, flat desert we spotted a number of vehicles ahead of us. We pulled over and observed them with our scopes and binoculars. Bingo! They were Iraqi military transporters, so the boss ordered us to head towards them. When we were within 600m we could identify the target – a Scud launcher and a missile trailer. The Iraqis were in the process of camouflaging the vehicles and had forgotten to post any sentries. Big mistake.

'We quickly held a briefing and decided to divide our firepower between the two targets. A hand signal from the boss would begin the attack. We edged forward and the signal was given. The next moment several Milan missiles streaked across the desert and slammed into the enemy vehicles. A fireball engulfed the Iraqis as explosives combined with fuel to form a lethal cocktail. And then it was all over. Elation. We roared off at full speed, our minds racing with thoughts of what the Iraqi commander would do; we are trained to think like the enemy so you can take effective evasive action. We were on top of the world, but we had no time to gloat. We had to get away from the area as fast as possible, re-group and arrange a rendezvous with our supply vehicles.

'Later in the war some American A-10 aircraft strafed some British Army vehicles by mistake, killing nine soldiers. After this incident one of our SOPs was to lay out a Union Jack flag, pegged out with stones, on the ground whenever we stopped so it could be seen by aircraft overhead (there were no enemy aircraft operating by this stage of the war).'

Occasionally, SAS fighting columns would be reinforced with additional troops flown in by helicopter. A member of one such 12-man team remembers an operation against Iraqi Scuds that took place in January:

'The Regiment did well against Hussein's Scuds, but it wasn't all plain sailing. I remember there was a lot of fierce firefights between our "mobiles" and enemy troops. The sector of Iraq assigned to the SAS was described by our men as being "toppers with targets", on account of the area being a prime location for the huge rocket sites and mobile launchers. In January, one of our mobile columns had identified a Scud position and called down an air strike on it. The immediate area was saturated with enemy troops, which meant our team legged it quickly after checking the damage done by the F15s. While they were reporting back to Saudi, however, they were informed that one of the launchers was still intact.

'In a hastily drawn-up plan we were flown in by helicopter to rendezvous with the mobile column, which was going to have another crack. We were then given an on-the-ground briefing for the attack on the launcher site. The boss decided to try and lure the Iraqis from their defended positions by using "come ons": small charges planted roughly one kilometre from their camp. Hopefully they would venture forth to investigate, leaving us to destroy their site while their minds were on other things. We didn't fancy taking on the Iraqis where they were, as they had set up a host of machine-gun nests and they might have had heavier stuff, such as artillery, which we couldn't see.

'The heliborne team was split into two and deployed on the flanks. It was bloody freezing as dawn broke over the arid terrain, and no one spoke a word as we waited for the charges to detonate. I remember casting a quick glance at the other guys. They were wrapped up like it was the arctic. Then we heard the thump, thump of the charges going off one by one. Then the Iraqis started to fire, not aimed shots but wild bursts that sprayed everywhere. They weren't going to leave the safety of their camp. Oh well, if Mohammed won't come to the mountain...

'Now it was our turn. The plan was for the main force of Land Rovers to conduct the main attack against the Scud site, while the Milans on the flanks would concentrate on the launchers. A steady and well-aimed stream of SAS GPMG and Browning .5in rounds poured into the Iraqi position as the camp began to catch fire. I didn't know what was burning, but it made an excellent point of reference for all the gunners. Then the Milans opened up, the missiles racing across the ground and slamming into their targets. A fireball erupted as a fuel tanker was hit. The launchers disappeared in a pall of smoke, and Iraqi soldiers began to flee their positions, only to be cut down by our withering fire.

'Then there was silence, interspersed by the sound of ammunition being ignited by the flames or fuel exploding in vehicles. The Scuds site was now totally immobilised. The commander quickly surveyed the scene and then gave the order to bug out. We left the area at speed and reported in our position and direction. As the sun started to climb into the desert sky, we congratulated ourselves on a job well done,'

The SAS also continued hitting enemy communications systems. After one such attack, on 21 February, a column from A Squadron was involved in running battles with an Iraqi force. The British soldiers managed to beat off their assailants with a combination of Milans and Browning machine guns, but an SAS motorcyclist, Lance-Corporal David Denbury, was mortally wounded. Nevertheless, the Regiment made a sizeable contribution to the war against Saddam Hussein's communications systems.

A little-known part of the SAS campaign during the Gulf War concerned the collation of intelligence gained from Kuwaiti sources. In

Above: 'Mohammed', who risked his life to transmit messages to the Allies from Kuwait City.

Riyadh, several SAS soldiers worked alongside US Special Forces intelligence personnel to produce detailed information concerning Iraqi troop strengths in Kuwait. The operation was manned by three SAS linguists, who worked with three American counterparts. Their initial task was to locate and secure a source of regular and reliable information inside Kuwait City that could provide intelligence about the enemy to

contribute towards the liberation of the city. In its efforts, the SAS struck gold:

'The SAS team targeted radio hams, and through a "third player" in Geneva were able to make contact with "Mohammed", a school teacher and computer expert who lived in Kuwait City and who had transmitted around the globe as a radio ham for 10 years. Elements of the Kuwaiti resistance were supplying information via Sat-Com [satellite communications], but the latter relied on high-frequency transmissions and the Iraqis were often able to identify the source of the sets and arrest their users.

'The kit used by "Mohammed" emitted a low pulse which was much more difficult to pinpoint. To add to his security he only operated at certain times of the day from his basement cellar, where he had three computer terminals linked to his radio transmitter, which he used to send messages straight to western Europe. He had a small generator outside the house which he used to boost the two huge industrial batteries that formed his power source. His information was spot on most of the time. One of our guys and an American visited him three days after the war had ended to thank him personally on behalf of all the Allied special forces. He was a very brave person.'

This, then, was the SAS in the 1991 Gulf War, undertaking intelligence gathering duties and hunting down Scud missiles to prevent Israel entering the war. What, in the final analysis, did the Regiment achieve? Perhaps the final verdict should belong to Schwarzkopf himself:

'I wish to officially commend the 22nd Special Air Service (SAS) Regiment for their totally outstanding performance of military operations during Operation Desert Storm...The performance of the 22nd Special Air Service (SAS) Regiment during Operation Desert Storm was in the highest traditions of the professional military service and in keeping with the proud history and tradition that has been established by that regiment.'

Right: One tragedy the SAS couldn't prevent – the oil fields set alight by retreating Iraqi forces.

THE FUTURE

SAS soldiers talk candidly about the tasks and difficulties the Regiment will face in the future, such as the battle against international drug gangs, and also the problems of resources and manpower that may adversely affect the world's most highly trained military unit.

On the face of it, the main wartime role of the SAS has disappeared. Up to the end of the 1980s, the Regiment was heavily involved in training for operations behind the lines in eastern Europe and the Soviet Union in the event of a military confrontation between the Warsaw Pact and NATO. However, with the collapse of the Soviet bloc and its fragmentation into a number of non-aligned states, the threat from the east has largely gone. The 'new world order' talked of by ex-president of the United States George Bush has theoretically made redundant such units as the SAS. Unfortunately, this 'new world order', far from ushering in a period of international peace and prosperity, has created uncertainty and de-stabilisation throughout many areas of the world. As a result, the SAS is needed more than ever. But to do what? One of the main priorities of the Regiment now is fighting international terrorism.

Practising parachute insertion techniques. SAS soldiers are multi-skilled operatives, but will future demands made on the Regiment result in less time for training?

The fact is that European and US counter-terrorist units are stretched to the limit, a situation not helped by the current trend to cut back on defence spending in the West as a result of the so-called 'peace dividend' (the facile assumption that now the Warsaw Pact has gone, all threat of conflict in the world has disappeared; meanwhile, the 1991 Gulf War witnessed the largest wartime deployment of Western forces since the Korean War):

'The weekly intelligence briefing at Stirling Lines highlights the current activities of leading international terror groups. There are currently more than 300 active terrorist cells operating worldwide,

Above: The SAS conducts cross-training with many units, such as these US Special Forces.

hawking violence and death as their trademark. In the area of Counter

Revolutionary Warfare (CRW), the Regiment works alongside German, French, Spanish and American units, sharing ideas and concepts.'

The international nature of terrorism has resulted in close cooperation between the organisations set up to fight it. A cursory look at current terrorist activity does not make happy reading. In Germany, the Red Army Faction has been in existence since the late 1960s. Although now tiny due to a determined campaign against it by the police, it is still active. In 1989, for example, it assassinated the chairman of the Deutsche Bank, Alfred Herrhausen, using a remote-controlled bomb. In Italy, the Red

Since the 1970s, national governments in Europe have established a number of dedicated counter-terrorist units. In Germany, *Grenzschutzgruppe 9* (GSG 9) was set up after the 1972 Munich Olympics; in Italy, *Nucleo Operativo Centrale di Sicurezza* (NOCS) was trained in counter-terrorist tactics by the SAS; France established the counter-terrorist unit *Groupement d'Intervention de la Gendarmerie Nationale* (GIGN); and in the United States Delta Force was created in 1977 following GSG 9's successful operation at Mogadishu. All these groups, including the SAS, undertake frequent cross-training with each other, resulting in a constant interchange of information about specialist weapons, equipment and tactics. However, cross-training has presented a number of problems to the Regiment:

'The SAS is facing a major problem with regard to meeting growing demands with fewer resources. What people don't realise is that the Regiment is quite small. Its "badged" men – those who have passed Selection and Continuation – number around 350 men. Support units of vital tradesmen such as medics and signallers serve alongside the Regiment and wear the beige beret with their own cap badge, but it is the "badged" men who form the Sabre Squadrons. Each SAS trooper can serve up to eight months out of every year "deployed" away from Hereford on operational duties and training commitments. In 1992, for example, one trooper spent just seven weeks out of the whole year at Stirling Lines.

'To boost the available manpower to meet the growing demands, it has been proposed that the Royal Marines Special Boat Squadron (SBS) join forces with the SAS, thus reducing overheads and centralising the skills of both formations. However, the merger idea was abandoned in early 1990 after fierce lobbying by the Royal Marines to keep their "swimmer

Brigades, though now greatly diminished, still have a number of active cells, and in Spain the Basque group ETA continues its terror campaign to win self-determination for the Basque homeland. In addition, the easing of border controls as a result of the strengthening of the European Community has made it easy for terrorist groups to transport arms across the continent.

canoeists" within the Corps, and thus retain its beach reconnaissance capacity for amphibious landings. For the moment it appears that the two formations will remain separate, but in the current climate of financial restraints the prospect of merger is by no means remote, and in 1994 there will be the first joint SAS/SBS Selection course. If it is successful, it will herald the closure of the SBS's training base at Portland, Dorset.

'Despite the uncertainty with regards to organisational changes, some things don't change. There will always be the fight against the IRA, for example. At the same time, the Regiment always trains for the unexpected, such as a Gulf War scenario or a hostage-rescue situation.'

In a world of change one thing is certain: there will not be peace in the short term in Northern Ireland. Both the British and Irish governments have tried hard to bring about a peaceful solution to the conflict, most notably the Anglo-Irish agreement of November 1985, which gave the Irish Republic a direct role in Northern Ireland affairs for the first time. The British know that the likelihood of defeating the IRA is remote, but they hope the Provos will eventually lose support as the lot of Catholics in the Province is improved, which, combined with a general war-weariness, will result in a de facto ceasefire. To date, however, this scenario shows no sign of happening.

This being the case, the SAS continues its war against the terrorists. For its part the IRA has, since the 1970s, become ever more proficient and deadly. Sophisticated weapons were supplied to the Provisionals from the United States and the Middle East in the 1980s, for example, and the money raised for the Republican cause has meant that IRA terrorists have received the very best with regards to training and equipment. Libyan arms and American money, plus cash raised through extortion, has resulted in the IRA becoming a 'slick' organisation, one which has become expert at using violence as an instrument to further its aims, and the war has spread beyond Ulster's shores. In

1989, for example, the IRA killed 10 Royal Marines at Deal, Kent, and shot an RAF corporal and his six-month-old child in Germany; in 1990, the Tory MP Ian Gow was killed by a car bomb and the London stock exchange was bombed; in 1991, there was a bombing campaign in London and the Prime Minister's home in Downing Street was mortar bombed; in 1992 more bombs went off in London; and in the latest outrage, in April 1993, the Bishop's Gate area of the City of London was wrecked by IRA explosives.

The SAS continues to fight back in the deadly cat-and-mouse game. Since 1990 it has killed a number of IRA terrorists in numerous ambushes: Martin Corrigan, killed in Armagh in April 1990 while attempting to murder an Army reservist; Desmond Grew, nicknamed the 'Widow Maker', shot at Loughall in October 1990 while moving a consignment of Kalashnikov rifles; Alexander Patterson, a man responsible for the deaths of numerous civilians, including women and children, killed in November 1990 while firing on the house of a UDR reservist in Strabane; Peter Ryan, shot by the SAS in June 1991 in Coagh while on his way to murder someone; and Kevin Barry O'Donnell, Sean O'Farrell, Patrick Vincent and Peter Clancy, all ambushed in Clonoe, Coalisland, after machine gunning a police station. Though there is only troop operating in the Province – Ulster Troop – the SAS's commitment in Northern Ireland shows no sign of ending, a fact that will further tax the Regiment's resources.

The SAS is one of the best special forces units in the world. This fact is not lost on the allies and friends of Great Britain, who often request SAS advice on a host of matters. As a result, there has been an increase in 'advisory' roles undertaken by SAS soldiers:

'There is a long list of security tasks, as well as the increasing requirement for training teams. The latter provide military instruction to "friendly forces" in the Middle East and elsewhere, and they keep the Regiment's calendar fully booked. At any one time there are SAS advisors in

Above: The Land Rover SOV, one of the new vehicles currently entering service with the SAS.

Ulster, Belize, Brunei, the USA and the Middle East. Then there are the one-off jobs that crop up. In one month, for example, there were some of our blokes testing the defences of the Falklands and Ascension Island, as well as checking the security of two key military locations in the UK and preparing for an exercise in Gibraltar.

'Because of the pressure on manpower, many of these "jobs" are filled by men from R Squadron, the reserve squadron which is based at Hereford. Unlike the other two Territorial Army units, 21 and

23 SAS, the men who serve in R Squadron must all have previous military service. Indeed, they attend the same Selection courses as the regulars. Because of this they are all highly regarded.'

Special forces traditionally employ sophisticated equipment in their operations. This being the case, the SAS has an Operations Research Wing that continually tests and evaluates new equipment and weapons for the Regiment.

Transportation, for example, has always been an important part of SAS operations:

Below: A vulnerable target – a North Sea oil rig. The SAS is now responsible for their safety.

'A development unit is constantly working on new concepts and methods of operation for the Mobility, Air, Mountain and Boat Troops within each Sabre Squadron. Mobility has been a major part of SAS operations since its formation, and new vehicles are regularly tested by the development staff to ensure they meet future requirements with regards to utmost reliability and performance. Currently, the Regiment has two main requirements with regard to its vehicles: mobility on the battlefield and fast and effective transport capable of ferrying the "on call" CRW assault teams from Hereford to the scene of a major incident anywhere in the United Kingdom.

'Range Rovers form the nucleus of the fast-reaction force, being big enough to carry a four-man team, all their equipment and an extensive communications package, while Land Rovers have for years been the Regiment's main off-road vehicle. However, prior to the 1991 Gulf War the land mobility of the Regiment was being given special attention after the request for a purpose-built vehicle had been approved. The resulting trials and development project produced the Light Strike Vehicle (LSV), a two-man, four-wheel drive, all-terrain vehicle. It was undergoing the last phase of its trials in Oman when the Gulf War broke out. Several LSVs are currently being further enhanced, while a second project has concentrated on the procurement of a custom-built Land Rover following its excellent performance in the Gulf. Other vehicles currently under evaluation include a Land Rover Special Operations Vehicle (SOV), a six-wheeled Land Rover used by the Australian SAS, and numerous four-wheel drive vehicles from Europe.'

Land Rovers have been used by the SAS since the 1960s, and they have proved to be remarkable vehicles. Rugged, reliable and able to carry heavy payloads, the Land Rover will continue to serve with the Regiment well into

179

the next century. Pictures of SAS Land Rovers in the Gulf War showed them festooned with a variety of weapons, including Stinger anti-aircraft missiles, Browning heavy machine guns, Milan anti-tank missiles, grenade launchers and general purpose machine guns. The SOV, which is capable of carrying up to six men and all their equipment, also has the capacity to mount a number of weapons, such as machine guns front and rear, an 81mm mortar, a 51mm mortar and personal weapons. In addition, Milan, TOW or a 25mm cannon can be mounted on the pulpit weapons platform.

Though seaborne operations are mainly the preserve of the SBS, SAS Boat Troops also have a maritime brief. This being the case, Hereford is always looking at ways to upgrade the capabilities of its Boat Troops:

'Maritime Counter Measures (MCM) are the priority of the Boat Troops. Working closely with the SBS, their key tasks are the protection of Britain's oilfields from terrorist attacks and the safeguarding of UK shipping anywhere in the world. This is the one area of responsibility the

Left: Practising Maritime Counter Measures. In this the SAS works closely with the SBS.

practised in the North Sea in a series of so-called "purple" exercises.

'Among the new developments being examined in the maritime field are heated diving suits and sub-sea vehicles, which are used when exiting a submarine in freezing waters, such as around northern Norway.'

The sub-sea vehicle talked about above is the subskimmer, a piece of equipment that makes a clandestine approach to a hostile shore much easier. The great advantage with this craft is that it can operate as a high-speed surface craft or as a submersible, and can switch from one role to another with ease. On the surface it is powered by an ordinary outboard motor, while below the waves propulsion is provided by two electric underwater motors. An additional feature of the subskimmer is its ability to be 'parked' on the sea bed while the crew completes their mission. Having a maximum surface speed of 25 knots and a top underwater speed of 2.5 knots, the subskimmer will be a great asset to SAS Boat Troops on future operations.

David Stirling believed that his men should be able to arrive at their target by land, sea or air, and ever since the SAS was founded aircraft and parachuting have been an integral part of its operations. Today, the provision of long-range transport aircraft is provided by an RAF Special Forces Flight based at RAF Lyneham, Wiltshire. The principle fixed-wing aircraft used to support SAS operations is the C-130 Hercules long-range transport. There are several attributes that make the Hercules an excellent aircraft for special forces missions. Apart from the fact that it can be refuelled in midair by way of a probe located above the cockpit, it has turboprop propulsion, which means more power for less weight. In addition, high-strength alloys are used in the construction of the aircraft, its tricycle landing gear means it can take off and land from rough airstrips, its radar and full-span thermal de-icing give it an all-weather capacity, and the rear ramp door can be opened in flight for heavy dropping.

Regiment believes is still untested. To date there has been only one major "incident": in 1972, when a combined SAS/SBS team parachuted into the Atlantic Ocean to deal with a bomb threat to the luxury liner *Queen Elizabeth II*. However, the threat turned out to be a hoax, and since then only exercises have been carried out. Nevertheless, the growth in maritime traffic has increased the likelihood of a terrorist incident, and so new security measures have been introduced to prevent this from happening. They are regularly

The Regiment has been trying a number of parachuting concepts in recent years:

'The air wing of development operations is looking towards the twenty-first century with a concept of airborne insertion that will allow a trooper to exit a Hercules at a high altitude up to 80km away from the target. The procedure is called HAHO (high altitude, low opening) and it is already in service. However, at the moment the parachutist has a maximum ceiling of 7600m for leaving the aircraft, and to drift for up to 80km would require him to wear a sophisticated oxygen system and an astronaut-type heated suit to survive the extremely cold temperatures.

'Computer-simulated trials have indicated that such a drop would take up to an hour before the trooper landed, which means the aircraft could remain at a considerable distance away from any enemy detection sources, thus reducing the chances of the operation being com-promised. Using a "flat bed", nine-cell steerable canopy, it would be possible to glide across country and land with great accuracy.

'At present the Regiment is also main-taining its HALO (high altitude, low opening) skills, though operationally this form of insertion was turned down by force commanders in the Falklands and the Gulf because they considered it too risky. This being the case, HALO may be down-graded in the future.

'Another futuristic idea being reviewed by the SAS is Icarus, a powered microlight hand glider. The machine, designed by a former RAF officer and first seen at the 1992 Farnborough Air Show, has attracted major interest from the Americans. The concept behind the hi-tech glider is the rescue of special forces soldiers cut off and separated from their teams deep behind enemy lines, a scenario which became a

Left: HAHO parachuting. Such techniques will give the SAS even greater flexibility for future missions.

reality for several SAS soldiers during the 1991 Gulf War. Powered by a 100cc engine, two gliders can be packed into the 2500 litre drop tank of a Tornado aircraft. When assembled and in flight, the Icarus has a top speed of 80km/hr.'

One new form of operations the SAS is being involved in is the fight against drug trafficking:

'The Regiment's role in the 1990s includes an undercover war against international drug gangs. To date the SAS has worked with a number of American drug agencies, such as the Drug Enforcement Agency (DEA), whose personnel have visited Hereford on a number of occasions. Exchange operations have seen SAS men assisting US Coastguard anti-drug patrols. On the domestic front, the Regiment has been involved in drug-busting missions in London, and in one notable case MP5-armed troopers stormed a sea-going tug in docklands and seized a massive narcotics haul. However, in the UK the SAS's greatest interest in the drugs world is in stopping the IRA, who, in the mid-1980s, masterminded a worldwide chain of drug operations to fund its terrorist activities. It also claimed it would defeat the British authorities by undermining the economy with cheap drugs, which would destroy society and cost millions of pounds to put right. This harebrained scheme, needless to say, didn't work, but the IRA's involvement with drug trafficking is real and is one of the SAS's hardest challenges.'

The battle against drugs is a worldwide one and is being fought by many agencies in Europe and the United States. It is a war that is escalating in intensity: world production of opium doubled between 1986 and 1989, and the cocaine trade has wrecked many governments in Latin America, most notably Colombia. The main market for drugs is still the United States, which seems to have an insatiable desire for cocaine, heroin and marijuana, but increasingly Europe is attracting the attention of the world's drug

Above: The new Icarus glider, which, if it had been in service, might have prevented the deaths of SAS soldiers during the 1991 Gulf War with Iraq.

barons. As a consequence, drugs have started to pour onto the continent, and the inner cities of western Europe in particular have become major distribution points for narcotics. At long last the state's agencies have been mobilised, and they include the SAS. But the enemy is powerful

The Colombian cocaine trade developed from a small cottage industry in the early 1970s into a multi-billion dollar concern by the beginning of the 1990s, with its own distribution network and armies of 'narco-terrorists' to ensure the trade continued undisturbed. The

chief villain of the piece is the Medellin Cartel, a loose association of drug producers and smugglers who have combined to share the market, ward off rivals and intimidate the government. The Cartel's profits are immense, and with this wealth has come the power to kill the country's presidents, judges, senior army officials and a multitude of civilians with impunity. To be fair to the Colombian government, measures have been taken against the Cartel, but it has proved to be an intractable foe. In the late 1980s Western leaders, such as President George Bush of the United States and Prime Minister Thatcher of the UK, tried to help the Colombians against the Cartel. Thatcher, for example, sent an SAS team to

Above: No one doubts that international drug gangs pose a threat to Western democracy, and so units such as the SAS have been tasked to fight them. But is it a case of too little too late?

assist in the war against cocaine production in the Colombian jungle. It was an astute move: the SAS has a fine pedigree in jungle warfare. The troopers trained a unit called the Anti-Narcotics Police in the art of jungle warfare, teaching them such things as carrying rifles when on patrol crooked in the forearms, in a position known as the 'Belfast cradle', that allows a quicker response when a surprise contact with the enemy occurs. In a significant victory over the drug barons, an SAS-led team found and killed one of Colombia's leading cocaine barons, Gonzalo Rodriquez Gacha, along with his son and five bodyguards. As ever, though, there were other ruthless drug lords to replace Gacha. One of the major drug barons, Pablo Escobar, surrendered to the government, but on his own terms. In effect both sides declared a draw, but the export of cocaine to the United States and Europe goes on. The SAS, for its part, continues to train Colombian police and military units in the art of jungle warfare, but one wonders how long this deployment will go on for in the face of UK defence cuts and the continuing over-stretching of the Regiment's resources. One thing is certain: the SAS's campaign against international drug gangs is just beginning.

SAS OPERATIONS 1941 TO THE PRESENT

1941
Axis airfields raided:
14 December:
Agheila   Enemy vehicles destroyed

21 December:
Agedabia   37 Axis aircraft destroyed

1942
Axis airfields raided:
8 March:
Barce   One aircraft and some trucks destroyed
Berka   15 aircraft destroyed

25 March:
Benina   Five aircraft destroyed

13 June:
Benina   Two aircraft destroyed
Berka   11 aircraft destroyed

7 July:
Bagoush   37 Axis aircraft destroyed
El Daba   Failed to destroy any aircraft
Fuka   14 aircraft destroyed

12 July:
Fuka   22 aircraft destroyed

26 July:
Sidi Haneish   40 aircraft destroyed

1943
12 July:
Operation 'Chestnut'   2 SAS
Abortive operation in northern Sicily intended
to support the Allied invasion of the island

3 September:
Operation 'Baytown'   Special Raiding
Squadron (1 SAS temporarily renamed)
Capture of the Italian port of Bagnara

7 September:
Operation 'Speedwell'   2 SAS
Successful mission in northeast Italy

2-6 October:
Operation 'Begonia'   2 SAS
Evacuation of British POWs from Italy

27 October:
Operation 'Candytuft'   2 SAS
Railway line cut on east Italian coast

1944
7 January:
Operation 'Maple'   2 SAS
Abortive attempt to support the Anzio landings

30 January:
Operation 'Baobab'   2 SAS
Support of the Anzio landings in Italy

6 June:
Operation 'Titanic'   1 SAS
Unsuccessful mission in Normandy

6 June-3 July:
Operation 'Bulbasket'   1 SAS
Railway lines cut and trains destroyed in
southern France

6 June:
Operation 'Dingson'   4 SAS
Abortive mission in Brittany, France

6-9 June:
Operation 'Samwest'   4 SAS
Mission in Brittany that was disrupted by
German forces

6-21 June:
Operation 'Houndsworth'   1 SAS
Railway lines cut west of Dijon, France

6 June-15 August:
Operation 'Gain'   1 SAS
German commuications severed
southwest of Paris

7 June:
Operation 'Cooney'   4 SAS
Severing railway lines in Brittany, France,
before joining up with the 'Dingson' party

Above: David Stirling, whose vision and drive
established the world's most effective special
forces unit. Stirling himself died in 1990.

23 June-18 July:
Operation 'Lost'   4 SAS
A very successful mission in Brittany, France,
which resulted in over 2000 enemy casualties
and a large number of *Maquis* being armed

8 July-11 August:
Operation 'Haft'   1 SAS
Intelligence gathering in northwest France

16 July-7 October:
Operation 'Dickens'   3 SAS
Disruption of rail communications around
Nantes, France.

19 July-23 August:
Operation 'Defoe'   2 SAS
Ineffectual reconnaissance of the Argentan area
of Normandy

23 July-10 September:
Operation 'Rupert'   2 SAS
Unsuccessful attempt to destroy rail lines in
eastern France

25 July:
Operation 'Gaff'   2 SAS
Abortive attempt to kill Erwin Rommel

27 July-1 September:
Operation 'Hardy'   2 SAS
Aggressive raiding around Dijon

28 July-15 August:
Operation 'Chaucer'   5 SAS
General harassment of German forces in
northwest France

31 July-15 August:
Operation 'Shakespeare'   5 SAS
Harassment of German forces west of Paris

3-15 August:
Operation 'Bunyan'   5 SAS
Harassing German forces west of Paris

3-24 August:
Operation 'Dunhill'   2 SAS
Intelligence gathering in
northwest France

5-18 August:
Operation 'Derry'   3 SAS
German forces hindered as they tried
to move towards Brest

10-23 August:
Operation 'Haggard'   1 SAS
Fighting German forces around the River Loire

10 August-27 September:
Operation 'Samson'   3 SAS
Moderately successful mission in southern
France

11-24 August:
Operation 'Marshall'   3 SAS
Offensive operations in France

12 August-9 October:
Operation 'Loyton'   2 SAS
Intelligence gathering in eastern France

13-24 August:
Operation 'Snelgrove'   3 SAS
Arming Resistance forces in southern France

13 August-19 September:
Operation 'Barker'   3 SAS
Protecting flank of US Third Army
as it advanced through France

13 August-24 September:
Operation 'Harrod'   3 SAS
Disrupting enemy movements in
central France

13 August-26 September:
Operation 'Kipling'   1 SAS
Large jeep operation in central France which
resulted in the surrender of 3000 Germans

15 August-9 September:
Operation 'Jockworth'   3 SAS
Disrupting enemy forces in
southeast France

16 August-13 September:
Operation 'Noah'   5 SAS
Intelligence gathering in the French Ardennes

19 August-11 September:
Operation 'Newton'   3 SAS
Successful harassing mission of German forces
in central France

19 August-19 September:
Operation 'Wallace'   2 SAS
Large, successful jeep operation around
Dijon, western France

26 August-3 September:
Operation 'Wolsey'
Intelligence gathering in northeast France

28 August-1 September:
Operation 'Benson'   5 SAS
Intelligence gathering in northeast France

29 August-14 September:
Operation 'Spenser'   4 SAS
Much damage inflicted in the Germans in
central France

2 September-15 September:
Operation 'Brutus'   5 SAS
Intelligence gathering in Belgian Ardennes

6-11 September:
Operation 'Caliban'   5 SAS
Severing enemy communications in
northeast Belgium

**Above: SAS jeeps in northwest Europe, 1945. One
of the largest SAS jeep missions in this period was
Operation 'Archway', which involved 75 jeeps.**

15 September-3 October:
Operation 'Pistol'   2 SAS
Cutting rail lines in eastern France

16 September-14 March 1945:
Operation 'Fabian'   5 SAS
Intelligence gathering around
Arnhem, Holland

27 September-17 March 1945:
Operation 'Gobbo'   5 SAS
Intelligence gathering around
Drente, Holland

24 December-25 January 1945:
Operation 'Franklin'   4 SAS
Supporting US forces during German
Ardenness offensive

27 December-14 February 1945:
Operation 'Galia'   2 SAS
Intelligence gathering in northern Italy

27 December-15 January 1945:
Operation 'Regent'   5 SAS
Blunting the German Ardennes offensive

1945
March-May 1945:
Operation 'Archway'   1 and 2 SAS
Assisting advance of British 21st Army Group
into Germany

4 March-24 April:
Operation 'Tombola'   2 SAS
Successful offensive mission in north Italy

3-18 April:
Operation 'Keystone'   2 SAS
Jeep mission in Holland

3 April-8 May:
Operation 'Larkswood'   5 SAS
Jeep offensive into northern Germany

6 April-6 May:
Operation 'Howard'   1 SAS
Jeep operation in northwest Germany

May:
Operation 'Apostle'
Disarming German garrison in Norway

1950-60
Malaya
Campaign against communist guerrillas in
the jungle which resulted in the
reformation of 22 SAS

November 1958-January 1959
Jebel Akhdar, Oman
Successful campaign against rebels
in northern Oman

1963-1966
Borneo   A, B, D and G Squadrons
Victorious jungle campaign against rebel
guerrillas and Indonesian forces

April 1964-November 1967
Aden   A, B and D Squadrons
Campaign against tribesmen in the Radfan area

of the interior, and guerrillas in the port of
Aden itself (so-called 'Keeni Meeni' operations)

1969-
Northern Ireland
On-going campaign against terrorists in Ulster

1970-76
Oman
Successful campaign against communist
guerrillas, included very effective SAS 'hearts
and minds' policy

19 July 1972
The Battle of Mirbat
Nine-man SAS team defeats large guerrilla
force in Oman during one-day battle

5 May 1980
Iranian Embassy, London
Operation 'Nimrod'
Successful SAS hostage-rescue operation

July 1981
The Gambia
SAS helps to restore President Jawara to power

April-June 1982
The Falkland Islands
Intelligence gathering and raiding operations
against Argentinian positions

8 May 1987
Loughall, Northern Ireland
SAS wipes out East Tyrone Brigade in ambush

6 March 1988
Gibraltar
SAS team shoots dead three IRA terrorists

1989-
Columbia
22 SAS committed to the anti-cocaine war. This
commitment is on-going

August 1990-February 1991
Arabian Gulf
Large SAS contingent involved in operations
behind the lines in Iraq and Kuwait

INDEX

Jane Hudson

Series Adviser **Catherine Walter**

Audio CD included

Navigate

Workbook
with key

Beginner → **A1**

OXFORD
UNIVERSITY PRESS

Contents

Oxford 3000™ *Navigate* has been based on the Oxford 3000 to ensure that learners are only covering the most relevant vocabulary.

1 First meetings

1.1 On business or on holiday?

Vocabulary introductions

1 Complete the sentences. Use the phrases in the box.

> on business ~~on holiday~~ on holiday to study

I'm Aneta. I'm here _on holiday_.

I'm Haluk. I'm here _____.

I'm Sachi. I'm here _____.

I'm Ryan. I'm here _____.

2 Match beginnings 1–8 to endings a–h.

1 Hello,	a business?
2 Hi, I'm	b you.
3 Nice	c I'm not.
4 And	d I am.
5 Are you here to	e I'm Luz.
6 No,	f Murat.
7 Are you here on	g study?
8 Yes,	h to meet you.

3 Complete the conversation between Chris and David. Use the words in the box.

> And ~~Hello~~ Hi holiday Nice No study Yes you

Chris ¹ _Hello_ , I'm Chris.
David ² _____, I'm David. ³ _____ to meet you.
Chris ⁴ _____ you. Are ⁵ _____ here on holiday?
David ⁶ _____, I'm not. I'm here to ⁷ _____. And you? Are you here on ⁸ _____?
Chris ⁹ _____, I am.

Grammar verb *be* (I/you)

4 Complete the sentences with *I* or *you*.

1 _I_ 'm Lola.
2 Are _____ on holiday?
3 _____'m not Ahmet.
4 _____'m here to study.
5 Are _____ Sarah?
6 _____'m not on business.

5 Complete the conversations.

1 **Viktor** Hi, _I'm_ Viktor.
   Amy _____ Amy.
2 **Kemal** Hello, _____ Kemal.
   Susie Hi, _____ Susie.
3 **Amy** _____ _____ on business?
   Susie No, _____ _____.
4 **Viktor** _____ on holiday. And you?
   Kemal _____ here to study.
5 **Viktor** _____ _____ Susie?
   Susie Yes, _____ _____.
6 **Amy** Hello. _____ _____ Viktor?
   Kemal No, _____ Kemal.

6a Circle the correct options.

1 ___ Will.
   a I'm **b** Am I
2 ___ Sabine.
   a Am I **b** I'm not
3 ___ here on business?
   a You aren't **b** Are you
4 ___ Frida?
   a You're **b** Are you
5 ___ to study.
   a Am I **b** I'm here
6 ___ on holiday?
   a Are you **b** You aren't
7 ___ Ben.
   a I'm not **b** Am I
8 ___ here to study.
   a Are you **b** You're

b 1.1))) Listen and check your answers.

c 1.1))) Listen again and repeat.

I can …	Very well	Quite well	More practice
introduce myself.	○	○	○
ask questions with *be*.	○	○	○

1.2 Where are you from?

Vocabulary numbers 1–10, countries

1 Complete the crossword.

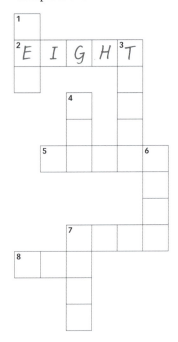

Across ▶
2 8
5 7
7 5
8 2

Down ▼
1 10
3 3
4 1
6 9
7 4

2 Complete the series.

1 one   two   _three_
2 two   four   _____
3 three six   _____
4 one   three _____
5 five   six   _____
6 six   eight _____
7 three two   _____
8 ten   nine   _____

3 Label the photos with the names of the countries.

1 Moscow, _Russia_
2 Sydney, _____
3 Beijing, _____

4 Rio de Janeiro, _____
5 Istanbul, _____
6 New York, _____ _____

7 Tokyo, _____
8 Java, _____
9 Madrid, _____

PRONUNCIATION saying names of countries

4a Complete the table with the countries in the box.

~~Australia~~ Brazil China Japan Russia Turkey

Stress on syllable one	Stress on syllable two
	Australia

b **1.2))** Listen and check your answers.

c **1.2))** Listen again and repeat.

Grammar verb *be* (we/you)

5 Complete the sentences with *I'm* or *We're*.

1 _I'm_ from Turkey.	**2** _____ from Spain.	**3** _____ from Russia.
4 _____ from Indonesia.	**5** _____ from Brazil.	**6** _____ from Australia.

6a Make the sentences negative. Use the words in (brackets).

1 We're from the UK. (the USA)

   We aren't from the USA.

2 I'm from Japan. (China)

   I_____

3 We're here on holiday. (on business)

   We _____

4 I'm Susie. (Amy)

   I_____

5 You're here to study. (on holiday)

   You _____

6 We're from Washington. (New York)

   We _____

7 You're from Brazil. (Spain)

   You _____

b 1.3))) Listen and check your answers.

7 Complete the conversation between Igor (I), Ratu (R) and Nuray (N).

I   Hello, **1** _I'm_ Igor.

R   Hi, **2**_____ Ratu.

N   And **3**_____ Nuray.

I   Nice to meet you. Where **4**__ _____ _____ from, Ratu?

R   **5**_____ from Indonesia.

I   And you, Nuray?

N   **6**_____ from Turkey.

I   **7**_____ _____ here to study?

R, N No, **8**__ _____ _____. **9**_____ on holiday.

8 Put eight more capital letters in the correct places.

_M_y name is _M_arisol. i'm from seville in spain. javier and i are on holiday in turkey. we are in a hotel in istanbul.

_____

_____

_____

_____

I can …	Very well	Quite well	More practice
say countries and numbers 1–10.	○	○	○
talk about where I'm from.	○	○	○

1.3   How do you spell that?

Vocabulary   the alphabet

1a   Circle the letter with a different sound.

1	A	G	H	J	5	D	P	T	Y
2	C	F	M	S	6	L	N	R	X
3	B	E	I	V	7	C	G	K	T
4	O	Q	U	W	8	E	F	M	Z

b   1.4))) Listen and check your answers.

2a   1.5))) Listen and write what you hear.

1 _U_ _S_ _A_   5 __ __ __
2 __ __ __   6 __ __ __
3 __ __ __   7 __ __ __
4 __ __ __   8 __ __ __

b   Match numbers 1–8 in exercise **2a** to photos A–H.

A

B

C

D

E 1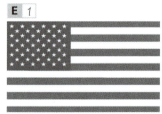

F

G

H

➔ **PRONUNCIATION TIP** To remember *A, E, I, O, U*:
A = day
E = meet
I = hi
O = no
U = you

PRONUNCIATION   the alphabet

3a   Complete the table with the words in the box.

address   are   bye   day   hi   home   meet   name
phone   see   spell   you

/eɪ/	/iː/	/e/	/aɪ/	/əʊ/	/juː/	/ɑː/
		address				

b   1.6))) Listen and check your answers to exercise **3a**.

Grammar question words

4a (Circle) the correct word.

1 ___ 's your name?
 a What   **b** How   **c** Where

2 ___ do you spell that?
 a What   **b** How   **c** Where

3 ___ are you from?
 a What   **b** How   **c** Where

4 ___ in Russia?
 a What   **b** How   **c** Where

5 ___ 's your phone number?
 a What   **b** How   **c** Where

b Match answers a–e to questions 1–5 in exercise **3a**.

a _3_ I'm from Russia.
b ___ Vladivostok.
c ___ My name's Viktor.
d ___ 007 495 23005799
e ___ V-I-K-T-O-R

5a Write the questions.

 A ¹ _What's your name?_ _____
 B My name's Amy.
 A ² _____
 B My last name's Chang.
 A ³ _____
 B C-H-A-N-G
 A ⁴ _____
 B I'm from China.
 A ⁵ _____
 B 0086 189 9820334

b **1.7**))) Listen and check your answers.

c **1.7**))) Listen again and repeat.

6a Put lines a–i in the correct order to make a conversation.

a Hi, I'm Tymon. What's your name? _1_
b How do you spell that? ___
c K-E-I-R-A? ___
d I'm from Gdańsk in Poland. ___
e Hello. My name's Keira. ___
f I'm from Bristol in the UK. And you? ___
g Yes, that's right. ___
h K-E-I-R-A. ___
i Where are you from, Keira? ___

b **1.8**))) Listen and check your answers to exercise **6a**.

I can …	Very well	Quite well	More practice
say the alphabet.	○	○	○
use question words.	○	○	○

1.4 Speaking and writing

Speaking *hello* and *goodbye*

1 Complete the table with the words and phrases in the box.

> Bye   Goodbye   ~~Good morning~~   Have a nice day   Hello
> Hi   How are you?   Morning   See you later

Hello	Goodbye
Good morning	

2 Complete the conversations. Write one word.

1 **A** Hello.
  B *Hi* .

2 **A** Goodbye.
  B _____.

3 **A** _____ are you?
  B _____, thanks. And you?
  A Great, _____.

4 **A** Have a nice _____.
  B Thanks. You, _____.

5 **A** _____ morning.
  B _____.

6 **A** Bye.
  B _____ you later.

Writing filling in a form

3 Match words 1–6 to information a–f.

1 First name   a Avenida Lusitana, 13, Granada
2 Last name   b Spain
3 Country   c 0034 758 3902281
4 Home address   d *Eva Sanz*
5 Phone number   e Eva
6 Signature   f Sanz

4 Read the information and complete the student registration card.

> " Hello, I'm Faruk Akkaya from Turkey. I'm here to study English. My address is 39 Beykoz Sokak, Ankara. My phone number is 0090 508 99200437. "

Student Registration Card

First name	¹ *Faruk*
Last name	² _____
Home address	³ _____, Ankara
Country	⁴ _____
Phone number	⁵ _____
Signature	*Faruk Akkaya*

I can …	Very well	Quite well	More practice
say *hello* and *goodbye*.	○	○	○
fill in a form.	○	○	○

1.5   Listening for pleasure

Murder in Kingston

1   Look at the illustrations. Put them in order 1–4.

2a   **1.9**))) Listen to an extract from a radio play. Tick (✓) the woman you believe.

Mrs Penelope R. Hoffman ___

Mrs Fiona D. Wright ___

b   **1.9**))) Listen to the extract again. Turn to page 84 and read along.

3   What do you think happens next? Look at the illustrations and choose one.

4   **1.10**))) Listen to the next part of the radio play and check your answer to exercise **3**. You can read along on page 85.

Questions

2.1   What's this in English?

objects; numbers 11–100

1a Complete the objects with the missing vowels (*a, e, i, o, u*) and write *a* or *an* if necessary.

1 *a* t*a*bl*e*t   2 *-* b*o* *o*ks   3 ___ ph_n_s   4 ___ n_t_p_d   5 ___ p_ns

6 ___ l_pt_p   7 ___ k_ys   8 ___ _ppl_s   9 ___ _mbr_ll_   10 ___ w_ll_t

b **2.1**))) Listen and check your answers.

2 Complete the series.

1 eight, nine, ten, *eleven*
2 thirteen, fourteen, fifteen, _____
3 thirty-one, thirty-two, thirty-three, _____
4 ninety-seven, ninety-eight, ninety-nine, _____
5 six, eight, ten, _____
6 fourteen, sixteen, eighteen, _____
7 forty-three, forty-five, forty-seven, _____
8 fifty, sixty, seventy, _____

PRONUNCIATION word stress: *-teen* and *-ty*

3a **2.2**))) Listen and write the numbers you hear.

1 ___*30*___   6 _____
2 _____   7 _____
3 _____   8 _____
4 _____   9 _____
5 _____   10 _____

b **2.2**))) Listen again and repeat.

Grammar   *this/that/these/those*; verb *be* (it/they)

4   Circle the correct options.

1   What's *this* / *that* / *these* / *those* in English?

2   What's *this* / *that* / *these* / *those* in English?

3   What are *this* / *that* / *these* / *those* in English?

4   What are *this* / *that* / *these* / *those* in English?

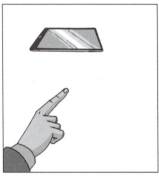

5   What's *this* / *that* / *these* / *those* in English?

6   What are *this* / *that* / *these* / *those* in English?

7   What's *this* / *that* / *these* / *those* in English?

8   What are *this* / *that* / *these* / *those* in English?

5a   Complete the sentences with *It's* or *They're*.

a   _They're_ apples.
b   _____ a book.
c   _____ a laptop.
d   _____ wallets.
e   _____ a tablet.
f   _____ pens.
g   _____ an umbrella.
h   _____ notepads.

b   Match answers a–h in exercise **5a** to questions 1–8 in exercise **4**.

1 _g_   3 ___   5 ___   7 ___
2 ___   4 ___   6 ___   8 ___

6   Complete the conversations with *'s*, *is*, *'re* or *are*. Use the contractions where possible.

1   A   What_'s_ that?
    B   It _____ my pen.
2   A   _____ those your keys?
    B   Yes, they _____ .
3   A   _____ this a phone?
    B   Yes, it _____ .
4   A   What _____ these?
    B   They _____ apples.
5   A   _____ those your books?
    B   Yes, they _____ .
6   A   What _____ that?
    B   It _____ my laptop.

I can ...	Very well	Quite well	More practice
use singular and plural forms.	○	○	○
say numbers 11–100.	○	○	○
use *this*, *that*, *these*, *those* and use the verb *be* (it/they).	○	○	○

2.2　What's your job?

Jane

Gregor

Hannah

Vocabulary jobs

1　Look at the photos and complete the puzzle. What is the mystery word?

Carmelo

¹S H O P A S S I S T A N T

Mike

Carmen

Phei

2　Complete the sentences about the people and their jobs from exercise **1**.

1　Jane's _a shop assistant._
2　Mike's _____.
3　Phei's _____.
4　Carmelo's _____.
5　Carmen's _____.
6　Gregor's _____.
7　Hannah's _____.

➡ **STUDY TIP** Try to write down vocabulary in groups, e.g.
numbers: *one, two, three*, etc.
countries: *Australia, Brazil, China*, etc.
objects: *apple, book, key*, etc.
jobs: *doctor, engineer, nurse*, etc.

PRONUNCIATION word stress: jobs

3a　Complete the table with the words in the box.

~~doctor~~　shop assistant　student　taxi driver　teacher
waiter

Two syllables	Four syllables
●●	●●●●
doctor	

b　2.3))) Listen and check your answers.

c　2.3))) Listen again and repeat.

Grammar verb *be* (he/she/it/they)

4a Complete the sentences with *He's*, *She's*, *It's* or *They're*.

1   _It's_ from Japan.   2 _____ a doctor.

3 _____ on holiday.   4 _____ from France.

5 _____ students.   6 _____ a taxi driver.

7 _____ from Spain.   8 _____ a shop
assistant.

b 2.4)) Listen and check your answers.

c 2.4)) Listen again and repeat.

5a (Circle) the correct options.

1   What ___ that?
    a ('s   **b** are
2   ___ Natasha a teacher?
    a Is   **b** Are
3   Where ___ Bagus from?
    a 's   **b** are
4   ___ those your pens?
    a Is   **b** Are
5   Where ___ Olga from?
    a 's   **b** are
6   ___ this your phone?
    a is   **b** are
7   What ___ these?
    a 's   **b** are
8   ___ Fabio a waiter?
    a Is   **b** Are

b Match answers a–h to questions 1–8 in exercise **5a**.

_3_   a   He's from Indonesia.
___   b   Yes, it is.
___   c   No, he isn't. He's unemployed.
___   d   It's my notepad.
___   e   She's from Russia.
___   f   They're apples.
___   g   No, she isn't. She's an engineer.
___   h   Yes, they are.

6 Complete the conversation with the correct form of *be*.
Use contractions where possible.

A Hi. I ¹_m_ Rob. What ² _____ your name?
B I ³ _____ Philippa.
A ⁴ _____ you a doctor, Philippa?
B Yes, I ⁵ _____.
A Who ⁶ _____ that?
B That ⁷ _____ my friend. Her name ⁸ _____
Tina.
A ⁹ _____ she a doctor, too?
B Yes, she ¹⁰ _____.
A Who ¹¹ _____ those people with Tina?
B They ¹² _____ Dan and Eddie.
A ¹³ _____ they doctors, too?
B No, they ¹⁴ _____. They ¹⁵ _____ nurses.

I can …	Very well	Quite well	More practice
talk about jobs.	○	○	○
use the verb *be* (he/she/it/they).	○	○	○

2.3 Where are they?

1 (Circle) the correct options.

1 This in Mark. _____ 's a taxi driver.
  a He   **b** She

2 Maksym and Agata are from Poland. _____ 're doctors.
  a She   **b** They

3 Where's my wallet? _____ isn't in my bag.
  a He   **b** It

4 I'm an engineer. _____ 'm from Brazil.
  a I   **b** You

5 Thorsten and I are from Germany. _____ 're waiters.
  a We   **b** They

6 Nice to meet you, Julio. Are _____ from Spain?
  a he   **b** you

7 Isabelle is from Australia. _____ 's a teacher.
  a He   **b** She

8 Those are nice apples. _____ 're from France.
  a It   **b** They

2 Complete the conversations with the correct pronouns.

1 **A** Are you a doctor?
  B No _I_ 'm not.

2 **A** Is that your laptop?
  B Yes, _____ is.

3 **A** Are Sam and Ella here to study?
  B No, _____ aren't.

4 **A** Is Paolo from Germany?
  B No, _____ isn't.

5 **A** Are those your keys?
  B Yes, _____ are.

6 **A** Is Maria from Spain?
  B Yes, _____ is.

7 **A** Are you and Markus friends?
  B Yes, _____ are.

8 **A** Are you here on holiday?
  B Yes, _____ am

3a Complete the phone conversation.

A Hi, Chris. Louise here. How are ¹_you_?
B ²_____ 'm fine, thanks. And ³_____ ?
A Great, thanks. Are ⁴_____ at home?
B No, ⁵_____ 'm on business in the USA with Jack.
A Where in the USA?
B ⁶_____ 're in New York.
A Is Ellen in New York with you?
B No, ⁷_____ isn't. ⁸_____ 's on holiday with friends.
A Really? Where are ⁹_____ ?
B ¹⁰_____ 're in Izmir.
A Where's that?
B ¹¹_____ 's in Turkey.
A Is Tommy in Turkey, too?
B No, ¹²_____ isn't. ¹³_____ 's at home with my mother.

b **2.5**))) Listen and check your answers.

Vocabulary   prepositions of place

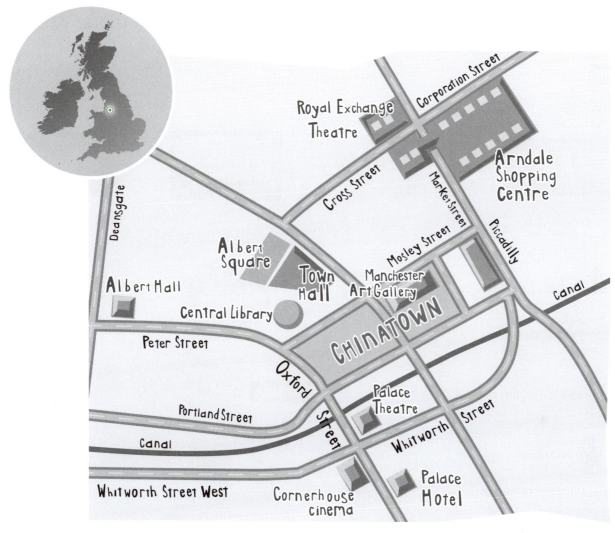

4 Look at the map of Manchester. Match questions 1–6 to answers a–f.

1 Where's Manchester? _d_
2 Where's the Arndale Shopping Centre? ___
3 Where's the Central Library? ___
4 Where's the Palace Theatre? ___
5 Where's Manchester Art Gallery? ___
6 Where's The Albert Hall? ___

a It's next to the Town Hall.
b It's in Chinatown.
c It's on Peter Street.
d It's in the UK.
e It's near the canal.
f It's in Manchester.

5 Look at the map and complete the sentences with the correct prepositions.

1 Manchester is _in_ the north west of England.
2 The Cornerhouse cinema is _____ the Palace Hotel.
3 The Manchester Art Gallery is _____ Mosley Street.
4 The Arndale Shopping centre is _____ Market Street.
5 The Royal Exchange Theatre is _____ the Arndale Shopping Centre.
6 The Palace Theatre is _____ Oxford Street.

I can …	Very well	Quite well	More practice
use subject pronouns.	○	○	○
use prepositions of place.	○	○	○

2.4 Speaking and writing

Speaking the time

1a Write the times.

1 `3.10`

It's three ten.

2 `8.55`

3 `10.15`

4 `2.00`

5 `9.20`

6 `4.45`

7 `11.05`

8 `5.30`

b 2.6)) Listen and check your answers.

c 2.6)) Listen again and repeat.

2a Circle the correct options.

1 **A** What time is it?
  B (It's) / It's at one twenty-five.

2 **A** What time is _it / your bus_?
  B It's at eleven fifty.

3 **A** What time's the meeting?
  B It's _at / from_ six o'clock to seven thirty.

4 **A** What time is _it / the class_?
  B It's two thirty-five.

5 **A** What time's your train?
  B _It's / It's at_ twelve forty.

6 **A** What time is _it / the party_?
  B It's from eight fifteen to eleven forty-five.

7 **A** What time's the film?
  B _It's / It's at_ six fifteen.

8 **A** What time is _it / the next class_?
  B It's at two thirty.

b 2.7)) Listen and check your answers.

Writing a blog

3 Rewrite the sentences using contractions.

1 My name is Fabiana.   _My name's Fabiana._
2 I am not a student.   _____
3 He is from Indonesia.   _____
4 We are here to study.   _____
5 He is not on business.   _____
6 She is a friend.   _____
7 We are not at home.   _____
8 It is a company in Berlin.   _____
9 She is not a doctor.   _____
10 In this photo I am with Paola.   _____

4 Complete the profile with the missing words. Some of the words are contractions.

> My ¹ _name's_ Liana. I'm 23 and I'm ² _____ Italy.
> I'm a nurse ³ _____ a hospital. In this photo
> ⁴ _____ with Matteo. ⁵ _____ on holiday
> in Greece. Matteo is 25 and he's ⁶ _____ shop
> assistant. The shop is a flower shop and ⁷ _____
> near the hospital. Matteo's my friend and ⁸ _____
> a really nice guy.

I can …	Very well	Quite well	More practice
tell the time.	○	○	○
write a blog.	○	○	○

Review: Units 1 and 2

Grammar

1 Complete the sentences with the correct form of *be*. Use contractions where possible.

1 It*'s* a pen.
2 _____ you from Germany?
3 He _____ an engineer. He's a teacher.
4 Hi, I _____ Sophie.
5 _____ she a student?
6 We _____ on holiday. We're on business.

2 Complete the conversations with the question words in the box. You can use the words more than once.

| How What Where Who |

1 **A** __*What*__'s your name?
   B Hannah.
2 **A** _____ are you from?
   B From Turkey.
3 **A** _____ do you spell 'clock'?
   B C-L-O-C-K.
4 **A** _____'s that?
   B It's Charlie. He's my friend.
5 **A** _____'s this in English?
   B It's a notepad.

3 Circle the correct options.

1 **A** What are *this* / *these*?
   B They're apples.
2 **A** Who's *that* / *those*?
   B It's Sam. He's in my class.
3 **A** What are those buildings?
   B *It's* / *They're* the Parliament Buildings.
4 **A** What's *this* / *these*?
   B It's a tablet.
5 **A** Who are *that* / *those* people?
   B They're students.

4 Rewrite the sentences with the correct subject pronoun.

1 John's a waiter.   __*He's a waiter.*__
2 George and Millie are friends. _____.
3 Jakarta's in Indonesia.   _____.
4 Laura's from Australia.   _____.
5 You and Robbie are late.   _____.

Vocabulary

5 Write the numbers.

1 12 __*twelve*__   4 58 _____
2 36 _____   5 40 _____
3 19 _____   6 100 _____

6 Complete the jobs with *a, e, i, o* or *u*.

1 d o c t o r   4 sh_p __ss__st__nt
2 __ng__n__ __r   5 t__x__ dr__v__r
3 n__rs__   6 t__ __ch__r

7 Label the photos with *a/an* and the names of the objects.

1 __*an apple*__   2 _____   3 _____   4 _____

8 Circle the correct prepositions.

1 Cape Town's *in* / *on* South Africa.
2 Buckingham Palace is *on* / *near* St James' Park.
3 The Museum of Modern Art is *next to* / *on* 53rd Street.
4 The Parliament Building is *near* / *in* the river Spree.
5 The gardens are *on* / *in* Chinatown.
6 Wat Pho is *on* / *in* Bangkok.

Functional language

9 Look at the clocks and complete the conversations.

1 **A** What time is it?
   B It's __*one forty-five.*__

2 **A** What time's the meeting?
   B It's _____
      _____

3 **A** What time's the next bus?
   B It's _____

4 **A** What time's your English class?
   B It's _____

5 **A** What time is it?
   B It's _____

6 **A** What time's the next train?
   B It's _____

1 1.45
2 9.30 – 11.00
3 3.30
4 6.15 – 7.45
5 4.25
6 12.05

3 People and possessions

3.1 My neighbours

Vocabulary adjective + noun phrases (1); irregular plurals

1 Complete the phrases with the words in the box.

> book   dog   funny   ~~great~~   hard   waiter

1   a _great_ song

2   a friendly _____

3   a _____ film

4   a clever _____

5   a _____ job

6   a lovely _____

2 Rewrite the sentences with the word in (brackets).

1   That's a phone. (nice)
    That's a nice phone.

2   Ireland is a country. (friendly)
    _____

3   Judith Polgár is a woman. (clever)
    _____

4   Noma's a restaurant. (great)
    _____

5   Prague is a city. (lovely)
    _____

6   Jonah Hill is a man. (funny)
    _____

3a Rewrite the sentences using the plural.

1   She's a good friend.
    They're good friends.

2   He's a clever child.
    _____

3   He's an old man.
    _____

4   She's a friendly neighbour.
    _____

5   She's a funny woman.
    _____

6   It's an interesting house.
    _____

7   He's a lovely person.
    _____

8   It's a great book.
    _____

b 3.1))) Listen and check your answers.

c 3.1))) Listen again and repeat.

Grammar   *have got, has got*

4 (Circle) the correct options.

1 I *'s got* / *'ve got* two phones.
2 You *'s got* / *'ve got* a lovely flat.
3 He *'s got* / *'ve got* a hard job.
4 This hotel *'s got* / *'ve got* twenty-five rooms.
5 We *'s got* / *'ve got* nice neighbours.
6 Emma *'s got* / *'ve got* a restaurant.
7 They *'s got* / *'ve got* four dogs.

5a Write sentences about the people in the table. Use a subject pronoun and the correct form of *have got*.

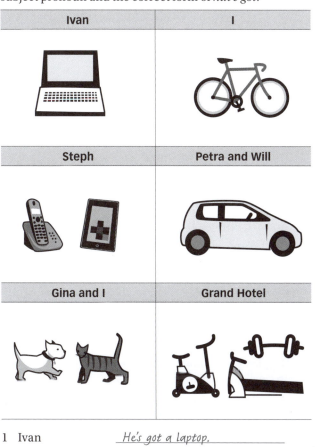

Ivan	I
Steph	**Petra and Will**
Gina and I	**Grand Hotel**

1 Ivan   *He's got a laptop.*
2 Petra and Will   _____
3 Gina and I   _____
4 Steph   _____
5 Grand Hotel   _____
6 I   _____

b   **3.2** 》 Listen and check your answers.

c   **3.2** 》 Listen again and repeat.

6 Complete the sentences with the correct form of *have got*. Use contractions.

1 You *'ve got* a nice house.
2 My flat _____ three rooms.
3 We _____ two children.
4 I _____ an umbrella in my bag.
5 My neighbour _____ a friendly dog.
6 They _____ a lovely garden.

7 Complete the text with the correct form of *have got*. Use contractions.

Neighbours

Xavier and I are from Spain. We ¹ *'ve got* a house in a quiet village near Madrid. It ² _____ four rooms and a lovely garden. Xavier is a waiter in a restaurant in the village and I ³ _____ a job in the city centre. The people in the village are very friendly, especially Adele and Damian. Adele ⁴ _____ a bicycle shop. Damian ⁵ _____ a hard job – he's an engineer. He's at work from 7 a.m. to 8 p.m. They ⁶ _____ two children, Oscar and Lauren. Oscar's five and Lauren's two.

I can …	Very well	Quite well	More practice
use adjective + noun phrases.	○	○	○
use irregular plurals.	○	○	○
talk about possessions with *have got*.	○	○	○

3.2 Possessions

Grammar *have got* negatives and questions

1 Write negative sentences.

1 I've got a bank account.
   I haven't got a bank account.

2 Kim's got an interesting job.
   _____

3 We've got nice neighbours.
   _____

4 Ali's got a mobile phone.
   _____

5 Yola and Paul have got a new TV.
   _____

6 My village has got a hospital.
   _____

2a Write questions with *have got* or *has got*.

1 you / children   *Have you got children* ?
2 your friends / cars _____ ?
3 your house / a garden _____ ?
4 you / my number   _____ ?
5 your neighbour / a dog _____ ?
6 Kate / a job   _____ ?

b Complete the answers with the words in the box.

~~has~~ has hasn't have haven't (x2) 's 've (x2)

a Yes, she _has_. She's a nurse.
b Yes, it _____. It's lovely.
c No, he _____. He _____ got a cat.
d Yes, we _____. We _____ got two.
e No, they _____. They _____ got bicycles.
f No, I _____. It isn't on my phone.

c Match questions 1–6 in exercise **2a** to answers a–f in exercise **2b**.

1 _d_   3 ___   5 ___
2 ___   4 ___   6 ___

PRONUNCIATION stress in *yes/no* questions and answers

3a **3.3**))) Listen and mark the stress. There is one stressed word in each sentence or question.

A Have you got a car?
B No, I haven't. And you?
A Yes, I have. I've got a Mini.

b **3.3**))) Listen again and repeat.

Vocabulary opposite adjectives

4a Match adjectives 1–8 to their opposites a–h.

1	expensive	a	bad
2	cold	b	cheap
3	big	c	hot
4	good	d	old
5	happy	e	poor
6	new	f	sad
7	old	g	small
8	rich	h	young

b 3.4)) Listen and check your answers.

c 3.4)) Listen again and repeat.

→ **VOCABULARY TIP** Make a note of adjectives with their opposites in your notebook. That way, you learn two adjectives at the same time.

5a Complete the phrases with an adjective from exercise **4**.

1 a _happy_ child   2 a _____ city

3 an _____ man   4 a _____ bag

5 a _____ wallet   6 an _____ pen

7 a _____ friend   8 a _____ woman

b 3.5)) Listen and check your answers.

6 Complete the sentences. Write *a/an*, an adjective from **A** and a noun from **B**.

A	big expensive good ~~hot~~ old rich sad young

B	building car city ~~country~~ man person story
	woman

1 Mali is _a hot country._
2 The Colosseum in Rome is _____.
3 A Maserati is _____.
4 Mark Zuckerberg is _____.
5 Istanbul is _____.
6 Katniss Everdeen is _____.
7 My best friend is _____.
8 *Les Misérables* is _____.

I can …	Very well	Quite well	More practice
talk about possessions using *have got*.	○	○	○
use opposite adjectives.	○	○	○

3.3 Family

Vocabulary family

1a Look at the photos and complete the missing letters.

grandfather and
gr_ _ _ _ _ _ _ _ _ _ =
gr_ _ _ _ _ _ _ _ _ _

br_ _ _ _ _ _ and
s_ _ _ _ _ _

f_ _ _ _ _ _ and
m_ _ _ _ _ _ =
p_ _ _ _ _ _ _

h_ _ _ _ _ _ _ and
w_ _ _ _

s_ _ and d_ _ _ _ h_ _ _ _ = ch_ _ _ _ _ _ _ _

b 3.6))) Listen and check your answers.

c 3.6))) Listen again and repeat.

2 Look at Miriam's family tree and complete the text. Use plurals where necessary.

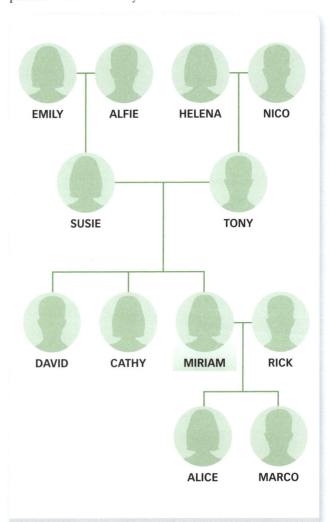

Hi! My name's Miriam and this is my family tree.
I'm married. My ¹ _husband_ is Rick. We've got
two ² _____ : a ³ _____ , Alice, and a
⁴ _____ , Marco. Susie and Tony are my
⁵ _____ . I've got a ⁶ _____ , David, and
a ⁷ _____ , Cathy. My grandparents are old.
Alfie and Nico are my ⁸ _____ and my
⁹ _____ are Emily and Helena.

Grammar possession

3 (Circle) the correct possessive determiner.

1 We're from Greece. (Our) / *Their* names are Iris and Athena.
2 He's from Russia. *Her* / *His* name's Boris.
3 They're from Indonesia. *Our* / *Their* names are Candra and Surya.
4 She's from Germany. *Her* / *His* name's Inge.
5 You're from Turkey. *My* / *Your* name's Ozkan.
6 I'm from China. *My* / *Your* name's Daisy.

4 Complete the conversations with possessive determiners.

1 **A** Hi. I'm Katia. What's __your__ name?
  B It's Sebastian. Nice to meet you.
2 **A** Where's Luc from?
  B He's from France, and _____ wife's from Indonesia.
3 **A** Who are those people?
  B They're Jenny and Phil and that's _____ daughter, Charlotte.
4 **A** Is your sister a nurse?
  B Yes, she is, and _____ husband's a doctor.
5 **A** Hi, Laila.
  B Hello, Vicky. This is _____ brother, Charlie.
6 **A** Hello. What are your names, please?
  B We're Chris and Sam Rodgers, and this is _____ son, Oliver.

5a Look at the family tree in exercise **2**. Complete the sentences. Use possessive *'s* where necessary.

1 Susie is __Tony's__ wife.
2 Alfie is _____ husband.
3 Alice is _____ sister.
4 David is _____ and _____ brother.
5 Emily is _____ mother.
6 Tony is _____ and _____ son.
7 Alice and Marco are _____ and _____ children.
8 Helena and Nico are _____ parents.
9 David, Cathy and Miriam are _____ and _____ children.
10 Emily and Alfie are _____ parents.

b 3.7))) Listen and check your answers.

6a 3.8))) Listen and write six sentences.

1 __That laptop's expensive.__
2 _____
3 _____
4 _____
5 _____
6 _____

b Look at sentences 1–6 in exercise **6a**. What is the meaning of *'s*? Complete the table with 1–6.

is	1	
has		
possession		

c 3.8))) Listen again and repeat.

I can …	Very well	Quite well	More practice
use possessive determiners and possessive *'s*.	○	○	○
talk about family.	○	○	○

3.4 Speaking and writing

Speaking everyday expressions

1a Circle the correct responses.

1 Thanks very much.
  a Bless you.
  b Sorry, I don't know.
  c You're welcome.

2 Can I sit here?
  a Oh, I'm so sorry.
  b Yes, of course.
  c Oh, thanks.

3 Sorry, I'm late.
  a That's OK. Don't worry.
  b Bless you.
  c You're welcome.

4 Tea?
  a Yes, of course.
  b Sorry, I don't know.
  c Yes, please.

5 Excuse me. That's my seat.
  a Oh, I'm so sorry.
  b You're welcome.
  c Oh, thanks.

6 Atishoo!
  a Yes, please.
  b Bless you.
  c That's OK. Don't worry.

7 Excuse me. Where's the toilet?
  a Oh, I'm so sorry.
  b Yes, of course.
  c Sorry, I don't know.

8 After you.
  a That's OK. Don't worry.
  b Oh, thanks.
  c Yes, please.

b 3.9))) Listen and check your answers.

c 3.9))) Listen again and repeat.

Writing a social media message

2 Join the sentences. Use *and* or *but*.

1 My grandparents have got a lovely house. It's got a big garden.
My grandparents have got a lovely house _and it's got a big garden._

2 Tim and Olga are very rich. They've got an expensive car.
Tim and Olga are very rich _____.

3 I've got two cats. I haven't got a dog.
I've got two cats, _____.

4 We've got three neighbours. They aren't our friends.
We've got three neighbours, _____.

5 Wilma is married. She's got two daughters.
Wilma is married _____.

6 My partner's got a hard job. He's very happy.
My partner's got a hard job, _____.

3 Complete the social media message with phrases a–f.

  a Bye for now   **d** I'm here in Istanbul on holiday
  b Hi Debbie,   **e** Message me soon
  c I hope you're well   **f** Our hotel is near the centre

MESSAGE ✉️³

¹ _b_

² ___. ³ ___. It's a very big and beautiful city. The buildings are very old, and they're very interesting.
⁴ ___. It's small, but our room is very nice. The people in the hotel are very friendly and our guide is very funny. The food in Istanbul is great and it's very cheap.

⁵ ___.

⁶ ___. xx

I can …	Very well	Quite well	More practice
use everyday expressions.	○	○	○
write a social media message.	○	○	○

3.5   Listening for pleasure

Unusual collections

1   Match the photos to the words in the box. Use a dictionary to help you, if necessary.

collect   collection   collector

1 _____

2 _____

3 _____

2   **3.10**))) Look at the photos and listen to a radio documentary about unusual collections. Number the pictures 1–3 in the order you hear them. Which do you find unusual? Why?

A

fridge magnets

B

comics

C

dolls

3   **3.10**))) Listen to the radio documentary again. Turn to page 86 and read along.

4   Answer the questions.

1   Which of the collections in the documentary do you like best?

2   Have you or somebody you know got a collection? What is it?

4 My life

4.1 About me

Grammar present simple positive

1 Complete the table with the present simple form of the verbs.

I/You/We/They	He/She/It
go	**1** _goes_
have	**2** _____
3 _____	likes
live	**4** _____
5 _____	plays
study	**6** _____
7 _____	teaches
watch	**8** _____
9 _____	works

2a (Circle) the correct verb forms.

1 My parents ___ in New Zealand.
   a (live) **b** lives
2 Elsa ___ in a charity shop.
   a work **b** works
3 Greg and Selma ___ Chinese at school.
   a study **b** studies
4 Sophie and I ___ to the beach every day.
   a go **b** goes
5 My best friend ___ the guitar and the piano.
   a play **b** plays
6 My sister ___ maths in her free time.
   a teach **b** teaches
7 I ___ a lot of videos on my tablet.
   a watch **b** watches
8 Petra ___ the newspaper every morning.
   a read **b** reads

b 4.1))) Listen and check your answers.

c 4.1))) Listen again and repeat.

3 Complete the text with the correct form of the verbs in (brackets).

Hi! I'm Yasmin. I'm from India, but I **1** _live_ (live) in Portugal. I'm a teacher, and I **2**_____ (teach) art at an art school in Lisbon. I **3**_____ (love) books and I **4**_____ (read) a lot in my free time. I'm married to Paulo. He's Portuguese, and he **5**_____ (work) for a software company. Paulo **6**_____ (like) sport, and he **7**_____ (play) tennis every weekend. He **8**_____ (watch) a lot of sport on television, too. Our daughter Rebeca **9**_____ (study) sociology at university in New York. Paulo and I sometimes **10**_____ (go) to the USA to see her.

PRONUNCIATION present simple with *he/she/it*

4a 4.2))) Listen to the pronunciation of the present simple ending -*(e)s*. Put a tick (✓) if the sound is the same and a cross (✗) if it is different.

1 goes   plays   ✓
2 lives   watches ✗
3 helps   works   ___
4 likes   teaches ___
5 reads   studies ___

b 4.2))) Listen again and repeat.

Vocabulary   common verbs

5 Match verbs 1–9 to words a–i.

1	watch	a	basketball
2	go	b	cars
3	live	c	engineering
4	play	d	a film on TV
5	read	e	for a charity
6	study	f	in a flat
7	teach	g	a newspaper
8	work	h	to Indonesia
9	like	i	young people

➡ **VOCABULARY TIP** Write verbs in your vocabulary notebook as part of a phrase, e.g. *go abroad*, *live in a flat*, *teach in a school*. That way, they are easier to learn.

6 Underline the option in each line 1–9 that doesn't go with the verb.

1	go	abroad / job / to work / to Hawaii
2	like	children / old buildings / to the beach / tennis
3	live	in a city / near a park / North Street / in a house
4	play	phone / tennis / the violin / music
5	read	books / comics / films / newspapers
6	study	at university / English / school / maths
7	teach	at a school / Australia / Japanese / children
8	work	in a hospital / for a company / restaurant / in an office
9	watch	a book / a DVD / television / a film

7 Complete the sentences with the verbs in exercise **6**.

1 My husband and I __like__ opera.
2 My children and I _____ films in English.
3 Fatima and Debbie _____ books in their free time.
4 Michel's parents _____ in a house in a small village.
5 Mr and Mrs Briggs _____ English to poor children.
6 My friends _____ for a charity.
7 Alex and Beth _____ German at university.
8 We _____ to France every year.
9 Ray and Mark _____ football in their free time.

8 Complete the text with the verbs in the box.

| go | goes | have | ~~likes~~ | live | love | play | plays | works |

This is Usain Bolt. He's an athlete. His brother Sadiki ¹ __likes__ sport too, but he ² _____ cricket. Usain and Sadiki ³ _____ the same father, but different mothers. Their father ⁴ _____ in a shop. The two brothers ⁵ _____ in Jamaica, but Usain often ⁶ _____ abroad for international competitions. They both ⁷ _____ reggae music, and they often ⁸ _____ to clubs. In their free time, they ⁹ _____ dominoes or video games.

I can …	Very well	Quite well	More practice
use the present simple positive with common verbs.	○	○	○
talk about my life.	○	○	○

4.2 Journeys

transport

1 Complete the table with the words in the box.

~~bus~~ cycle drive ferry go motorbike train walk

Nouns	Verbs
bus	

2 Complete the gaps with words for transport from exercise **1**. Add *by* where necessary.

1 I _go_ to work _by train_ .

2 We _____ on the beach every evening.

3 We _____ to Ireland _____ _____.

4 I _____ to the centre every day.

5 We _____ to university every morning.

6 I _____ to my office _____ _____.

3 Look at the graph and complete the text with nouns and verbs for transport.

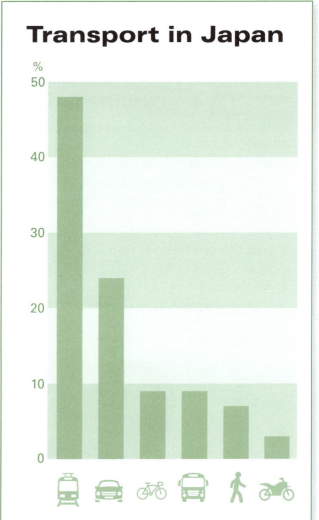

Transport in Japan

Japan isn't a very big country, but a lot of people live there. Every day, about sixty-three million people go to work. Public transport is very good, so 9% of people go to work by **1** _bus_ and 48% go by **2**_____. Workers use private transport, too. 24% of people **3**_____ to work every day, 9% of people **4**_____ and only 3% go by **5**_____. About 7% of workers live near their place of work and so they **6**_____ to work every morning.

Grammar   present simple negative

4a Complete the sentences with the negative form of the verbs.

1 Alex plays football. He _doesn't play_ basketball.
2 Gina teaches art. She _____ music.
3 We live in a village. We _____ in the city centre.
4 I study in the morning. I _____ at night.
5 My brother works for a charity. He _____ for a big company.
6 I like cats. I _____ dogs.
7 My parents watch films on TV. They _____ DVDs.
8 My partner goes to work by bus. He _____ by train.

b **4.3**)) Listen and check your answers.

c **4.3**)) Listen again and repeat.

5 Look at the table and complete the sentences.

Audrey and her friends

	Audrey	Audrey's friends
study music	✓	✓
play the guitar	✓	✗
play the violin	✓	✓
like sport	✗	✓
watch football on TV	✗	✓
watch films on TV	✓	✗
drive to university	✓	✗
cycle to university	✗	✓

Audrey ¹ _studies_ music at university. She
² _____ the guitar and the violin. Her friends
³ _____ the violin, too, but they ⁴_____
the guitar. Audrey ⁵_____ sport, but her
friends ⁶_____ it a lot. They ⁷_____ a lot
of football on TV. Audrey ⁸_____ football on
TV; she ⁹_____ films. Audrey's got a car and
so she ¹⁰_____ to university every morning.
Her friends ¹¹_____ because they haven't got
cars. They've got bicycles and so they
¹² _____.

6a **4.4**)) Listen and write six negative sentences.

1 _I don't play golf._
2 _____
3 _____
4 _____
5 _____
6 _____

b **4.4**)) Listen again and repeat.

c Look at sentences 1–6 in exercise **6a**. Complete the table with 1–6.

be		
have got		
Other verbs	1	

I can …

	Very well	Quite well	More practice
use the present simple negative.	○	○	○
talk about journeys.	○	○	○

4.3 My day

Vocabulary daily activities

1a Label photos 1–8 with the daily activities in the box.

check emails	get dressed	get home	~~get up~~	go to bed
have breakfast	have dinner	start work		

1 _get up_   2 _____

3 _____   4 _____

5 _____   6 _____

7 _____   8 _____

b 4.5))) Listen and check your answers.

c 4.5))) Listen again and repeat.

2 Complete the text with the daily activities in exercise **1a**.

Hi! I'm Seline and I'm a nurse. I only work three days a week, but my days are very long – I work twelve hours! On a work day I ¹ _get up_ at 6.30 a.m. because I ² _____ at 8 o'clock. I have a shower and I ³ _____, and then I go to work. I ⁴ _____ in the hospital with the other nurses – usually a sandwich and coffee. Then I work for six hours. I have lunch at 2 p.m. – usually a salad. After lunch I ⁵ _____ on my office computer and help patients . I finish work at 8 p.m. and I ⁶ _____ at about 8.30 p.m. I ⁷ _____ with my husband and then we watch TV. I ⁸ _____ early, at about 10 p.m., because I'm very tired.

3 Complete the crossword with the days of the week.

```
¹T H U R ²S D A Y        ³F
                         
              ⁴M         
         ⁵              
                        
    ⁶                   
                        
                        
  ⁷S
```

Grammar present simple *yes/no* questions

4 Read the information about Tim Armstrong. Match questions 1–6 to answers a–f.

Name	Tim Armstrong
Job	CEO of AOL
Home	New York
Family	Married with three children

From Monday to Friday, Tim gets up at 5 a.m. His daughter gets up early, too, so Tim has a coffee and talks to his daughter about her life. Then he checks emails. He goes to work by car, but he has a driver, so he doesn't drive. He finishes work at 7 p.m. and gets home at 8 p.m. In the evening, he reads a book to his children. His wife cooks and they have dinner together. He goes to bed at about 11 p.m. On Friday nights, he watches a film on TV with his family. On Saturdays and Sundays, he plays basketball with his children. On Saturday nights, he goes out with his wife, and on Sunday night he works from home.

1 Does Tim Armstrong work for AOL? __d__
2 Does he have four children? ____
3 Does his daughter get up late? ____
4 Does his wife cook dinner? ____
5 Do he and his family go to the cinema on Fridays? ____
6 Do he and his children play basketball at the weekend? ____

a No, they don't.
b Yes, she does.
c No, she doesn't.
d Yes, he does.
e Yes, they do.
f No, he doesn't.

5a Write questions about Tim Armstrong. Use the prompts.

1 Tim Armstrong / live in London
   Does Tim Armstrong live in London?
2 he / get up early
   _____
3 he / have a coffee in the morning
   _____
4 he / go to work by train
   _____
5 he / read a book to his children in the evening
   _____
6 he / go to bed at 10 p.m.
   _____
7 he and his wife go out on Friday nights
   _____
8 he and his children / like sport
   _____

b Read the information about Tim Armstrong again. Write short answers for the questions in exercise **5a**.

1 *No, he doesn't.*
2 _____
3 _____
4 _____
5 _____
6 _____
7 _____
8 _____

PRONUNCIATION stress in present simple *yes/no* questions and answers

6a **4.6** Listen and mark the stress. There are two stressed words in each line.

A Do you have coffee for breakfast?

B Yes, I do. And you?

A No, I don't. I have tea.

b **4.6** Listen again and repeat.

I can …	Very well	Quite well	More practice
ask present simple *yes/no* questions.	○	○	○
talk about my day.	○	○	○

4.4 Speaking and writing

Speaking in a shop

1 Match questions 1–6 to answers a–f.

1 Can I help you? _d_
2 Excuse me. Do you have any comics? ___
3 How much is this bicycle? ___
4 Is that everything? ___
5 How much are the wallets? ___
6 Do you have an English dictionary? ___

a They're €15.
b Yes, it's over there.
c No, I need a newspaper too.
d No, thanks. Just looking.
e Yes, they're over there.
f It's €350.

2a Put the lines in order to make a conversation.

_1_ Can I help you?
___ Yes, do you have any comics?
___ How much is the *Spider-Man* comic?
___ Is that everything?
___ It's €2.75.
___ The magazines are here.
___ OK. I'll take it.
___ Yes, they're over there.
___ No, I need a car magazine, too.
_10_ Great. Thank you.

b 4.7))) Listen and check your answers.

c 4.7))) Listen again and repeat.

Writing an informal email

3 Complete the email with the correct punctuation. Use:

- 4 full stops
- 2 question marks
- 2 commas
- 1 exclamation mark
- 2 apostrophes

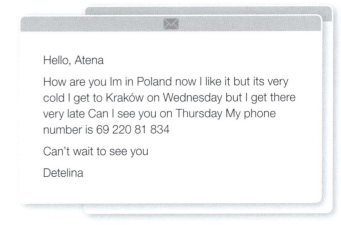

Hello, Atena

How are you Im in Poland now I like it but its very cold I get to Kraków on Wednesday but I get there very late Can I see you on Thursday My phone number is 69 220 81 834

Can't wait to see you

Detelina

4 Complete the reply to the email in exercise **3** with phrases a–f.

a Call me when you get to the museum
b My mobile number is 01148 50 823019
c See you on Thursday afternoon
d Hi, Detelina
e Love
f Thanks for your email

¹ _d_ ,

² ___. I work on Thursdays, but I finish at 3 o'clock. The tourist bus goes to the National Museum. You buy your ticket on the bus or online. ³ ___. It's very near my house. ⁴ ___.

⁵ ___.

⁶ ___,

Atena

I can …	Very well	Quite well	More practice
ask for things in a shop.	○	○	○
write an informal email.	○	○	○

Review: Units 3 and 4

Grammar

1 Complete the sentences with the correct form of *have got*. Use contractions where possible.

1 My parents _have got_ a lovely house. (+)
2 This village _hasn't got_ a shop. (–)
3 I _____ _____ two children. (+)
4 _____ your daughter _____ a pet?
5 We _____ _____ a car. (–)
6 Mario_____ _____ a smartphone. (+)

2 Put the words in order to make sentences.

1 brother / My / engineer / is / wife's / an .
   My wife's brother is an engineer.
2 don't / neighbour's / like / I / my / cat .
   _____
3 his / hasn't / tablet / got / Alex / sister's .
   _____
4 drives / mother's / her / Tina / car .
   _____
5 friends / and / very / Maya / are / Yusef's / nice .
   _____

3 Write sentences using the prompts.

1 I / go to work / bus (–) _I don't go to work by bus._
2 My friends and I / watch films / weekend (+)
   _____
3 Anisa / work / a hospital (–)
   _____
4 Sonny and Monica / live / a village (+)
   _____
5 We / go abroad / holiday (–)
   _____

4 Complete the conversations with *do, does, don't* or *doesn't*.

1 **A** _Do_ you like English?
  B Yes, I _do_. I like it a lot.
2 **A** _____ your husband work in an office?
  B No, he _____. He works at home.
3 **A** _____ your friends read comics?
  B Yes, they _____. They like comics.
4 **A** _____ Greta cycle to university?
  B Yes, she _____. She cycles there every day.
5 **A** _____ Blanca and Elena get up late?
  B No, they _____. They get up early.

Vocabulary

5 Complete the sentences with the opposite adjectives.

1 That hotel isn't cheap. It's _expensive_.
2 I'm not sad. I'm _____.
3 My phone isn't old. It's _____.
4 It isn't hot today. It's _____.
5 Those people aren't rich. They're _____.

6 Complete the text with members of the family. Use plurals where necessary.

Charlie and the Chocolate Factory is a famous book by Roald Dahl. Charlie Bucket lives in a small, old house with his [1] m_other_ and [2] f_____, and his [3] gr_____ – all four of them! He hasn't got any [4] br_____ or [5] s_____. Charlie is a lovely boy, and his [6] p_____ want their [7] s_____ to be happy. One day Charlie goes to the chocolate factory with his [8] gr_____, Joe. There he meets four horrible [9] ch_____ and his adventures begin …

7 Complete the sentences with the words in the box.

~~bus~~ cycle drive ferry motorbike train

1 I've got a stop near my house so I go to work by _bus_.
2 We've got a car, so we _____ to the shops.
3 We've got bicycles so we _____ to the beach.
4 They live near a station, so they go to work by _____.
5 When it isn't cold, I go to university by _____.

Functional language

8 Complete the conversation. Write one word only in each space.

A Can I [1] _help_ you?
B Yes, do you have [2] _____ bags?
A Yes, they're over [3] _____.
B How [4] _____ is the small bag?
A It's €35.99.
B OK. I'll [5] _____ it.
A Is that everything?
B No, I [6] _____ a book, too.

5 Style and design

5.1 Clothes style

Grammar adverbs of frequency

1a Put the words in order to make sentences.

1 to work / wears / usually / Krzysztof / a jacket .
   Krzysztof usually wears a jacket to work.

2 play / always / on Saturdays / tennis / We .
   _____

3 doesn't / My wife / often / clothes shopping / go .
   _____

4 sometimes / a bath / I / in the evening / have .
   _____

5 is / cold / It / in my house / never .
   _____

6 buy shoes / usually / online / don't / I .
   _____

b **5.1** ⟩⟩ Listen and check your answers.

c **5.1** ⟩⟩ Listen again and repeat.

2 Complete the two texts with a verb and an adverb of frequency, using the information in the chart.

	100%	85%	75%	40%	0%
wear casual clothes	●		●		
wear a T-shirt and jeans		●		●	
wear smart clothes		●			●
wear fashion clothes	●			●	
buy clothes online			●		●
be happy	●				

Raif works at home. He ¹ _always wears_ casual clothes when he works. He ² _____ _____ a T-shirt and jeans; he ³ _____ _____ smart clothes. When he goes out, he ⁴ _____ _____ fashion clothes. Raif ⁵ _____ _____ clothes online. He ⁶ _____ _____ happy when he buys nice, but cheap clothes on the internet.

Aida and Lotty work in an office. They ⁷ _____ _____ smart clothes to work because they have important jobs. They ⁸ _____ _____ casual clothes to work on Fridays; they ⁹ _____ _____ jeans and a T-shirt. They ¹⁰ _____ _____ fashion clothes when they go out. They ¹¹ _____ _____ clothes online because they love going to the shops. They ¹² _____ _____ happy when they go shopping together.

Vocabulary   colours and clothes

3   Complete the crossword with seven more colours.

```
          ¹B
          ²R        □
           O
      ³Y    W
  ⁴G  □  □  N
  □           ⁵B
         ⁶B  □  □  □
  □
      ⁷W  □  □  □
```

4   Complete the table with the words in the box. Write *a/an* with the singular words.

> ~~dress~~ hat jacket jeans jumper shirt shoes skirt
> top trainers trousers T-shirt

Singular	Plural
a dress _____	_____ _____
_____ _____	_____ _____
_____ _____	
_____ _____	

PRONUNCIATION   word stress: clothes

5a   Circle the word that is different in each group and say why.
1   top / trainers / trousers   _one syllable_
2   jacket / jeans / jumper   _____
3   fashion / shirt / shoes   _____
4   skirt / smart / T-shirt   _____
5   casual / clothes / dress   _____

b   **5.2**))) Listen, check and repeat.

➡ **STUDY TIP** The stress on two-syllable words is on the first syllable, e.g. *jumper*, or the second syllable, e.g. *hotel*. When you write two-syllable words in your notebook, always mark the stress.

6   Look at the illustrations and complete the sentences with the words from exercise **4**. Write *a/an* where necessary.

1   She has _trainers_, _____ and _____ .

2   He has _____ and _____ .

3   She has _____, _____ and _____ .

4   He has _____ and _____ .

7   Complete the text about Gisele Bündchen with *and*, *because* or *but*.

> Gisele Bündchen is a very important woman in the world of fashion ¹ _because_ she is a super-model. She is also an actress and a singer ² _____ she does a lot of charity work. Gisele is from Brazil, ³ _____ she lives in Los Angeles. She's married to Tom Brady ⁴ _____ they've got two small children. She often watches American football ⁵ _____ her husband plays for the New England Patriots.

I can …	Very well	Quite well	More practice
use adverbs of frequency.	○	○	○
talk about clothes.	○	○	○

Amazing architecture

1a Look at the photos and complete the adjectives with the missing letters.

Taj Mahal

1 It's b *i* g and b_ _ _ t_ _ _ _l.

Torre Galatea

2 It's m_ _d_ _ _ _ and u_ _ _s_ _ _l.

Hang Nga Guesthouse

3 It's d_ _f_ _ _r_ _ _ _ and e_ _ _ _t_ _ _g.

Leaning Tower of Pisa

4 It's o_ _ _ and i_ _ _ _r_ _ _t_ _ _ _ .

b **5.3**))) Listen and check your answers.

c **5.3**))) Listen again and repeat.

2 Read the texts and choose the correct options.

This is the Upside Down House. It's in Szymbark, Poland. It's an ¹ *old* / *unusual* house because it isn't for people to live in. It's from the year 2007, so it's ² *beautiful* / *modern*, but it's completely ³ *different* / *interesting* from normal houses. It's got a new design, so it's very ⁴ *big* / *exciting*.

This is the Winter Palace in St Petersburg, Russia. It's a ⁵ *beautiful* / *different* building near the Neva River. It's very ⁶ *big* / *exciting* – it's got 1,500 rooms. The palace is from the 1730s, so it's ⁷ *unusual* / *old*. It's ⁸ *modern* / *interesting* because it's got a lot of important paintings. Part of the palace is the Hermitage Museum.

Grammar *Wh-* questions

3a Circle the correct options.
1 *What* / *When* / *Why* is that building?
2 *When* / *Where* / *Why* do you live?
3 *What* / *When* / *Where* is the museum open?
4 *What* / *Where* / *Why* do you get up early?
5 *When* / *Where* / *Why* is your hotel?
6 *What* / *When* / *Why* do you have for breakfast?
7 *What* / *Where* / *Why* is the bookshop closed?
8 *What* / *When* / *Where* do you finish work?

b Match answers a–h to questions 1–8 in exercise **3a**.
_1_ a It's a hospital.
___ b Because I like mornings.
___ c From 10.00 to 18.00.
___ d In Johannesburg.
___ e I only have a coffee.
___ f At 5.30 p.m.
___ g Because it's late.
___ h It's on Oxford Road.

4a Complete the questions with *is*, *are*, *do* or *does*.
1 When _are_ the gardens open?
2 When _____ you check emails?
3 Why _____ Dominic buy expensive clothes?
4 What _____ your address?
5 Where _____ you and your family go on holiday?
6 Where _____ my keys?
7 What _____ your partner do?
8 Why _____ your grandmother in hospital?

b 5.4 》 Listen and check your answers.

c 5.4 》 Listen again and repeat.

5a Read the text about a big house.

This is Longleat House. It's a big and beautiful house in the south of England. It's the home of the 7th Marquess of Bath. His name is Alexander Thynn and he's a very rich man. A lot of people visit Longleat House and its park and gardens because there is a lot to do. Some people go there to visit the house, and others to drive through the safari park. The safari park has got a lot of animals, including lions and tigers. Longleat is open from February to December. It's closed in January because it's cold.

b Read the answers and complete the questions. Use a question word and *is*, *does* or *do*.
1 **A** _What is_ the name of the house?
  B Its name is Longleat House.
2 **A** _____ _____ the house?
  B It's in the south of England.
3 **A** _____ _____ Alexander Thynn live?
  B He lives in Longleat House.
4 **A** _____ _____ he live in a big house?
  B He lives there because he's rich.
5 **A** _____ _____ people do at Longleat?
  B They visit the house and drive through the safari park.
6 **A** _____ _____ people see animals?
  B They see animals in the safari park.
7 **A** _____ _____ Longleat open?
  B It's open from February to December.
8 **A** _____ _____ it closed in January?
  B It's closed because it's cold.

I can …	Very well	Quite well	More practice
ask *Wh-* questions.	○	○	○
talk about a building I like.	○	○	○

5.3 Styles around the world

Grammar present simple (all forms)

1a Complete the texts with the positive or negative present simple forms of the verbs in (brackets).

Scotland is famous for its kilts. These are skirts that men **1** _wear_ (wear). A lot of Scottish men **2**_____ (have) a kilt, but they only wear it on special days, like weddings, for example. Usually, they **3**_____ _____ (not go) to work in them. Traditionally, Scottish women **4**_____ _____ (not wear) kilts, but they sometimes wear long skirts or dresses in a similar style.

The traditional clothing for an Indian woman is the sari. This is a long colourful piece of cloth that a woman **5**_____ (wear) like a dress. A young woman **6**_____ _____ _____ (usually, not wear) a sari every day, but it is typical on special days. When a girl **7**_____ _____ (not know) how to wear a sari, her grandmother or her mother **8**_____ (teach) her. Men wear something similar called a dhoti.

b 5.5))) Listen and check your answers.

2a Use the prompts to write questions about the clothes in exercise **1**.

1 What / Scottish men / wear ?
 What do Scottish men wear?

2 When / they / wear kilts ?
 _____

3 Scottish women / wear kilts ?
 _____

4 What / an Indian woman / wear ?
 _____

5 a young woman / wear a sari / every day ?
 _____

6 When / a mother / help her daughter / with a sari ?
 _____

b Match questions 1–6 in exercise **2a** to answers a–f.

_1_ a They wear kilts.

___ b No, she doesn't.

___ c They wear them on special days.

___ d She helps when a girl doesn't know how to wear it.

___ e No, they don't.

___ f She wears a sari.

3a Complete the conversation with *do, does, don't* or *doesn't*.

A **1** _Do_ you and your partner like the same styles?

B No, we **2**_____.

A Oh. What clothes **3**_____ you like?

B I like casual clothes. And I always wear black.

A **4**_____ you always buy black clothes?

B Yes, I **5**_____.

A And what clothes **6**_____ your partner like?

B She wears long colourful dresses and long skirts.

A **7**_____ she like your clothes?

B No, she **8**_____.

A **9**_____ she sometimes buy clothes for you?

B Yes, she **10**_____. But I never wear them.

b 5.6))) Listen and check your answers in exercise **3a**.

Vocabulary   parts of the body

4   Look at the photos and complete the phrases with the words in the box.

arm   body   ~~face~~   feet   hair   hands   head   legs

1   a sad _face_   2   white _____

3   bare _____   4   a big _____

5   long _____   6   a woman's _____

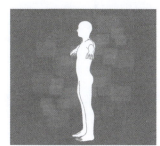

7   small _____   8   a man's _____

5a   Write plural phrases.

1   a white arm   _white arms_
2   a small head   _____
3   a beautiful body   _____
4   a happy face   _____
5   a brown leg   _____
6   a big hand   _____

b   **5.7** 》 Listen and check your answers. In which plural body part is the ending pronounced /ɪz/?

c   **5.7** 》 Listen again and repeat.

Vocabulary   adjective modifiers

6   Look at the information in the table and complete the sentences.

+ = very ++ = really	Harry	Grace and Anais
have got / expensive clothes	++	+
be / rich	+	++
buy / beautiful jackets	++	+
wear / nice hats	+	++

Harry's got [1] _really expensive_ clothes because he's
[2] _____ rich. He always buys
[3] _____ jackets and he sometimes
wears [4] _____ hats.

Grace and Anais are also [5] _____.
They usually buy [6] _____ jackets
and they often wear [7] _____ hats.
They've both got [8] _____ clothes.

I can ...	Very well	Quite well	More practice
use the present simple.	○	○	○
talk about body parts.	○	○	○
talk about style and fashion.	○	○	○

5.4 Speaking and writing

1a Put the words in order to make questions.

1 to / much / airport / is / How / it / the ?
How much is it to the airport?

2 I / a / do / Where / ticket / buy ?
_____?

3 train / airport / go / this / to / Does / the ?
_____?

4 next / time / the / What / train / is ?
_____?

5 time / arrive / does / What / it ?
_____?

6 does / go / it / from / Where ?
_____?

b Complete the answers with one word.

a It goes _from_ platform 7.
b You _____ your ticket from the ticket machine.
c _____ leaves at 11.45.
d _____ €15.
e It arrives _____ 12.30.
f No, it _____ to the city centre.

c Match questions 1–6 in exercise **1a** to answers a–f in exercise **1b**.

1 _d_   3 ___   5 ___
2 ___   4 ___   6 ___

d **5.8** 》 Listen and check your answers.

Writing making arrangements by text

2 Complete the conversation with the phrases in the box.

| Are you busy | Can we meet | Do you like | Do you want |
| I'm not busy | See you there | What time | Where do you |

Jane Hi, Karen. **1** _Are you busy_ on Friday?
Karen No, **2**_____. Why?
Jane **3**_____ to meet for dinner?
Karen OK. **4**_____ want to meet?
Jane **5**_____ Chinese food?
Karen Yes, I like it a lot.
Jane **6**_____ in Bamboo?
Karen OK. **7**_____ do you want to meet?
Jane Can we meet at 7.30?
Karen OK. **8**_____.

3 Make the conversation in exercise **2** short.

> **Yesterday 14:25**
>
> Hi, Karen. Are you busy on Friday?
>
> No, **1**_not busy._ Why?
>
> Do you want to meet for dinner?
>
> OK. **2**__ ____ ____?
>
> Do you like Chinese food?
>
> Yes, **3**__ ____.
>
> **4**___ _____?
>
> OK. **5**____ _____?
>
> **6**__ . ___?
>
> OK. See you there.

I can …	Very well	Quite well	More practice
ask for travel information.	○	○	○
make arrangements by text.	○	○	○

5.5   Reading for pleasure

The Girl with Red Hair

1 Read the first paragraph from a short story called *The Girl with Red Hair*.

What's Mark Sellers's job? He's a ...

a shop assistant   **b** driver   **c** security person

2 Read the rest of the story. Do you think his job is interesting? Why/Why not?

3 What do you think happens next? Use the illustrations to help you.

4 Read the summary and check your answers.

The Girl with Red Hair

My name is Mark Sellers. I'm twenty-two years old, and I work in security in Mason's store. You can get everything here – books, TVs, hats, flowers, sandwiches, beds, bicycles … It's interesting work, and I like it. Sometimes, I walk around in the store, and sometimes I work in the office.

Leon and Shami work in security, too. I like working with them.

'Look at this woman,' Leon says. 'Which hat is best for her – blue or black?'

I look at the woman on the screen.

'Oh – the black hat,' I say.

'No!' says Shami. 'The blue hat is nicer.'

We watch and wait. In the end, the woman takes the blue hat.

'Hurray!' says Shami. 'You two know nothing about hats.'

Yes, it's interesting work.

Today I'm watching the screens. I'm looking at a man with a big bag. He's got a clock in his hand. He looks around slowly. Now he's got a clock in his bag. The man walks to the door. I talk on the radio. Shami walks quietly behind the man. When he gets to the door, she puts her hand on his arm.

'Please come with me,' she says.

Good. I go back to the screens.

And then I see her.

'Wow! Who's that girl?'

'What girl. I can see lots of girls,' Leon says.

Now the picture on the screen is bigger.

'That girl there – with red hair.'

Leon looks at the screen.

'Hmm – yes, she's OK. But who is she? I don't know. Why don't you go and ask her, Mark?'

He laughs and walks away, but I can't stop looking at the screen. Who is that beautiful girl? What is her name?

I want to meet her.

Text extract from *Oxford Bookworms: The Girl with Red Hair*

SUMMARY

The girl with the red hair comes to the store every Wednesday. The next Wednesday, there's a little boy with her. His name is Greg. The third Wednesday, Greg takes a red plane from the store. Mark stops him and speaks to the girl with red hair. He likes her a lot. The fourth Wednesday, the girl is with another man. Mark is very sad. Mark's friend Leon sees his sad face, and invites him to Ocean Blue that night. Mark goes to the club with Leon and his girlfriend. He sees the girl with red hair in the club. She's with another girl with red hair. The girl from the store sees Mark and they start talking. The second girl is her sister. 'And Greg's mother! The girl with red hair is called Kate and she hasn't got a baby, or a husband. Mark is very happy.

43

Places and facilities

6.1 Two towns

Vocabulary places in a town

1 Look at the icons and complete the crossword.

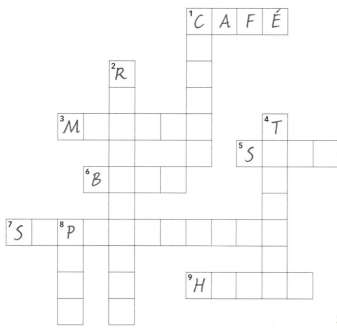

Across ▶

1 ☕

3 🏛

5 🛍

6 🏦

7 🛒

9 🛏

Down ▼

1 🎬

2 🍽

4 🎭

8 🌳

2a Answer the questions with the places from exercise **1**.

Where do people ...?

1 buy clothes   in a *shop*
2 watch films   in a _____
3 have dinner   in a _____
4 stay when they're on holiday in a _____
5 look at paintings or old things in a _____
6 buy food for a week   in a _____
7 walk or play football   in a _____
8 get money   from a _____
9 see a Shakespeare play   in a _____
10 have a coffee   in a _____

b 6.1))) Listen and check your answers.

c 6.1))) Listen again and repeat.

3 Complete the sentences with the words in exercise **2**.

1 We go to the _supermarket_ on Saturday mornings to buy food.
2 My grandparents walk in the _____ near their house every afternoon.
3 There's a _____ near my office where I usually get money.
4 The shoes in that _____ are very cheap.
5 Where do you watch films – on TV or at the _____?
6 I sometimes meet my friends for a snack at the _____ in the square.
7 My boyfriend is an actor and he works in a _____ in London.
8 The Louvre is a _____ on the River Seine in Paris.
9 They love their _____ because their room is very big.
10 We often have lunch at the Chinese _____ on my street.

Grammar *there is/there are*

4 Look at the map of Lacock village. Write sentences with *There's* or *There are*.

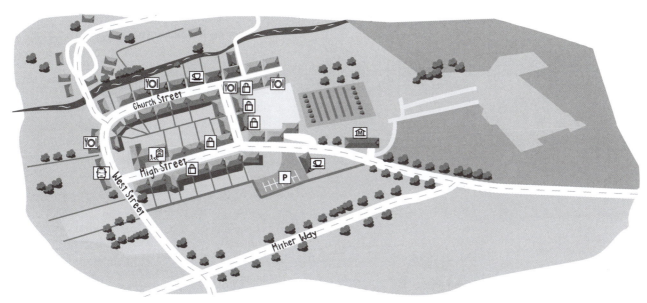

1 car park   *There's a car park.*
2 café   *There are two cafés.*
3 museum   _____
4 restaurant _____
5 river   _____
6 bus stop   _____
7 school   _____
8 shop   _____

5a Write negative sentences. Use the word in (brackets).

1 There are a lot of bicycles on the road. (cars)
   There aren't any cars.

2 There are expensive houses in the centre. (cheap flats)
   _____

3 There's a shop in the village. (supermarket)
   _____

4 There are nice shoes in that shoe shop. (trainers)
   _____

5 There's a station in the city. (airport)
   _____

6 There's a pharmacy in our town. (hospital)
   _____

b 6.2))) Listen and check your answers.

c 6.2))) Listen again and repeat.

6 Complete the text with *there's*, *there are*, *there isn't* or *there aren't*.

Torcross is a small village in the south-west of the UK. It's very near the beach. In Torcross ¹ *there are* nice houses and ² _____ a small shop. ³ _____ a restaurant in the village, but ⁴ _____ any hotels. ⁵ _____ big hotels in Kingsbridge, a town near Torcross. In Kingsbridge, ⁶ _____ a lot of shops and restaurants. ⁷ _____ one cinema in the town, but ⁸ _____ a theatre. People drive to Kingsbridge or go by bus because ⁹ _____ a station. ¹⁰ _____ a bus to Torcross, too.

I can ...	Very well	Quite well	More practice
use *there is/there are*.	○	○	○
talk about places in a town.	○	○	○

6.2 Is there Wi-fi?

Vocabulary hotel facilities

1a Look at the illustrations and complete the words with the missing letters.

1 a_ir_ c_ondi_t_io_ning

2 l _ _ _

3 r_fr_ _ _m_ _ _s

4 g_ _

5 W_-_ _

6 c_ _ p_ _ _

7 i_ _ _

8 s_ _ _

9 t_w_ _ _

10 b_ _ _

b 6.3))) Listen and check your answers.

c 6.3))) Listen again and repeat.

2 Complete the sentences with words from exercise **1a**.

1 I want to have a shower, but there aren't any _towels_ .
2 It's hot in our room. There isn't any _____.
3 I want to check my emails. Has the hotel got _____?
4 I've got a lot of money, but there isn't a _____.
5 I want to have a drink. Are there any _____ in the room?
6 There's a special place for motorbikes in the _____.
7 Look at your clothes! You need an _____!
8 There's a _____ in the hotel, so we can do some sport.
9 There isn't a _____ in the room, but there's a shower.
10 There's a _____ to the rooms on the first and second floors.

3 Complete the text with words from exercise **1a**.

Grandhotel Pupp

The Grandhotel Pupp is a beautiful old hotel in Karlovy Vary, a spa town in the Czech Republic. The hotel has 228 rooms and there are four [1] _lifts_ for the rooms upstairs. Each room has an en-suite bathroom with a [2]_____ and a shower. There are clean [3]_____ in the cupboard every day. There is a [4]_____ in the room for passports and money, and there are [5]_____ in the minibar. All the rooms have free [6]_____ for the internet and there's [7]_____, so it's never too hot. There isn't an [8]_____ for clothes because the hotel has a washing and ironing service. The hotel has a pool for swimming and a [9]_____ for exercise. Guests who drive to Karlovy Vary pay €15 to use the [10]_____.

4 Complete the questions with *a*, *an* or *any*.

1 Are there _any_ cars in the car park?
2 Is there _____ bank in the village?
3 Are there _____ old buildings in the centre?
4 Is there _____ iron in the room?
5 Is there _____ museum in the town?
6 Are there _____ cheap T-shirts in the shop?

➔ **GRAMMAR TIP** Remember that the first word in a *yes/no* question is usually the verb *be* (*am/is/are*) or an auxiliary verb (*have/has, do/does*), e.g. *Are you from Canada? Have you got a car? Do you live in a flat? Is there a bath?*

5a Read the text and tick (✓) the facilities in the hotel.

Alfina Cave Hotel

The Alfina Cave Hotel is in Ürgüp, Cappadocia, in Turkey. It's got 41 rooms, lots of meeting areas and a lovely restaurant with a free breakfast buffet. There's free Wi-fi in the hotel. Each room has got a balcony, a safe and a minibar. The hotel hasn't got a swimming pool, but each room has got a private bathroom with a jacuzzi. There isn't any air conditioning, but the rooms aren't hot. There's a free car park for guests at the hotel.

1	a restaurant / hotel	✓
2	meeting areas / hotel	___
3	air conditioning / rooms	___
4	refreshments / rooms	___
5	free Wi-fi / hotel	___
6	swimming pool / hotel	___

b Look at the information in exercise **5a** and write questions about the hotel.

1 _Is there a restaurant in the hotel?_
2 _____
3 _____
4 _____
5 _____
6 _____

c Write answers for the questions in exercise **5b**.

1 _Yes, there is._
2 _____
3 _____
4 _____
5 _____
6 _____

PRONUNCIATION *Is there …?/Are there …?*

6a **6.4**)) Listen to the questions and short answers and mark the stress. One word in each line is stressed.

1 **A** Is there a lift?   3 **A** Are there any toilets?
   B Yes, there is.   **B** Yes, there are.
2 **A** Is there a safe?   4 **A** Are there any parks?
   B No, there isn't.   **B** No, there aren't.

b **6.4**)) Listen again and repeat.

I can …	Very well	Quite well	More practice
ask questions with *Is there …?/Are there …?*	○	○	○
talk about hotel facilities.	○	○	○

6.3 Has each flat got a kitchen?

Vocabulary rooms and furniture

1a Complete the words for rooms and areas in a house or flat.

1 You usually have a snack in the k*itchen* .
2 You usually watch TV with the family in the l_____ r_____.
3 You usually have a shower in the b_____.
4 You usually get dressed in the b_____.
5 You usually have lunch in the d_____ a_____ .
6 You usually sit in the sun on the b_____.
7 You usually have a barbecue in the g_____.

b **6.5**)》 Listen and check your answers.

2 Look at illustrations 1–8 and complete the sentences with the words in the box.

| bed chair fridge ~~microwave~~ shower |
| sofa table TV |

1 There's food in the *microwave* .
2 There are books near the _____.
3 There's a man in the _____.
4 There's a woman on the _____.
5 There are drinks in the _____.
6 There are clothes on the _____.
7 There's a cat on the _____.
8 There's a phone on the _____.

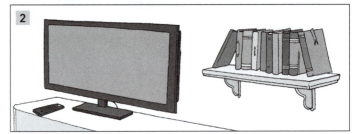

Grammar   *all the* and *each*

3 (Circle) the correct options.

1 (All the) / *Each* houses have a garden.
2 *All the / Each* flat has a bathroom with a shower.
3 *All the / Each* beds are new.
4 *All the / Each* balcony has a table and four chairs.
5 *All the / Each* bedroom has a TV.
6 *All the / Each* rooms are very big.

4 Complete the text with *each* or *all the*.

CAPSULE HOTELS

This is a capsule hotel in Japan. ¹ _All the_ rooms
in the hotel are small capsules. ² _____ capsule
has a bed and a TV. ³ _____ beds are
very comfortable and there's air conditioning in
⁴ _____ capsule. ⁵ _____ floor of the
hotel has an area with free Wi-fi. In this hotel,
⁶ _____ guests are men. ⁷ _____ guest pays
for his room when he arrives and then he either
goes to bed or uses the facilities in the hotel. The
hotel has a swimming pool, a jacuzzi and a sauna.
Some guests use ⁸ _____ facilities in one night!

5a Mark the linked words in sentences 1–6. Two words are linked in each sentence.

1 There isn't a bath.
2 Is there a fridge in the kitchen?
3 There's an old sofa in the living room.
4 Have all the rooms got air conditioning?
5 The room has got a phone and free Wi-fi.
6 Has each flat got a microwave?

b **6.6** ⟩⟩ Listen and check your answers.

c **6.6** ⟩⟩ Listen again and repeat.

6 **6.7** ⟩⟩ Listen and write six sentences. Mark the linked words.

1 _There aren't any towels._
2 _____
3 _____
4 _____
5 _____
6 _____

7 Choose the correct words to complete the sentences.

1 Diana works _from_ nine to five.
  a form   **b** from
2 There are _____ chairs in the garden.
  a for   **b** four
3 My grandparents live near the _____.
  a sea   **b** see
4 Monday's a _____ day.
  a bad   **b** bed
5 I know those women, but I can't remember _____ names.
  a there   **b** their
6 I like your _____ trousers.
  a read   **b** red
7 Each room's got _____ beds.
  a too   **b** two
8 _____ do you go to work every day?
  a How   **b** Who
9 The flat has got a _____ and a sofa.
  a bad   **b** bed
10 I _____ the newspaper every morning.
  a read   **b** red

I can …	Very well	Quite well	More practice
use *each* and *all the*.	○	○	○
describe rooms and furniture	○	○	○

1a Put the words in order to make sentences explaining problems in a hotel.

1 room / noisy / is / Our / very .

Our room is very noisy.

2 is / heater / broken / The .

_____

3 very / My / is / hot / room .

_____

4 refreshments / aren't / There / any .

_____

5 the safe / the code / I / for / don't know .

_____

b Complete solutions a–e with the phrases in the box.

> I'll send someone ~~It's~~ The switch is Try in the fridge
> You can have

a _It's_ 9159.

b There's air conditioning. _____ next to the door.

c Oh, I'm sorry. _____ to look.

d I'm so sorry. _____ another room.

e Hmmm … _____ under the table.

c Match problems 1–5 in exercise **1a** to solutions a–e in exercise **1b**.

1 _d_   3 ___   5 ___

2 ___   4 ___

d **6.8**))) Listen and check your answers.

Writing a hotel review

2 Match subjects 1–6 to the rest of the sentence a–f.

1 The hotel   a have big windows.

2 The rooms   b goes every hour.

3 The air conditioning   c is near the sea.

4 The food   d isn't open in the morning.

5 The bus   e is broken.

6 The gym   f is very good.

3 Complete the hotel review with the subjects in the box.

> Buses The bathroom the food a heater the lift
> ~~This hotel~~ The rooms the TV

| HOTEL | REVIEWS | FACILITIES | PRICE | CONTACT |

Review by JessB

2 weeks ago

¹ _This hotel_ is cheap, but it isn't very good. It's very big – it's got five floors, but ² _____ is always broken. ³ _____ are small and cold. There's ⁴ _____ in each room, but it's very noisy. ⁵ _____ is a bit dirty – there's only one for all the rooms! Another problem is that there aren't a lot of things to do. There isn't a gym or a swimming pool, and ⁶ _____ has only one channel. You can have breakfast in the hotel, but ⁷ _____ is terrible! The only good thing is that the hotel is near a bus stop. ⁸ _____ go to the centre every five minutes.

I can …	Very well	Quite well	More practice
explain problems.	○	○	○
write a hotel review.	○	○	○

Review: Units 5 and 6

Grammar

1 Rewrite the sentences with the adverb of frequency in (brackets) in the correct position.

1 My partner goes to the gym at the weekend. (never)
  My partner never goes to the gym at the weekend.

2 Andy wears jeans to work. (sometimes)
  _____

3 I don't get dressed in the bathroom. (usually)
  _____

4 Do you buy your clothes from the same shop? (always)
  _____

5 Amara doesn't have baths; she prefers showers. (often)
  _____

2 Complete the conversation with the present simple form of the verbs in (brackets). Where there isn't a verb, write *do*, *does*, *don't* or *doesn't*.

A Where ¹ _do_ you _live_, Wendy? (live)
B I ² _____ in the city centre. (live)
A ³ _____ you _____ it? (like)
B No, I ⁴ _____.
A Why not?
B Because I ⁵ _____ my partner very often. (not see)
A Where ⁶ _____ he _____? (live)
B He's got a house in the country. He ⁷ _____ from home. (work)
A ⁸ _____ he _____ to the city to see you? (go)
B No, he ⁹ _____. He's very busy.

3 Complete the sentences and questions with the correct form of *there is* or *there are*.

1 _There's_ a shop in the museum. (+)
2 _____ _____ any cafés in the park?
3 _____ _____ a bath in the bathroom. (–)
4 _____ _____ a pharmacy in the centre?
5 _____ _____ any chairs in the kitchen. (–)

4 Complete the sentences with *Each* or *All the*.

1 _All the_ rooms have got windows.
2 _____ door has a different key.
3 _____ old buildings are in the centre.
4 _____ house has a lovely garden.
5 _____ hotels are very expensive.

Vocabulary

5 Circle the word that is different.

1 jeans / dress / trousers
2 jacket / trainers / shoes
3 green / interesting / white
4 café / park / restaurant
5 beautiful / interesting / red
6 hotel / cinema / theatre
7 fridge / table / gym
8 bath / lift / towels

6 Complete the sentences with the body parts in the box.

| face | feet | hair | hand | head | ~~leg~~ |

1 Hans is in hospital because his _leg_ is broken.
2 Selina's always got a pen in one _____ and a notepad in the other.
3 People like my mother because she's got a friendly _____.
4 I wear a hat on my _____ when it's cold.
5 My grandparents are old so they've got white _____.
6 These shoes are too small for my _____.

Functional language

7 Complete the conversations.

1 A _What time_ is the next bus to Kinshasa?
  B It leaves at 10.30.
2 A Where does the train _____ _____?
  B Platform 3.
3 A _____ _____ is it to the hospital?
  B It's €1.50.
4 A The air conditioning in our room _____ _____.
  B I'll send someone to look at it.
5 A My room's _____ _____.
  B There's a heater. The switch is next to the door.
6 A I _____ _____ the code for the door.
  B It's AB1993.

7.1   She can paint

Vocabulary skills

1a Look at the photos and complete the phrases with the verbs in the box.

> ~~drive~~ paint play remember ride speak understand
> use

1 _drive_ a car

Здравствуйте

2 _____ Russian

3 _____ the piano

4 _____ a phone

5 _____ instructions

6 _____ a picture

7 _____ somebody's birthday

8 _____ a bike

b **7.1**))) Listen and check your answers.

c **7.1**))) Listen again and repeat.

2a Circle the word in each line that doesn't go with the verb.

1	drive	a bus / a car / a bike
2	paint	a book / a flat / a picture
3	play	the guitar / the internet / the piano
4	remember	names / people / television
5	ride	a bike / a motorbike / a car
6	speak	a language / maths / Spanish
7	understand	faces / instructions / questions
8	use	an iron / a jacket / a paintbrush

b Look at the words you circled in exercise **2a**. Which verbs in the box can you use with these words?

> drive read ~~ride~~ remember study use watch wear

1 You _ride a bike._ _____
2 You _____ .
3 You _____ .
4 You _____ .
5 You _____ .
6 You _____ .
7 You _____ .
8 You _____ .

3 Complete the text with the verbs in the box.

> drive paint play ~~remember~~ understand use

Elephants are very clever animals. They **1** _remember_ things and they also **2**_____ easy instructions. But elephants aren't usually good artists or musicians; they don't often **3**_____ pictures or **4**_____ a musical instrument.

Karishma is an Asian elephant at Whipsnade Zoo in the UK. She's different from other elephants because she can **5**_____ a paintbrush. Her pictures are very famous and a lot of people **6**_____ to Whipsnade Zoo to see them. Karishma's paintings are in the zoo shop. The money from the pictures is for helping elephants all over the world.

4   Look at the photos and circle the correct options.

1   She can / can't sing.

2   It *can* / *can't* swim.

3   He *can* / *can't* drive.

4   They *can* / *can't* fly.

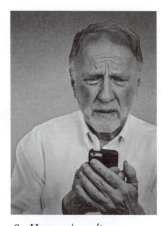

5   He *can* / *can't* walk.

6   He *can* / *can't* use a phone.

5   Complete the text with *can* or *can't* and the verbs in the box.

~~fly~~   run (x2)   see   sing   swim

Most birds ¹ _can fly_ , but there are some birds that can't, for example penguins and ostriches.

Penguins usually live in cold places and they like water. They ² _____ _____ at 24 km an hour. When they aren't in the sea, they stay on the land. They can walk, but they ³ _____ _____ very fast because they have short legs.

Ostriches live in hot places, where there isn't a lot of water. They've got very long legs, so they ⁴ _____ _____ very fast – at 70 km an hour! They have long necks and very big eyes, so they ⁵ _____ _____ far away.

Most birds are nice to listen to, but not penguins and ostriches. They ⁶ _____ _____ like other birds.

6a **7.2**)) Listen and write six sentences.

1   _I can swim._

2   _____

3   _____

4   _____

5   _____

6   _____

b   Circle the schwa sound /ə/ in the sentences in exercise **6a**. There is one example in each sentence.

I c(a)n swim.

c   **7.2**)) Listen again and check your answers.

d   **7.2**)) Listen again and repeat.

I can …	Very well	Quite well	More practice
use *can* and *can't*.	○	○	○
talk about my abilities.	○	○	○

7.2 Can you help?

1a Put the words in order to make questions.

1 you / a / Can / bike / ride ?
   Can you ride a bike?

2 your / Can / read / daughter ?
   _____

3 a / paint / Adam / picture / Can ?
   _____

4 guitar / play / friends / your / Can / the ?
   _____

5 Can / a / grandparents / computer / your / use ?
   _____

6 your / and / sister / Can / you / sing ?
   _____

b Complete the answers to the questions in exercise **1a**.

1 Yes, *I can.*
2 Yes, _____.
3 No, _____.
4 No, _____.
5 Yes, _____.
6 No, _____.

2 Read the advert for a volunteer job. Tick (✓) the abilities the volunteer needs.

cook ___   speak Spanish ___
drive ___   swim ___
use a computer ✓   teach people about animals ___

3 Complete an interview for the job in exercise **2**. Write questions and short answers with *can* using the verbs in (brackets).

Interviewer So, Leyla ¹ *can you speak* (speak) Spanish?
Leyla Yes, ² _____.
Interviewer Um, we have a lot of visitors from Brazil.
³ _____ (speak) Portuguese, too?
Leyla No, ⁴ _____. But I ⁵ _____ (learn) some Portuguese phrases, I'm a fast learner.
Interviewer Great! Now, I know you like animals, but
⁶ _____ (teach) other people about them?
Leyla Yes, ⁷ _____. I love animals, and I'm a really good teacher.
Interviewer That's great. What about computers?
⁸ _____ (use) a computer?
Leyla Yes, ⁹ _____. I'm very good with computers.
Interviewer OK, that's fine, Leyla. Can we talk about your studies now?

PRONUNCIATION *can, can't* in questions and statements

4a **7.3**))) Listen and mark the stress. There is one stressed word in each line.

1 Can you drive?   4 No, I can't.
2 Yes, I can.   5 I can cook.
3 Can you swim?   6 I can sing.

b **7.3**))) Listen again and repeat.

Volunteers wanted for Galapagos Giant Tortoise Conservation Project

The Galapagos Giant Tortoise Conservation Project works with the giant tortoises in the Galapagos National Park.

Most of the work is outside in the hot sun. Volunteers feed the tortoises, record on a computer how big they are and give information about the tortoises to Spanish tourists.

In their free time, volunteers can go to the beach and visit the other islands.

Duration: 2–12 weeks

Cost: €970 for 2 weeks

■ **feed** give food to a person or animal

Galapagos Islands

giant tortoise

Vocabulary adverbs of manner

5 Complete the sentences with adverbs from the adjectives in the box. Use each adverb twice.

bad fast good slow

1 My teacher teaches English very _well_ .

2 That car goes very _____.

3 She can walk _____.

4 Your friend cooks _____.

5 He can run very _____.

6 Tommy can't ride a bike very _____.

7 That artist paints _____.

8 Lettie can write _____.

6a Rewrite the sentences with the verbs in (brackets). Use adverbs of manner.

1 I'm a slow driver. (drive)
   I drive slowly .

2 My sister's a good painter. (paints)
   She _____.

3 We're bad cooks. (cook)
   We _____.

4 Michael's a fast swimmer. (swims)
   He _____.

5 You and Jan are slow walkers. (walk)
   You _____.

6 Christina's a good speaker. (speaks)
   She _____.

7 Those men are fast runners. (run)
   They _____.

8 Nadia and I are bad tennis players. (play)
   We _____.

b **7.4**))) Listen and check your answers.

c **7.4**))) Listen again and repeat.

7 Read the texts and circle the correct form, adjective or adverb.

Fast or Slow?

claws

a sloth

Sloths are very **1** slow / slowly animals from Central and South America. They don't go very **2** fast / slowly in the trees where they live – they do four metres a minute! When they're on the ground, they walk very **3** bad / badly because their hands and feet have very long claws. But sloths are happy in the water and they are very **4** good / well swimmers.

Octopuses are very clever sea animals; they're very **5** fast / badly learners. They can swim very **6** good / well, but they usually walk **7** slow / slowly over the rocks. Octopuses are very **8** bad / badly pets because they don't stay in their tanks.

an octopus

I can …	Very well	Quite well	More practice
use *Can* to ask and answer about abilities.	○	○	○
use adverbs of manner.	○	○	○

7.3 I like going out

Vocabulary hobbies

1 Answer the questions with the words and phrases in the box.

> cook   go out with friends   go to the cinema   play sport
> read   ~~take photos~~   travel

What can you do when you want to ...?

1 remember a beautiful place   _take photos_
2 watch a good film   _____
3 see another country   _____
4 have dinner at home   _____
5 dance   _____
6 do exercise   _____
7 learn interesting things   _____

2 Match the words in **A** to the words in **B** to make hobbies. Then complete the sentences.

> **A**   go on   listen to   play   shop   take   watch   ~~work~~

> **B**   Facebook   ~~in the garden~~   online   photos   to music
> TV   video games

1 A lot of British people _work in the garden_ when the weather's good.
2 Young people often _____ online with people they don't know.
3 Internet users often _____ when they want to speak to friends.
4 Families sometimes _____ together in the evening.
5 Some people _____ when they want to buy clothes.
6 A lot of people _____ on the radio in their cars.
7 Today, people usually _____ with their mobile phones.

➡ **VOCABULARY TIP** Record verbs in context to help you remember them, e.g. *take photos, swim in the sea, watch a film*, etc.

Grammar *like + -ing*

3 Complete the table with the *-ing* form of the verbs in the box.

> cook   dance   eat   fly   get   ride   shop   sing   swim
> travel   use   write

listen + -ing = listening	**have + -ing** = having	**run + -ing** = running
cooking		

4a Look at the photos and complete the sentences with *like* + verb + *-ing*.

1 They _like_ _playing_ sport.

2 She _____ _____ photos.

3 They _____ _____ bikes.

4 He _____ _____ to music.

5   They _____
    _____ to the
    cinema.

6   She _____
    _____ TV.

7   He _____
    _____ online.

8   They _____
    _____ their phones.

b   **7.5**))) Listen and check your answers.

c   **7.5**))) Listen again and repeat.

5   Complete the conversation with the correct form of *like*
    and the *-ing* form of the verbs in (brackets).

Eve   Mel, ¹_do_ you _like running_ (like/run)?

Mel   Not really. I ²_____ (like/walk), but
          I don't often go running. Why?

Eve   I want to go running, but I haven't got a running
          partner.

Mel   What about your husband?

Eve   No, he ³_____ (not like/run).

Mel   What about a different sport? ⁴_____ he
          _____ (like/play) tennis ?

Eve   No, he doesn't play any sport. But he
          ⁵_____ (like/watch) it on TV.

Mel   What about you, Eve? ⁶_____ you _____
          _____ (like/play) tennis?

Eve   Yes, it's OK. Why?

Mel   I ⁷_____ (not like/run), but I can
          play tennis with you if you want.

Eve   OK, that sounds great! When is good for you?

6a   **7.6**))) Listen and write what you hear.

1   _What do you like doing?_

2   _____

3   _____

4   _____

b   Look at the *-ing* forms in the questions and sentences in
        exercise **6a**. Are the vowels linked with /w/ or /j/?

c   **7.6**))) Listen, check and repeat.

Vocabulary   *like, love, hate + -ing*

7   Look at the chart and complete the text. Use the correct
    form of *like*, *love* or *hate* and the *-ing* form of a verb.

	Poppy	Amir and Rose
☺☺		
☺		
☹		
☹☹		

Poppy ¹_loves going out_ with friends. When she
isn't with friends, she ²_____ TV.
She ³_____, so she hasn't got a lot
of books. She usually has dinner in a restaurant,
because she ⁴_____.

Amir and Rose ⁵_____ _____ in
their free time. When they're at home, they
⁶_____ in their garden. They
aren't very good with computers and they
⁷_____ online. They
⁸_____ video games because
they want to be outside.

I can …	Very well	Quite well	More practice
use *like + -ing*.	○	○	○
talk about my hobbies.	○	○	○

Speaking and writing

Speaking simple requests

1a Circle the correct option.

1 *Can I* / *Can you* take this chair, please?
2 *Can I* / *Can you* have an apple, please?
3 Excuse me. *Can I* / *Can you* call me a taxi?
4 *Can I* / *Can you* use your laptop, please?
5 Excuse me. *Can I* / *Can you* help me?
6 Excuse me. *Can I* / *Can you* tell me the way to the hospital?

b Complete answers a–f with the words in the box.

> I'm   It's   ~~no problem~~   of course   that way   you are

a Sure, _no problem_ .
b Of course. Here _____.
c Sorry. _____ taken.
d Sorry. _____ busy.
e Sure. It's _____.
f Yes, _____. Where do you want to go?

c Match questions 1–6 in exercise **1a** to answers a–f in exercise **1b**.

1 _c_   3 ___   5 ___
2 ___   4 ___   6 ___

d **7.7**))) Listen and check your answers.

Writing a post on a social media website

2 Put the word in (brackets) in the correct place in the sentence.

a My friend Fern is a photographer. (great)
   My friend Fern is a great photographer.

b I can speak English. (well)
   _____

c She helps me take photos. (amazing)
   _____

d I paint the flowers in my garden. (often)
   _____

e We have a lot of guests from abroad. (always)
   _____

f I paint. (badly)
   _____

3 Complete the post with the sentences in exercise **2**.

🏠 ✉ 💬   🔍

May (24) from Thailand

Hi!

I'm new to this site. I'm here because I love speaking English. **1** _b_ because I use it in my job. I'm a receptionist in an international hotel, and **2**___. My hobby is taking photos. **3**___ and we see each other every weekend. **4**___.

I also like painting, but **5**___. I sometimes paint from photos and **6**___. It helps me relax, but my paintings aren't very good.

Please write and tell me what you like doing. We can speak English to each other!

I can …	Very well	Quite well	More practice
make simple requests.	○	○	○
write a post on a social media website.	○	○	○

7.5   Reading for pleasure

Last chance

1a Read the introduction to a short story called *Last Chance*. Answer the questions.

1 What is Mike's job?
2 Is Mr Frank happy with Mike's work?
3 Why does Mike go to Hawaii?

> Mike is a cameraman and he works for SFX News. Mr Frank is Mike's boss. He is angry with Mike because he doesn't like Mike's work. Mike has one last chance to make a good film. He goes to Hawaii to film a volcano.

b Which of the items in the box do you think are in the story?

> camera   fire   laptop   plane   rock   smoke

2 Read an extract from the story and check your answers to exercise **1b**. Why doesn't Mike leave the volcano after he films it?

3 What do you think happens next? Use the illustrations to help you.

Last Chance

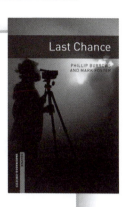

After two long hours, Mike is on the volcano. There is a lot of smoke and a lot of fire. Mike can't see any people.

'I must be quick', he thinks. Mike films the smoke and the fire. A big rock nearly hits him, but he films it. 'This film is good,' he thinks.

He is afraid but happy. 'How can Mr Frank be angry now?' Mike thinks. He is taking lots of film.

Another rock almost hits him. Mike feels hot and tired. 'It's time to go,' says Mike. 'Good job!' he says to his camera.

A bigger rock goes over his head. 'I don't like this. I must go now,' he says. Mike can smell the smoke. He can feel the fire.

Mike puts his camera under his arm. He starts to run. Just then, the volcano makes a noise. Mike runs faster. Suddenly, he hears a different noise.

'Is that a woman?' thinks Mike. 'It can't be. There is nobody here.'

He starts to run again, but then …

'Help!'

'It is somebody. They need me,' he thinks. 'Hello,' he says. 'Where are you?' Mike looks everywhere, but he can't see anybody.

'I'm here. Please help me!'

Mike sees something behind a rock. It moves. He goes to the rock and sees a young woman there. She can't move her leg because it is under the rock.

'Oh, thank you. Thank you,' she says to Mike. She starts to cry. 'My leg. I think it's broken.'

'Wait a minute,' says Mike. 'I can help.'

He pushes the rock. It is too big. There are small rocks in front. He pushes them away then pushes the big rock again. It moves a little. He pushes harder. It moves a little more.

'Aargh,' cries the woman.

Suddenly, the rock moves down the volcano.

The woman's face is white. She smiles slowly.

Text extract from *Oxford Bookworms: Last Chance*

4 Read the summary and check your answers.

> **SUMMARY**
> The woman's name is Jenny. Mike helps her down the volcano. But he forgets his camera! When they get to the town, they get into a helicopter. Mike tells a man in the helicopter about his camera, and then he goes to sleep. When he gets home, he doesn't go to work. But one day, Mike's boss phones him because he wants to talk to him. Mike goes into his boss's office. Mr Frank gives Mike his camera. It's from the man in the helicopter. The camera is broken, but they can watch the video of the volcano. Mike's boss is very happy with Mike and his film. And Mike is happy because Jenny now works for SFX News, too.

8 Our past

8.1 When we were seven

Grammar verb *be* past simple

1 (Circle) the correct options.

1 It (was) / *were* cold.
2 You *was* / *were* late.
3 Andreas *wasn't* / *weren't* at work.
4 We *was* / *were* at home.
5 The managers *was* / *were* in a meeting.
6 Liam and Ava *wasn't* / *weren't* in class.

2 Complete the conversations with the correct past simple form of *be*.

1 A __Was__ the concert good?
  B Yes, it _____.
2 A Where _____ you yesterday?
  B I _____ at the beach with my friends.
3 A _____ you and your partner at the party?
  B Yes, we _____.
4 A _____ your sister at home yesterday?
  B No, she _____.
5 A When _____ you and your family in Chile?
  B We _____ there in April.
6 A _____ your parents teachers?
  B No, they _____.

PRONUNCIATION *was* and *were*

3a 8.1))) Listen and mark the stress. The numbers in (brackets) are the number of stressed words.

1 I was a good student. (2)
2 My parents weren't rich. (3)
3 Were you clever? (1)
4 Yes, I was. (1)
5 Was she nice? (1)
6 No, she wasn't. (1)

b 8.1))) Listen again and repeat.

4 Complete the text with the correct past simple form of *be*.

Boyhood **1** __was__ a 2014 film about the life of a boy called Mason. The film **2**_____ unusual because filming **3**_____ very long – from 2002 to 2013. The actors **4**_____ the same for all that time; the same boy – Ellar Coltrane – **5**_____ Mason from the age of seven to the age of eighteen. But Coltrane and the other actors **6**_____ in the film studios every day for twelve years. They **7**_____ there for about a week every year making the film. *Boyhood* **8**_____ the best film of 2014, but many people say they like it.

Vocabulary   dates

5   Continue the series.

1   fourth, fifth, _sixth_
2   first, second, _____
3   ninth, tenth, _____
4   eighth, tenth, _____
5   fifth, tenth, _____
6   nineteenth, twentieth, _____
7   twenty-second, twenty-fifth, _____
8   tenth, twentieth, _____

6   Complete the months with the missing vowels (*a,e,i,o,u*).

1   J**a**n**u** **a**ry
2   F_br_ _ry
3   M_rch
4   _pr_l
5   M_y
6   J_n_

7   J_ly
8   _ _g_st
9   S_pt_mb_r
10   _ct_b_r
11   N_v_mb_r
12   D_c_mb_r

7   Match years 1–8 to words a–h.

1   1912
2   1920
3   1977
4   1990
5   2003
6   2009
7   2017
8   2030

a   two thousand and three
b   nineteen ninety
c   twenty seventeen
d   nineteen twelve
e   twenty thirty
f   nineteen seventy-seven
g   two thousand and nine
h   nineteen twenty

8   Write the years in numbers.

1   nineteen fourteen   _1914_
2   twenty fifteen   _____
3   two thousand and eight   _____
4   nineteen ninety-six   _____
5   two thousand and two   _____
6   twenty twenty   _____

9   Write the years in words.

1   1876   _____
2   2040   _____
3   1957   _____
4   2004   _____
5   1164   _____
6   2018   _____

10a   Answer the questions using the dates in the box.

26th January   23rd April   1st May   4th July   18th July
31st December

When is …
1   Australia Day?   _26th January_
2   New Year's Eve?   _____
3   International Workers Day?   _____
4   Independence Day (USA)?   _____
5   World Book Day?   _____
6   Nelson Mandela Day?   _____

b   **8.2**))) Listen and check your answers.

c   **8.2**))) Listen again and repeat.

I can …

	Very well	Quite well	More practice
use the verb *be* in the past.	○	○	○
talk about my life then and now.	○	○	○

8.2 Lives from the past

Vocabulary *was born/died*

1a Match the people in the photos to sentences 1–6.

Helen Keller

Leonardo da Vinci

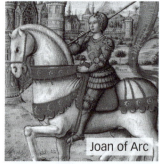
Joan of Arc

Genghis Khan

Jane Austen

Mahatma Gandhi

1 He was born in 1452 and he died in 1519.
   Leonardo da Vinci
2 She was born in 1412 and she died in 1431.

3 He was born in 1869 and he died in 1948.

4 She was born in 1880 and she died in 1968.

5 He was born in 1162 and he died in 1227.

6 She was born in 1775 and she died in 1817.

b **8.3**))) Listen and check your answers.

2 Write sentences using the information about the people.
1 Bob Marley (1945–1981)
   Bob Marley was born in 1945 and he died in 1981.
2 Pocahontas (1595–1617)

3 Marco Polo (1254–1325)

4 Anne Frank (1929–1945)

5 Albert Einstein (1879–1955)

6 Edith Piaf (1915–1963)

7 Charles Darwin (1809–1882)

8 Rosa Parks (1913–2005)

3a Use the words to write sentences. Try to choose the correct year.
1 Dante Alighieri / born / (1265 / 1365 / 1465)
   Dante Alighieri _was born in 1265._
2 Agatha Christie / died / (1776 / 1876 / 1976)
   Agatha Christie _____.
3 Christopher Columbus / born / (1451 / 1551 / 1651)
   Christopher Columbus _____.
4 Galileo Galilei / died / (1542 / 1642 / 1742)
   Galileo Galilei _____.
5 Alfred Hitchcock / born / (1699 / 1799 / 1899)
   Alfred Hitchcock _____.
6 Catherine the Great / died / (1796 / 1896 / 1996)
   Catherine the Great _____.
7 William Shakespeare / born / (1464 / 1564 / 1664)
   William Shakespeare _____.
8 Emmeline Pankhurst / died / (1728 / 1828 / 1928)
   Emmeline Pankhurst _____.

b **8.4**))) Listen and check your answers.

Grammar past simple regular verbs

4 Complete the sentences with the past simple form of the verbs in the box.

finish ~~paint~~ play study travel walk watch work

1 Matt *painted* the door yesterday.

2 My sister _____ to work.

3 My friends _____ tennis on Sunday.

4 Padma _____ TV yesterday.

5 They _____ work late yesterday.

6 Ali _____ in the garden.

7 We _____ to London yesterday.

8 I _____ German at school.

5 Complete the text about Ada Lovelace with the past simple form of the verbs in the box.

die help ~~live~~ love show study talk visit

ADA LOVELACE

Ada Lovelace was born in London in 1815. As a child, she [1] *lived* with her grandmother because her parents separated when she was a baby. She [2] _____ maths with a private teacher because she was often ill. Ada was very clever, and she [3] _____ the classes. When she was seventeen, she [4] _____ Charles Babbage, the father of the computer. Babbage [5] _____ Ada his new machine and she asked a lot of questions about it. When Babbage invented a computer, Ada [6] _____ him write the instructions for it. She had a lot of ideas about computers, and she [7] _____ about these ideas with Babbage. Today, people say that Ada Lovelace was the first computer programmer. She [8] _____ in London in 1852.

PRONUNCIATION regular past simple endings

The regular past simple ending -*ed* is pronounced /ɪd/ when the infinitive finishes in /t/ or /d/, e.g. *start → started, decide → decided.*

6a Circle the past simple form with a different pronunciation of -*ed*.

1 lived / started / studied / used
2 hated / loved / opened / travelled
3 helped / liked / visited / walked
4 finished / painted / talked / worked
5 died / married / showed / wanted

b 8.5))) Listen and check your answers.

c 8.5))) Listen again and repeat.

I can ...	Very well	Quite well	More practice
use past simple regular verbs to talk about the past.	○	○	○
describe a past life.	○	○	○

8.3 Special moments

Grammar object pronouns

1 Look at the photos and (circle) the correct object pronouns.

Il Divo

Leo Messi

big cities

sushi

Charlotte Dujardin

my grandparents

1 My partner and I like *her / him / it /* (*them*)
2 We like *her / him / it / them.*
3 We hate *her / him / it / them.*
4 We love *her / him / it / them.*
5 We like *her / him / it / them.*
6 We love *her / him / it / them.*

2 Complete the sentences with the object pronouns in the box.

~~her~~ him it me them us you

1 Marina likes Rashid, but he doesn't like _her_.
2 When you speak fast, I don't understand _____.
3 My parents live abroad. I call _____ every week.
4 This book's really interesting. I really like _____.
5 Excuse me. We have a problem. Can you help _____?
6 I often visit my brother, but he never visits _____.
7 My friend has a new boyfriend. She likes _____ a lot.

3 Complete the conversation between a reporter, Oscar, and Chloe with the correct object pronouns.

Oscar Hello. I'm Oscar from City Radio. Can I ask ¹_you_ some questions about exercise?

Chloe Yes, of course.

Oscar Um, first question. How much exercise do you do?

Chloe Well, I go walking every day.

Oscar Really? Do you go with your partner?

Chloe No, I don't. He doesn't like ²_____. But he likes jogging, so I go jogging with ³_____ every Sunday.

Oscar Right. Who do you go walking with, then?

Chloe I go with some friends. I meet ⁴_____ at 9 a.m. and we walk for about an hour.

Oscar OK. Do you always go with the same people?

Chloe No, not always. My sister sometimes comes with ⁵_____. She walks slowly, but we always wait for ⁶_____.

Oscar So ... walking with friends and sister, and jogging with partner. That's great. Thank you for talking to ⁷_____.

Chloe You're welcome.

O≡ Oxford 3000™

PRONUNCIATION linking (2)

4a 8.6))) Listen and write six sentences.

1   _I like it._
2   _____
3   _____
4   _____
5   _____
6   _____

b 8.6))) Listen again. Mark the linked words in exercise **4a**.

1   _I like⌣it._

c 8.6))) Listen again and repeat.

Vocabulary past time phrases

5 Correct the past time phrases in **bold**.

1   I helped my friend move house **last day**.   _yesterday_
2   My neighbour was in Beijing **past year**. _____
3   We watched a good film on TV **yesterday night**.

    _____
4   They visited the museum **in Saturday**. _____
5   Irina started work early **today morning**. _____
6   We were in Costa Rica **on June**. _____

6a Complete the text. Write one word in each space.

My wife and I were in Croatia for a week ¹ _last_ year
with a group of twelve people. It was cold because
we were there ² _____ February. We were in
Dubrovnik ³ _____ Wednesday and Thursday,
and then we travelled to Plitvice. It was great!
⁴ _____ week, I received an email from a woman
in the group called Fabiola. She invited us to lunch at
her house, so that's where we were ⁵ _____.
We had a great time, and we arrived home very late
⁶ _____ night. I called Fabiola ⁷ _____
morning to say thank you for a lovely day.

b 8.7))) Listen and check your answers to exercise **6a**.

I can ...	Very well	Quite well	More practice
tell a story about a photo.	○	○	○
use object pronouns.	○	○	○

8.4 Speaking and writing

Speaking special occasions

1a Circle the correct responses.

1 I've got an exam tomorrow.
   a Congratulations!
   b Good luck!
   c That's great!

2 I'm twenty-one today.
   a Never mind.
   b Cheers!
   c Happy birthday!

3 My brother's got a new girlfriend.
   a Good luck!
   b I'm sorry to hear that.
   c Really?

4 I've got a new job!
   a Cheers!
   b Congratulations!
   c Happy birthday!

5 I can't go out tonight.
   a Never mind.
   b That's great!
   c Good luck!

6 My mother's in hospital.
   a Congratulations!
   b That's great!
   c I'm sorry to hear that.

7 Here's to Keegan and Angie!
   a Cheers!
   b Really?
   c Never mind.

8 My sister's got a place at university!
   a Happy birthday!
   b That's great!
   c I'm sorry to hear that.

b 8.8))) Listen and check your answers.

Writing a biography

2 Complete the sentences with *after* or *then*.

1 Eddie studied medicine and _*after*_ that he worked in a hospital as a doctor.
2 I waited for my friend, and _____ we walked home together.
3 Gemma and I travelled around the world for a year. _____, we returned home.
4 We finished dinner and talked for a time. _____ that, they showed us some photos.

3 Complete the text with the missing phrases.

a Then, she started planning her own flight
b and then she worked to get money for more lessons
c and after that she was very famous
d After that, she wanted to learn to fly

Amelia Earhart

Amelia Earhart was born in the USA in July, 1897. She was the first woman to fly across the Atlantic alone. She wasn't very interested in planes when she was a child, but that changed when she was older. In December 1920, she travelled in a plane for the first time and she loved it! **1** _d_. Her first flying lesson was in January 1921, **2**___. At the end of the year, she passed her flying exams and she was a pilot! But there wasn't any work for a female pilot, so she worked in a lot of different jobs. In 1928, another pilot asked her to fly across the Atlantic with him … as a passenger. In June of that year, she crossed the Atlantic Ocean in a plane for the first time. **3**___. On 20th May 1932, Amelia Earhart was the first female pilot to fly across the Atlantic **4**___. Her last flight was around the world. She disappeared in a plane over the Pacific Ocean in July 1937, and nobody knows what happened to her.

I can …	Very well	Quite well	More practice
use expressions for special occasions.	○	○	○
show interest.	○	○	○
write a biography.	○	○	○

Review: Units 7 and 8

Grammar

1 Complete the questions and statements. Use *can* or *can't* and the words in (brackets).

1 I'm sorry, but _I can't remember_ your name. (I/not remember)
2 Simone's very clever. _____ six languages. (She/speak)
3 **A** _____? (your brothers/cook)
   B Yes, they're very good cooks.
4 Phei and I don't like going to the beach because _____. (we/not swim)
5 **A** _____? (you/sing)
   B No, I can't. I sing very badly.

2 Complete the sentences with the *-ing* form of the verbs in the box.

> dance   paint   ~~read~~   shop   take

1 Jo's got a lot of books because she loves _reading_ .
2 I don't like _____ online because I want to see the clothes.
3 Thom loves _____ photos with his new camera.
4 My friends and I like _____ in clubs.
5 Sabine loves _____ and she's a very good artist.

3 Write the sentences in the past tense.

1 We live in a village.
   We lived in a village.
2 Catrin studies languages at university.
   _____
3 Is it a good hotel?
   _____
4 Are those trousers expensive?
   _____
5 My partner starts work early.
   _____

4 Complete the sentences with the correct object pronoun (*me, you, him, her*, etc.).

1 Sorry, but I can't tell _you_ . It's a secret.
2 I like Ryan and he likes _____.
3 Our friends visited _____ last weekend.
4 David loves his wife and she loves _____, too.
5 My parents weren't at home yesterday – I called _____ three times!

Vocabulary

5 Match the verbs in **A** to the words in **B** to make verb phrases. Then complete the sentences.

A ~~drive~~   paint   play   remember   speak   use

B a camera   ~~a car~~   a picture   dates   French   the piano

1 I always cycle to work because I can't _drive a car_ .
2 Lolita isn't very good at history because she can't _____.
3 My children can _____. They were born in Paris.
4 Rory's good at music. He can _____ very well.
5 I'm not good at art, so I can't _____.

6 Rewrite the sentences using the word in (brackets) in the correct place.

1 Erik is a painter. (good)
   Erik is a good painter.
2 Helena and Leo are typists. (fast)
   _____
3 Tommy can write. (slowly)
   _____
4 I can't run. (fast)
   _____
5 Birgit and I speak English. (badly)
   _____

7 Complete the sentences with one word.

1 I finished the book _yesterday_ .
2 My mother was born _____ 1966.
3 You showed me your photos _____ week.
4 Yves started his new job _____ Monday.
5 I called the doctor _____ morning.

Functional language

8 8.9))) Listen and respond using phrases a–h.

1 _g_   a Happy birthday!
2 ___   b Sorry, I'm busy.
3 ___   c Never mind.
4 ___   d Sure. Here you are.
5 ___   e Sure. It's that way.
6 ___   f That's great!
7 ___   g Sorry, it's taken.
8 ___   h Good luck!

9 Unusual stories

9.1 Happy memories

Grammar past simple irregular verbs

1 Complete the past simple forms with the missing vowels (*a, e, i, o, u*).

1	be	w<u>a</u>s/w<u>e</u>re	9	write	wr_t_
2	meet	m_t	10	leave	l_ft
3	fall	f_ll	11	know	kn_w
4	get	g_t	12	sell	s_ld
5	lose	l_st	13	go	w_nt
6	say	s_ _d	14	come	c_m_
7	can	c_ _ld	15	see	s_w
8	have	h_d			

2 Write the sentences in the past.

1 We sometimes have lunch with our friends.
   We ___*had lunch*___ with our friends yesterday.
2 I see my parents every Saturday.
   I _____ on Sunday last weekend.
3 Ahmed can play golf very well.
   He _____ when he was five.
4 My partner comes home late every evening.
   She _____ early yesterday evening.
5 That shop sells cheap clothes in January.
   It _____ in February, too.
6 I often lose my keys.
   I _____ this morning.
7 My husband always says hello to our neighbours.
   He _____ to them this morning.
8 Kate sometimes writes an email to her brother.
   She _____ to him last night.

3 Complete Nadia's story with the past simple form of the verbs in (brackets).

'I already ¹ ___*knew*___ (know) Pedro because he was one of my students – I ² _____ (be) a teacher at a language school in Madrid at the time. But then I ³ _____ (leave) my job to go travelling for a year with a friend. In April, we ⁴ _____ (go) to Peru. We ⁵ _____ (be) in Machu Picchu when suddenly I ⁶ _____ (see) Pedro! We talked and we decided to meet again when we were back in Madrid. Five months later, we ⁷ _____ (meet) for a walk. We started going out together and we ⁸ _____ (fall) in love. We ⁹ _____ (get) married three years later and we now have a beautiful daughter called Hannah.'

Vocabulary   adjective + noun phrases (2)

4a   Put the words in order to make adjective + noun phrases.

1   easy / an / life
    an easy life

2   a / time / happy
    _____

3   ending / sad / a
    _____

4   new / a / friend
    _____

5   book / interesting / an
    _____

6   my / life / old
    _____

b   **9.1**))) Listen and check your answers.

c   **9.1**))) Listen again and repeat.

5   ⭕Circle the correct options.

1   That book tells an *unusual* / *easy* story about a girl and a chimpanzee.

2   I met *a new* / *an old* friend from school yesterday. It was lovely to see her again!

3   My grandparents had *an easy* / *a difficult* life because they were very poor.

4   I always feel good after seeing that film because it's got a *happy* / *sad* ending.

5   We had a *difficult* / *good* time at the party. It was fun!

6   When she was young, Isabel left her village to start *a new* / *an old* life in the big city.

6   Complete the text with the phrases in the box.

> a difficult life   an easy time   a happy ending
> an interesting story   a new friend   his new life

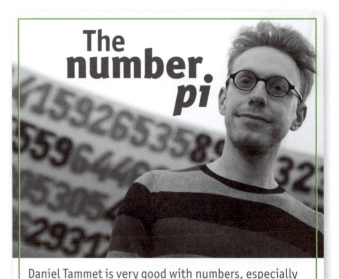

The number *pi*

Daniel Tammet is very good with numbers, especially the number *pi* (π). Most of us know *pi* as 3.14, but Daniel can remember 22,514 numbers of it. Daniel also writes books. His books tell ¹ *an interesting story* : the story of his life. As a child, Daniel had ² _____ because he was different. He didn't understand the other children, so he didn't have any friends. He didn't have ³ _____ at school, and he was very sad. But Daniel was clever, so he passed his exams and he learnt to understand people. When he left school, he met ⁴ _____ who helped him a lot. Daniel's story has ⁵ _____ because he has a lot of friends now. He likes ⁶ _____ a lot because he is more open and he feels good about meeting new people.

I can ...	Very well	Quite well	More practice
use past simple irregular verbs.	◯	◯	◯
talk about a memory.	◯	◯	◯

9.2 A good excuse

Grammar past simple negatives and questions

1 Write negative sentences using the words in (brackets).

1 I lost my wallet. (my phone)
I _didn't lose my phone._

2 Lucy studied languages. (science)
She _____

3 You got home early. (late)
You _____

4 We watched a film on TV. (the football)
We _____.

5 Solomon met his sister for lunch. (his girlfriend)
He _____

6 I visited family. (friends)
I _____

7 Emma and I had dinner in a restaurant. (at home)
We _____

8 Nihan and Maryam painted the living room. (bedroom)
They _____

2a Put the words in order to make questions.

1 you / book / like / Did / the ?
Did you like the book?

2 Galuh / work / yesterday / Did ?
_____

3 your / theatre / to / friends / Did / walk / the ?
_____

4 come / your / Did / Coline / party / to ?
_____

5 university / you / Did / in love / at / fall ?
_____

6 the / late / film / Did / finish ?
_____

b Complete the short answers with *did* or *didn't*.

a Yes, it _did_. We went to bed at 2 a.m.

b No, she _____. She was ill.

c No, he _____. It was a holiday.

d Yes, I _____. It was great.

e No, they _____. They went by car.

f Yes, we _____. We were in the same maths class.

c Match questions 1–6 in exercise **2a** to answers a–f in exercise **2b**.

1 _d_   3 ___   5 ___
2 ___   4 ___   6 ___

3 Complete the conversation. Write questions using the words in (brackets).

A Nicole, ¹ _where did you go_ on holiday last year? (where / go)

B We went to Menorca, in the Mediterranean Sea.

A I know Menorca. We went there last month.
² _____? (Where / stay)

B We stayed in a hotel in Ciutadella.

A Oh. We were near Mahón. ³_____ to Menorca? (How / get)

B We flew to Barcelona, and then we went to Menorca by ferry.

A Right. ⁴_____? (When / go)

B In August. I went for two weeks.

A Nice. ⁵_____? (Who / go with)

B My sister and her family. There were six of us.

A Really? ⁶_____ of Menorca? (What / think)

B I loved it. It's a beautiful island.

Vocabulary verb phrases (1)

4a Complete the phrases with the verbs in the box.

fall feel forget ~~go~~ have meet miss sleep

1 _go_ to the doctor

2 _____ badly

3 _____ an old friend

4 _____ my train

5 _____ in the shower

6 _____ a headache

7 _____ the time

8 _____ sick

b **9.2**))) Listen and check your answers.

c **9.2**))) Listen again and repeat.

5 Complete the excuses with the verb phrases in exercise **4a**. Use the past simple form of the verbs.

> ## Why are you late for work?

1 I ___met an old friend___ on the way to work.
2 I _____ because I ate something bad last night.
3 I _____ because it left early.
4 I _____ of the meeting.
5 I _____ because I felt ill.
6 I _____ because my neighbours had a party.
7 I _____ because I couldn't sleep.
8 I _____ when I was in the bathroom.

PRONUNCIATION sentence stress

6a **9.3**))) Listen and mark the stress on the past simple questions (2 words) and negatives (3 words).

1 Did you **know** the **answer**?
2 Did you buy any clothes?
3 Did you call your friend?
4 I didn't have a shower.
5 I didn't ride my bike.
6 I didn't go to work.

b **9.3**))) Listen again and repeat.

9.3 News stories

Grammar *ago*

1 Put the words in order to make sentences.

1 lost / ago / his wallet / Pierre / a week .
   Pierre lost his wallet a week ago.

2 saw / three days / a film / ago / We .
   _____

3 five minutes / got / ago / You / a text message .
   _____

4 ago / wrote / I / two hours / an email .
   _____

5 her car / Susie / ago / six months / sold .
   _____

6 on holiday / ago / They / a year / went .
   _____

2a It's 9 p.m. on 21st June 2016. Look at the timeline on Katia's profile. Complete the sentences using *ago*.

1 Katia cooked dinner *five minutes ago* .
2 She used her new bike _____ .
3 She met her friends _____ .
4 She saw her grandparents _____ .
5 She went to a concert _____ .
6 She bought a house _____ .

b **9.4 »** Listen and check your answers.

c **9.4 »** Listen again and repeat.

3 Complete the conversations with the questions. Use the words in (brackets).

1 A *When did you last leave a tip?* (when / last / leave)
   B About three days ago.
   A _____? (how much / leave)
   B €2.

2 A _____ a present? (when / last / get)
   B About two weeks ago.
   A _____ it from? (who / get)
   B I got some flowers from my husband.

3 A _____ a book? (when / last / read)
   B About six months ago.
   A _____? (what book / read)
   B I read *The Rosie Project* by Graeme Simsion.

4 A _____ Chinese food? (when / last / eat)
   B About a week ago.
   A _____ it? (where / eat)
   B In a restaurant near my house.

KATIA   FRIENDS   HOME

Katia Simms
20.55

Katia Simms
17.00

Katia Simms
19 June 20.00

Katia Simms
14 June 17.00

Katia Simms
20 March 19.30

Katia Simms
18 June 2015
15.00

4a Look at the photo and read the title of the news story. Answer the questions.

1 Who is the girl? _____ 2 What did she do? _____

Student helps man with no home

Art student Dominique Harrison-Bentzen went out with friends in December 2014. During the night she lost her bank card, so she couldn't get a taxi home. She started walking and she met a man. His name was Robbie, and he lived on the streets – he was homeless. Dominique told him about her bank card. Robbie only had £3, but he wanted to give the money to Dominique. She said, 'Thank you,' but she didn't take the money. The next morning, Dominique went on Facebook. She wrote about Robbie, and people wrote back. Everyone said he was an amazing person. Dominique decided to help Robbie, so she opened pages on Facebook and Twitter to get money for him. She decided to be homeless for a day and sleep on the street, so she asked people to give her £3.

A week later, Dominique slept on the street with six friends. They were cold and hungry, but they were happy. They got a lot of money from people all over the world. Dominique gave the money to a local charity to help Robbie and other homeless people like him.

b Read the news story. Answer the questions.

1 What was the name of the student?
   Her name *was Dominique Harrison-Bentzen.*

2 What did she lose when she went out with her friends?
   She _____.

3 Who did she meet on her way home?
   She _____.

4 How much money did Robbie have?
   He _____.

5 Where did Dominique write about Robbie?
   She _____.

6 What did people say about Robbie?
   They _____.

7 Where did she sleep for a night?
   She _____.

8 What did Dominique do with all the money?
   She _____.

word stress in two-syllable words

5a Circle the word with the stress on a different syllable.

1 answer / colour / correct

2 about / ago / fashion

3 address / meeting / lucky

4 forget / hotel / story

5 arrive / decide / marry

6 listen / return / study

7 happy / mistake / present

8 excuse / headache / waiter

b **9.5** Listen and check your answers.

c **9.5** Listen again and repeat.

I can …	Very well	Quite well	More practice
use *ago* to talk about when something happened.	○	○	○
talk about the last time.	○	○	○

9.4 Speaking and writing

the weather

1 Look at the illustrations and complete the crossword.

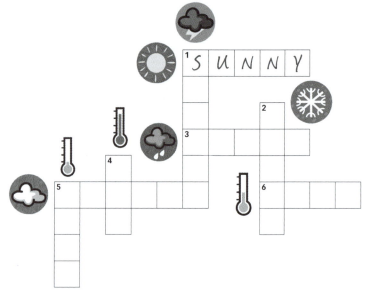

1 S U N N Y

2a Write present or past questions. Then circle the correct option in the answers.

1 what / weather / like / with you ?
  A _What's the weather like with you?_
  B (It's) / It was very stormy.

2 what / weather / like / yesterday ?
  A _____
  B It's / It was cloudy, but warm.

3 what / weather / like / now ?
  A _____
  B It's / It was very snowy.

4 what / weather / like / when you were on holiday ?
  A _____
  B It's / It was nice and warm.

5 what / weather / like / last summer ?
  A _____
  B It's / It was hot and sunny.

b 9.6))) Listen and check your answers.

Writing a review of an event

3 Look at the adjectives in the box. Circle the two words that have a negative meaning.

> amazing beautiful boring friendly funny great
> interesting small sunny terrible warm

4 Complete the review with phrases a–h.

a good songs   e amazing bands
b a boring time   f a big festival
c a beautiful walk   g friendly people
d a great atmosphere   h terrible weather

Summer in the City

Last year, I went to the Summer in the City festival in Manchester with a friend. It isn't ¹ _a big festival_ , but it isn't small, either – around 8,000 people go there. The festival is in an interesting part of the city called Castlefield and you can walk there from the station. It's ² _____ along the canal. Manchester is famous for its ³ _____, but it was warm and sunny when I was there.

Summer in the City is a music festival. A lot of the bands that play are from Manchester, but some of them are from other places in the UK and abroad. The year I went, we saw some ⁴ _____. They played a lot of ⁵ _____ and everybody danced.

I really liked the festival because there were a lot of ⁶ _____ there. We went there on two evenings for about six hours, but we never had ⁷ _____. There was ⁸ _____ at the festival and I loved it!

I can …	Very well	Quite well	More practice
talk about the weather.	○	○	○
write a review of an event.	○	○	○

9.5 Listening for pleasure

Kim Peek

1 **9.7**)) Listen to the first part of a radio programme about Kim Peek, a man with an amazing memory. What could Kim Peek remember?

2 **9.8**)) Listen to the rest of the radio programme. Choose the correct answer for each question.

1 Why do the speakers talk about the film *Rain Man*?
   a *Rain Man* tells the story of Kim Peek's life.
   b Kim Peek was an actor in *Rain Man*.
   c The director wrote *Rain Man* after he met Kim Peek.
   d *Rain Man* is Kim Peek's favourite film.

2 How did Kim Peek's life change after *Rain Man*?
   a He won an Oscar.
   b He acted in another film.
   c He met lots of people.
   d He met Tom Cruise.

3 Imagine you could meet Kim Peek. Write three difficult questions to ask him. Look at the examples and use the topics in the box to help you.

art cinema literature music news science sport theatre

1 _____
2 _____
3 _____

Which countries played in the final of the 1962 Football World Cup?

When was Albert Einstein born?

10.1 We're going to raise £5,000

1 Look at the photos. Circle the correct options.

1 *He's going to* / *He isn't going to* drive to work.
2 *She's going to* / *She isn't going to* buy clothes.
3 *They're going to* / *They aren't going to* play sport.
4 *He's going to* / *He isn't going to* go by bus.
5 *She's going to* / *She isn't going to* swim in the sea.
6 *They're going to* / *They aren't going to* see a film.

2 Write positive and negative sentences with *going to*. Use contractions where possible.

1 I / get up late .
   I'm going to get up late.
2 my husband / not / watch the football .
   _____
3 that shop / close .
   _____
4 I / not / play tennis .
   _____
5 Marta and Dino / travel to Brazil .
   _____
6 we / not / go out .
   _____

3 Read about Josh's project. Tick (✓) the things he and the volunteers are going to do.

Typhoon in the Philippines

'Hi! I'm Josh and I'm a student. Next summer, I want to go to the Philippines to be a volunteer. Some years ago, there was a typhoon in the country and 6,000 people died. A lot of houses and schools fell down. I want to work with a group called Projects Abroad to help build new schools. We're going to paint and clean the classrooms. The teachers need help too, so we're going to read with the children and play games with them. I need $6,500 to travel to the Philippines and stay there for eight weeks. Please help me to help them!'

Josh		The volunteers	
1	be a volunteer in the Philippines ✓	5	be teachers ___
2	work in a hospital ___	6	paint the classrooms ___
3	stay there for two months ___	7	cook for the children ___
4	live abroad for a year ___	8	play games with the children ___

4 Look at your answers in exercise **3**. Write sentences about Josh and the volunteers with the positive or negative form of *going to*. Use contractions where possible.

1 *Josh is going to be a volunteer in the Philippines.*
2 He _____
3 _____
4 _____
5 The volunteers _____
6 They _____
7 _____
8 _____

PRONUNCIATION *going to*

5a **10.1** 🔊 Listen and write six sentences.

1 *I'm going to check my emails.*
2 _____
3 _____
4 _____
5 _____
6 _____

b **10.1** 🔊 Listen again and repeat. Pay attention to the pronunciation of *to* in *going to*.

Vocabulary future time phrases

6 Complete the timeline with the words in the box.

in three days   next month   next week   next year
the day after tomorrow   this evening   ~~today~~   tomorrow

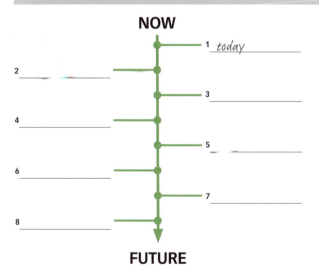

NOW
1 *today*
2 _____
3 _____
4 _____
5 _____
6 _____
7 _____
8 _____
FUTURE

7 Complete Amy's plans with the future time expressions from exercise **6**.

3rd June

3rd June
study for exam
Tom's party –
8pm

Amy

4th June
last exam!!!

5th June
buy plane
ticket

6th June
collect
passport

10th June
Spanish
course

3rd July
fly to Buenos
Aires

201_
come home
when???

'I'm Amy and these are my plans for the future.
¹ *Today* , I'm going to study for my exam. I'm not going to go to Tom's party ² _____ because I want to go to bed early. Good news – my exams finish ³ _____! After that, I need to plan my trip to South America. I'm going to buy my plane ticket ⁴ _____, and ⁵ _____ I'm going to get my new passport. I need to go to London for the day to collect it, but that's OK. ⁶ _____ I'm going to start a Spanish course – I've got three weeks to learn some of the language before I leave. I'm going to fly to Buenos Aires ⁷ _____ and I'm very excited. I'm going to come home sometime ⁸ _____, but I'm not sure when.'

I can …

	Very well	Quite well	More practice
use *going to* for future plans.	○	○	○
talk about a future project.	○	○	○

10.2 A new life

Vocabulary verb phrases (2)

1a (Circle) the word that isn't possible.

1
- a flat
- (jobs)
- a house

BUY

2
- abroad
- classes
- schools

CHANGE

3
- a baby
- exams
- school

FINISH

4
- a child
- a little girl
- university

HAVE

5
- a car
- a new language
- Chinese

LEARN

6
- English
- to another city
- to another country

MOVE

b Use the verbs in CAPITALS in exercise **1a** to write correct verb phrases with the words you circled.

1 _jobs – change jobs_
2 _____
3 _____
4 _____
5 _____
6 _____

2 Write sentences about Kay's plans. Use *going to* with *probably* or *probably not* where necessary.

0%

change jobs

learn Chinese

move abroad

buy a house

have a baby

100%

finish school

1 (learn Chinese)
   I'm probably not going to learn Chinese.
2 (finish school)
   I'm _____
3 (move abroad)
   _____
4 (buy a house)
   _____
5 (change jobs)
   _____
6 (have a baby)
   _____

Grammar *going to* questions and short answers

3a Put the words in order to make questions.

1 have a baby / Lou and Vicky / going to / Are ?
   Are Lou and Vicky going to have a baby?

2 Alec / move abroad / Is / going to ?
   _____

3 going to / Are / buy a flat / you ?
   _____

4 Is / going to / change jobs / your sister ?
   _____

5 you / Are / going to / learn a new language ?
   _____

6 next week / finish school / Matt / going to / Is ?
   _____

b Complete the short answers.

a No, he _isn't_ . He's going to live here.
b Yes, I _____. Two languages: French and Arabic.
c Yes, they _____. They think it's a boy.
d No, she _____. She's very happy where she is.
e No, we _____. We want a small house.
f Yes, he _____. His last exam is on Friday.

c Match questions 1–6 in exercise **3a** to answers a–f in exercise **3b**.

1 _C_   3 ___   5 ___
2 ___   4 ___   6 ___

4a Complete the conversation. Write questions with *going to* and the verbs in (brackets).

A Sam, what ¹ _are you going to do_ (do) when you finish university?
B I'm not really sure.
A Well, ² _____ (get) a job?
B Yes, of course, but first I want to go travelling.
A Really? Where ³ _____ (go)?
B I want to go to India.
A How interesting! What ⁴ _____ (see) in India?
B I don't really know. I want to travel around and see all the country.
A Great! Who ⁵ _____ (travel) with?
B That's the problem. My friends aren't interested.
A Oh. So, what ⁶ _____ (do)?
B I think I'm probably going to go on my own.
A Oh! Well, good luck and have fun!

b 10.2))) Listen and check your answers.

c 10.3))) Listen to the questions again and repeat.

Vocabulary prepositions of time

5 Complete the table with the time expressions in the box.

~~10.30~~ 15th August 2010 2nd March night 9 o'clock autumn February Saturday the afternoon the weekend Wednesday

in	on	at
		10.30

6 Complete the sentences with the correct prepositions.

1 I'm going to finish university _in_ 2020.
2 We're going to get married _____ the spring.
3 The new restaurant is going to open _____ 1st May.
4 Alonso's going to play basketball _____ the weekend.
5 The barbecue is going to be _____ the evening.
6 I'm going to leave work _____ 5.30 this evening.
7 My partner's going to go to the doctor _____ Monday.
8 Petra's going to have a baby _____ September.

I can …	Very well	Quite well	More practice
ask and answer questions using *going to*.	○	○	○
talk about a life change.	○	○	○

10.3 Café cities

café food

1 Look at the photos and complete the puzzle. What's the mystery word?

```
¹C  O  F  F  E  E
 2
 3
    4
   5
       6
  7
    8
        9
       10
   11
```

2 Match definitions 1–8 to the café food in exercise 1.
   1 It's a cold snack made with two pieces of bread.
      sandwich
   2 It's a cold drink with no colour. _____
   3 It's a cold or hot snack typical at breakfast.
      _____
   4 It's a cold drink that is white. _____
   5 It's a cold snack. You eat it alone or with other food.
      _____
   6 It's a hot drink, originally from China. _____
   7 It's a hot black drink. _____
   8 It's a cold snack typical at birthdays. _____

Grammar *would like*

➔ **STUDY TIP** We use *like* to ask for an opinion:
   Do you like coffee?
   Yes, I do. / No, I don't.
   We use *would like* to offer food or drink:
   Would you like a coffee?
   Yes, please. / No, thanks.

3 Circle the correct options.
   1 *I'd like* / *I'd like to* a cup of tea.
   2 *Would you like* / *Would you like to* see the menu?
   3 *I'd like* / *I'd like to* order now.
   4 *He'd like* / *He'd like to* a doughnut.
   5 *Would she like* / *Would she like to* an apple juice?
   6 *We'd like* / *We'd like to* go home now.
   7 *Would they like* / *Would they like to* try the cake?
   8 *Would you like* / *Would you like to* a salad?

4 Complete the questions and sentences with the correct form of *would like*.

1 <u>Would you like</u> a sandwich?

2 <u>I'd like</u> a croissant.

3 _____ a salad?

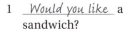

4 _____ a doughnut.

5 _____ an orange juice.

6 _____ a cake?

7 _____ an apple juice.

8 _____ a coffee?

5 Complete the conversations with the correct form of *would like*. Use contractions and write *to* where necessary.

1 **A** Good evening. Can I help you?
   B Hello. Yes, we<u>'d like</u> a table for two, please.

2 **A** _____ see the menu?
   B Yes, please. Thank you.

3 **A** Excuse me. We _____ order now.
   B Just a moment.

4 **A** Yes?
   B I _____ a coffee, please.

5 **A** Anything else?
   B Yes, I _____ a salad, please.

6 **A** _____ an orange juice?
   B No, thanks. That's fine.

7 **A** _____ try the cake?
   B No, thanks. I'm not hungry.

8 **A** Excuse me. We _____ the bill, please.
   B Yes, of course.

PRONUNCIATION silent letters

6 **10.4**)) Listen and repeat the questions.

1 Would you like a coffee?
2 Would you like a sandwich?
3 Would you like a biscuit?
4 Would you like an orange juice?
5 Would you like a doughnut?

cake salad salad coffee
orange juice salad cake
coffee cake orange juice
doughnut coffee sandwich
coffee croissant croissant
apple juice coffee

I can …	Very well	Quite well	More practice
use *would like* + noun/verb.	○	○	○
talk about a café.	○	○	○

10.4 Speaking and writing

Speaking ordering food and drink

1a Look at the two restaurants. Complete the two conversations with items a–l.

a Would you like to order?
b What can I get you?
c A burger, please.
d Yes, can I have a salad, please?
e Would you like anything else?
f Anything else?
g Yes, please. I'd like an orange juice.
h No, thanks. Just the burger.
i How much is that?
j Can I have the bill, please?
k £4.50.
l Of course. Just a moment.

Waiter   *a*
Customer   ___
Waiter   ___
Customer   ___
Customer   ___
Waiter   ___

Shop assistant   *b*
Customer   ___
Shop assistant   ___
Customer   ___
Customer   ___
Shop assistant   ___

b 10.5))) Listen and check your answers.

Writing invitations and thank-you notes

2 Complete the invitations and thank-you notes with phrases a–g.

a Please join us for lunch
b Many thanks for the invitation
c Would you like to come?
d Can you come?
e I'd love to come
f I'm so sorry, but I can't come
g Thanks! Sounds great.

Hi there, Melanie,
How are things?
1 _c_ to my house for coffee on Thursday morning?
I hope you've got time.
Love
Jane

Thanks! **2** ___.
What time is good for you?

Javi and I are forty this year!
3 ___ at the Country Club on Saturday 13th June at 1 o'clock.

4 ___. I can't believe you and Javi are forty!
5 ___ to the lunch. I'm on holiday in Portugal that week.
Have a lovely time!

Hi Réka! We're going to the cinema tonight. **6** ___

7 ___ What film are we going to see?

I can ...	Very well	Quite well	More practice
order food and drink.	○	○	○
write invitations and thank-you notes.	○	○	○

Review: Units 9 and 10

Grammar

1 Complete the sentences with the past simple form of the verbs in the box.

get up   go   ~~have~~   meet   leave   see

1 We _had_ lunch with friends yesterday.
2 I _____ a good film on TV last night.
3 Josh _____ his partner in Vietnam six years ago.
4 You _____ your phone in my car.
5 Millie _____ to Amsterdam last weekend.
6 We _____ late this morning.

2 Complete the conversations with the correct past simple form of the verbs in (brackets).

A Hi, Beth. [1] _Did you enjoy_ (enjoy) your trip to Thailand?
B Very much! I [2]_____ (not want) to come home.
A What [3]_____ you _____ (do) there?
B I [4]_____ (work) in a school. It was great!
A [5]_____ you _____ (see) a lot of the country?
B No, I [6]_____ (not have) time. I was only there for a month.

3 Complete the sentences with the correct form of *going to* and the words in (brackets).

1 _My parents are going to call_ tonight. (my parents / call)
2 _____ his old car? (Cal / sell)
3 What time _____ in Milan? (you / arrive)
4 _____ to the football match. (Kate / not go)
5 _____ friends next weekend. (I / visit)

4 Put the words in the correct order to make sentences.

1 like / biscuit / you / Would / a
   Would you like a biscuit?
2 would / drink / like / you / What / to ?
   _____
3 like / cake / to / I'd / the / try .
   _____
4 like / tea / cup / I'd / of / a .
   _____
5 you / else / like / Would / anything ?
   _____

Vocabulary

5 Match the verbs in **A** to the words in **B** to make verb phrases. Complete the sentences.

A	change go ~~have~~ miss move

B	abroad ~~a headache~~ jobs my train to the doctor

1 I usually drink a cup of tea when I _have a headache_.
2 Theo doesn't like his boss so he wants to _____.
3 Rosie felt sick, but she didn't _____.
4 We're sad because our best friends are going to _____.
5 The bus to the station was late, but I didn't _____.

6 Complete the text with the prepositions *in*, *on* or *at*.

[1] _In_ summer, the days are very long in countries like Norway. [2]_____ May, June and July, you can see the sun [3]_____ 12 o'clock [4]_____ night in the north of the country. That's why this time of year is called 'the midnight sun'. On the island of Svalbard, the midnight sun starts [5]_____ 20th April and continues until 22nd August. Of course, the opposite is true [6]_____ winter. The days are very short because there isn't much sun [7]_____ the morning or the afternoon. Some people find it very difficult to live in places like this.

Functional language

7 Circle the correct options.

1 **A** What *can I* / *would I* get you?
   B A large coffee, please.
2 **A** What's the weather like with *you* / *yesterday*?
   B It's very stormy.
3 **A** *Can I have* / *Would you like* a croissant, please?
   B Here you are.
4 **A** *Can I have* / *Would you like* anything else?
   B No, just the tea.
5 **A** *What's* / *What was* the weather like last weekend?
   B It was hot and sunny.
6 **A** *Would you like* / *Would you like to* see the menu?
   B Yes, please.

Audioscripts

Unit 1 First meetings

Page 4, Exercises 6b & c

1.1 🔊
1 I'm Will.
2 I'm not Sabine.
3 Are you here on business?
4 Are you Frida?
5 I'm here to study.
6 Are you on holiday?
7 I'm not Ben.
8 You're here to study.

Page 6, Exercises 4b & c

1.2 🔊
Stress on syllable one
China
Russia
Turkey

Stress on syllable two
Australia
Brazil
Japan

Page 7, Exercise 6b

1.3 🔊
1 We aren't from the USA.
2 I'm not from China.
3 We aren't here on business.
4 I'm not Amy.
5 You aren't here on holiday.
6 We aren't from New York.
7 You aren't from Spain.

Page 8, Exercise 1b

1.4 🔊
1 A G H J
2 C F M S
3 B E I V
4 O Q U W
5 D P T Y
6 L N R X
7 C G K T
8 E F M Z

Page 8, Exercise 2a

1.5 🔊
1 U S A
2 D V D
3 U H T
4 A T M
5 U S B
6 V I P
7 L C D
8 G M T

Page 8, Exercises 3b & c

1.6 🔊
/eɪ/ day   name
/iː/ meet   see
/e/ address   spell
/aɪ/ bye   hi
/əʊ/ home   phone
/juː/ you
/ɑː/ are

Page 9, Exercises 5b & c

1.7 🔊
1 What's your name?
2 What's your last name?
3 How do you spell that?
4 Where are you from?
5 What's your phone number?

Page 9, Exercise 6b

1.8 🔊
A Hi, I'm Tymon. What's your name?
B Hello. My name is Keira.
A How do you spell that?
B K-E-I-R-A.
A K-E-I-R-A.
B Yes, that's right.
A Where are you from, Keira?
B I'm from Bristol in the UK. And you?
A I'm from Gdańsk in Poland.

Page 11 Listening for pleasure, Exercises 2a & b

1.9 🔊
A Good morning. I'm Chief Inspector Thomas Abbot from the Kingston Police Department. I'm here to ask you some questions about the murder of William Hoffman. Madam, can you please answer some questions? Let's go in here.
B Of course.
A So ... What's your full name?
B Mrs Penelope R. Hoffman.
A Hoffman? Is that H-O-F-F-M-A-N?
B Yes, it is.
A Hmmm ... Mrs Hoffman, what's your home address, please?
B It's 75 Victoria Street, Brighton.
A 75 Victoria Street? Our records say 98 Sydney Street.
B Yes, of course. Sorry. It's 98 Sydney Street.
A Are you here on holiday, Mrs Hoffman?
B Yes, I am. I'm here with my friend, Mrs Fiona Wright. She's from Australia, you know.
A I see. What's your phone number, Mrs Hoffman?
B Um ... oh ... I can't remember. I'm sorry.
A That's OK. Thank you very much, Mrs Hoffman. Can you please send Mrs Wright in?
B Sure, no problem. Goodbye, Chief Inspector Abbot.

...

A Good morning, Mrs Wright. Please sit down.
B Thank you.
A Just a few questions ... Um, what's your full name, please?
B Mrs Fiona D. Wright.
A How do you spell 'Wright'?
B W-R-I-G-H-T
A Thank you. Now, I understand you're from Australia ...
B Sorry?
A Mrs Hoffman says that you're from Australia.

B Mrs Hoffman?

A Yes, Mrs Penelope Hoffman. The woman before you. She says that you're friends.

B Oh, is that Mrs Hoffman? I know her, but we aren't friends.

A Hmmm ... interesting. So, what's your address in Australia, Mrs Wright?

B Australia? I'm not from Australia, I'm from the USA. I live in Pheonix, Arizona.

A I see. And why are you here, Mrs Wright?

B I'm here on business, Chief Inspector. I'm a businesswoman.

A Thank you Mrs Wright. Can you please send Mrs Hoffman in again?

B Yes, of course.

Presenter Two different stories. One is true, and one is not. Who is lying? And why? Join us next time to find out more ...

Page 11 Listening for pleasure, Exercise 4

1.10 》)

A Thank you, Mrs Wright. Can you please send Mrs Hoffman in again?

B Yes, of course.
Chief Inspector Abbot! Mrs Hoffman isn't here! But I think I know why ...

Unit 2 Questions

Page 12, Exercise 1b

2.1 》)

1 a tablet
2 books
3 phones
4 a notepad
5 pens
6 a laptop
7 keys
8 apples
9 an umbrella
10 a wallet

Page 12, Exercises 3a & b

2.2 》)

1 30	6 15
2 16	7 90
3 70	8 14
4 40	9 60
5 18	10 13

Page 14, Exercises 3b & c

2.3 》)

Two syllables:

doctor
student
teacher
waiter

Four syllables:

shop assistant
taxi driver

Page 15, Exercises 4b & c

2.4 》)

1 It's from Japan.
2 She's a doctor.
3 They're on holiday.
4 It's from France.
5 They're students.
6 She's a taxi driver.
7 She's from Spain.
8 He's a shop assistant.

Page 16, Exercise 3

2.5 》)

A Hi Chris. Louise here. How are you?

B I'm fine, thanks. And you?

A Great, thanks. Are you at home?

B No, I'm on business in the USA with Jack.

A Where in the USA?

B We're in New York.

A Is Ellen in New York with you?

B No, she isn't. She's on holiday with friends.

A Really? Where are they?

B They're in Izmir.

A Where's that?

B It's in Turkey.

A Is Tommy in Turkey, too?

B No, he isn't. He's at home with my mother.

Page 18, Exercises 1b & c

2.6 》)

1 It's three ten.
2 It's eight fifty-five.
3 It's ten fifteen.
4 It's two o'clock.
5 It's nine twenty.
6 It's four forty-five.
7 It's eleven oh five.
8 It's five thirty.

Page 18, Exercise 2b

2.7 》)

1 **A** What time is it?
   B It's one twenty-five.
2 **A** What time is your bus?
   B It's at eleven fifty.
3 **A** What time's the meeting?
   B It's from six o'clock to seven thirty.
4 **A** What time is it?
   B It's two thirty-five.
5 **A** What time's your train?
   B It's at twelve forty.
6 **A** What time is the party?
   B It's from eight fifteen to eleven forty-five.
7 **A** What time's the film?
   B It's at six fifteen.
8 **A** What time is the next class?
   B It's at two thirty.

Unit 3 People and possessions

Page 20, Exercises 3b & c

3.1 》)

1 They're good friends.
2 They're clever children.
3 They're old men.
4 They're friendly neighbours.
5 They're funny women.
6 They're interesting houses.
7 They're lovely people.
8 They're great books.

Page 21, Exercises 5b & c

3.2 》)

1 He's got a laptop.
2 They've got a car.
3 We've got a dog and a cat.
4 She's got a phone and a tablet.
5 It's got a gym.
6 I've got a bike.

Page 22, Exercises 3a & b

3.3 》)

A Have you got a car?

B No, I haven't. And you?

A Yes, I have. I've got a Mini.

Page 23, Exercises 4b & c

3.4 》)

1 expensive – cheap
2 cold – hot
3 big – small
4 good – bad
5 happy – sad
6 new – old
7 old – young
8 rich – poor

Page 23, Exercise 5b

3.5)))
1. a happy child
2. a cold city
3. an old man
4. a big bag
5. a new wallet
6. an expensive pen
7. a good friend
8. a rich woman

Page 24, Exercises 1b & c

3.6)))
1. grandfather and grandmother, grandparents
2. brother and sister
3. father and mother, parents
4. husband and wife
5. son and daughter, children

Page 25, Exercise 5b

3.7)))
1. Susie is Tony's wife.
2. Alfie is Emily's husband.
3. Alice is Marco's sister.
4. David is Cathy and Miriam's brother.
5. Emily is Susie's mother.
6. Tony is Helena and Nico's son.
7. Alice and Marco are Miriam and Rick's children.
8. Helena and Nico are Tony's parents.
9. David, Cathy and Miriam are Susie and Tony's children.
10. Emily and Alfie are Susie's parents.

Page 25, Exercises 6a & c

3.8)))
1. That laptop's expensive.
2. Susie's got three children.
3. My mother's car is new.
4. Rick's children are on holiday.
5. Our son's an engineer.
6. His wife's got a good job.

Page 26, Exercises 1b & c

3.9)))
1. **A** Thanks very much.
   B You're welcome.
2. **A** Can I sit here?
   B Yes, of course.
3. **A** Sorry, I'm late.
   B That's OK. Don't worry.
4. **A** Tea?
   B Yes, please.
5. **A** Excuse me. That's my seat.
   B Oh, I'm so sorry.
6. **A** Atishoo!
   B Bless you.
7. **A** Excuse me. Where's the toilet?
   B Sorry, I don't know.
8. **A** After you.
   B Oh, thanks.

Page 27, Listening for pleasure, Exercises 2 & 3

3.10)))
Presenter Hello and welcome to the programme. Today we've got Frances in the studio. She's here to tell us about unusual collections in the world. Hi, Frances.
Frances Hello.
Presenter So Frances, tell us … What unusual things have people got in their homes?
Frances Well, our first collector is a thirty-six-year-old man from Singapore. His name is Jian Yang and he's got one of the largest private collections of Barbie dolls in the world. He's got a very small house, but he's got around 9,000 dolls in his home. Six thousand of the dolls are Barbie dolls. He buys his dolls from different countries, including Hong Kong and the USA. His first Barbie doll is from the early 1960s. But he's also got Grace Kelly, Frank Sinatra and Elizabeth Taylor dolls in his collection.
Presenter What a great collection! What has our next collector got, I wonder.
Frances Next on my list is an American woman. Her name is Louise J. Greenfarb, and she collects fridge magnets. Her first magnet is from the 1970s, and now she's got 45,000 of them from all over the world. She's got five or six hundred magnets on her fridge alone. The magnets are in all the rooms of her house – even on the front door. She's very happy with her collection because she says it's the photo album of her life.
Presenter That's nice, Frances. We've got time for one more.
Frances OK, then I'll tell you about Brett Chilman. He's from Perth, Australia, and he's got a very big collection of comics. Today, he's got around 100,000 of them, including the first *Spider-Man* comic and the first *X-Men* comic. Most of the comics are new and he's got them in boxes in two different houses. Brett has got three children and they've all got names from comics. His first son is Tristen, from the comic *Stardust*, his second son is Logan, from *Wolverine*, and his daughter is Isabelle, from *Beauty and the Beast*.
Presenter What a great guy! Frances, thank you for coming to the show.
Frances You're welcome.

Unit 4 My life

Page 28, Exercises 2b & c

4.1)))
1. My parents live in New Zealand.
2. Elsa works in a charity shop.
3. Greg and Selma study Chinese at school.
4. Sophie and I go to the beach every day.
5. My best friend plays the guitar and the piano.
6. My sister teaches maths in her free time.
7. I watch a lot of videos on my tablet.
8. Petra reads the newspaper every morning.

Page 28, Exercises 4a & b

4.2)))
1. goes   plays
2. lives   watches
3. helps   works
4. likes   teaches
5. reads   studies

Page 31, Exercises 4b & c

4.3)))
1. Alex plays football. He doesn't play basketball.
2. Gina teaches art. She doesn't teach music.
3. We live in a village. We don't live in the city centre.
4. I study in the morning. I don't study at night.
5. My brother works for a charity. He doesn't work for a big company.
6. I like cats. I don't like dogs.
7. My parents watch films on TV. They don't watch DVDs.
8. My partner goes to work by bus. He doesn't go by train.

Page 31, Exercises 6a & b

4.4 》))
1   I don't play golf.
2   That phone isn't cheap.
3   We haven't got a car.
4   My parents aren't old.
5   He doesn't live here.
6   My husband hasn't got a job.

Page 32, Exercises 1b & c

4.5 》))
1   get up
2   get dressed
3   check emails
4   have breakfast
5   start work
6   get home
7   have dinner
8   go to bed

Page 33, Exercises 6a & b

4.6 》))
A   Do you have coffee for breakfast?
B   Yes, I do. And you?
A   No, I don't. I have tea.

Page 34, Exercise 2b & c

4.7 》))
A   Can I help you?
B   Yes, do you have any comics?
A   Yes, they're over there.
B   How much is the *Spider-Man* comic?
A   It's €2.75.
B   OK. I'll take it.
A   Is that everything?
B   No, I need a car magazine, too.
A   The magazines are here.
B   Great. Thank you.

Unit 5 Style and design

Page 36, Exercises 1b & c

5.1 》))
1   Krzysztof usually wears a jacket to work.
2   We always play tennis on Saturdays.
3   My wife doesn't often go clothes shopping.
4   I sometimes have a bath in the evening.
5   It is never cold in my house.
6   I don't usually buy shoes online.

Page 37, Exercise 5b

5.2 》))
1   top   trainers   trousers
2   jacket   jeans   jumper
3   fashion   shirt   shoes
4   skirt   smart   T-shirt
5   casual   clothes   dress

Page 38, Exercises 1b & c

5.3 》))
1   It's big and beautiful.
2   It's modern and unusual.
3   It's different and exciting.
4   It's old and interesting.

Page 39, Exercises 4b & c

5.4 》))
1   When are the gardens open?
2   When do you check emails?
3   Why does Dominic buy expensive clothes?
4   What is your address?
5   Where do you and your family go on holiday?
6   Where are my keys?
7   What does your partner do?
8   Why is your grandmother in hospital?

Page 40, Exercise 1b

5.5 》))
Scotland is famous for its kilts. These are skirts that men wear. A lot of Scottish men have a kilt, but they only wear it on special days, like weddings, for example. Usually, they don't go to work in them. Traditionally, Scottish women don't wear kilts, but they sometimes wear long skirts or dresses in a similar style.

The traditional clothing for an Indian woman is the sari. This is a long colourful piece of cloth that a woman wears like a dress. A young woman doesn't usually wear a sari every day, but it is typical on special days. When a girl doesn't know how to wear a sari, her grandmother or her mother teaches her. Men wear something similar called a dhoti.

Page 40, Exercises 3b

5.6 》))
A   Do you and your partner like the same styles?
B   No, we don't.
A   Oh. What clothes do you like?
B   I like casual clothes. And I always wear black.
A   Do you always buy black clothes?
B   Yes, I do.
A   And what clothes does your partner like?
B   She wears long colourful dresses and long skirts.
A   Does she like your clothes?
B   No, she doesn't.
A   Does she sometimes buy clothes for you?
B   Yes, she does. But I never wear them.

Page 41, Exercises 5b & c

5.7 》))
1   white arms
2   small heads
3   beautiful bodies
4   happy faces
5   brown legs
6   big hands

Page 42, Exercise 1d

5.8 》))
1   A   How much is it to the airport?
      B   It's €15.
2   A   Where do I buy a ticket?
      B   You buy your ticket from the ticket machine.
3   A   Does this train go to the airport?
      B   No, it goes to the city centre.
4   A   What time is the next train?
      B   It leaves at 11.45.
5   A   What time does it arrive?
      B   It arrives at 12.30.
6   A   Where does it go from?
      B   It goes from platform 7.

Unit 6 Places and facilities

Page 44, Exercises 2b & c

6.1 》))
1   in a shop
2   in a cinema
3   in a restaurant
4   in a hotel
5   in a museum
6   in a supermarket
7   in a park
8   from a bank
9   in a theatre
10   in a café

Page 45, Exercises 5b & c

6.2 🔊
1 There aren't any cars.
2 There aren't any cheap flats.
3 There isn't a supermarket.
4 There aren't any trainers.
5 There isn't an airport.
6 There isn't a hospital.

Page 46, Exercise 1b

6.3 🔊
1 air conditioning
2 lift
3 refreshments
4 gym
5 Wi-fi
6 car park
7 iron
8 safe
9 towels
10 bath

Page 47, Exercises 6a & b

6.4 🔊
1 A Is there a lift?
  B Yes, there is.
2 A Is there a safe?
  B No, there isn't.
3 A Are there any toilets?
  B Yes, there are.
4 A Are there any parks?
  B No, there aren't.

Page 48, Exercises 1b & c

6.5 🔊
1 You usually have a snack in the kitchen.
2 You usually watch TV with the family in the living room.
3 You usually have a shower in the bathroom.
4 You usually get dressed in the bedroom.
5 You usually have lunch in the dining area.
6 You usually sit in the sun on the balcony.
7 You usually have a barbecue in the garden.

Page 49, Exercises 5b & c

6.6 🔊
1 There isn't a bath.
2 Is there a fridge in the kitchen?
3 There's an old sofa in the living room.
4 Have all the rooms got air conditioning?
5 The room has got a phone and free Wi-fi.
6 Has each flat got a microwave?

Page 49, Exercise 6

6.7 🔊
1 There aren't any towels.
2 There's an iron on the table.
3 Has each room got a safe?
4 Is there a shop in the hotel?
5 Are all the chairs in the kitchen?
6 Are there any refreshments in the room?

Page 50, Exercise 1d

6.8 🔊
1 A Our room is very noisy.
  B I'm so sorry. You can have another room.
2 A The heater is broken.
  B Oh, I'm sorry. I'll send someone to look.
3 A My room is very hot.
  B There's air conditioning. The switch is next to the door.
4 A There aren't any refreshments.
  B Hmmm ... Try in the fridge under the table.
5 A I don't know the code for the safe.
  B It's 9159.

Unit 7 Skills and interests

Page 52, Exercises 1b & c

7.1 🔊
1 drive a car
2 speak Russian
3 play the piano
4 use a phone
5 understand instructions
6 paint a picture
7 remember somebody's birthday
8 ride a bike

Page 53, Exercises 6a, 6c & 6d

7.2 🔊
1 I can swim.
2 I can't ride a bike.
3 I can't drive a car.
4 I can sing.
5 I can't play the guitar.
6 I can speak English.

Page 54, Exercises 4a & b

7.3 🔊
1 Can you drive?
2 Yes, I can.
3 Can you swim?
4 No, I can't.
5 I can cook.
6 I can't sing.

Page 55, Exercises 6b & c

7.4 🔊
1 I drive slowly.
2 She paints well.
3 We cook badly.
4 He swims fast.
5 You walk slowly.
6 She speaks well.
7 They run fast.
8 We play tennis badly.

Page 57, Exercises 4b & c

7.5 🔊
1 They like playing sport.
2 She likes taking photos.
3 They like riding bikes.
4 He likes listening to music.
5 They like going to the cinema.
6 She likes watching TV.
7 He likes shopping online.
8 They like using their phones.

Page 57, Exercises 6a, 6c & 6d

7.6 🔊
1 What do you like doing?
2 Do you like being at home?
3 I don't like going out.
4 I like seeing my family.

Page 58, Exercise 1d

7.7 🔊
1 A Can I take this chair, please?
  B Sorry. It's taken.
2 A Can I have an apple, please?
  B Of course. Here you are.
3 A Excuse me. Can you call me a taxi?
  B Yes, of course. Where do you want to go?
4 A Can I use your laptop, please?
  B Sure, no problem.
5 A Excuse me. Can you help me?
  B Sorry. I'm busy.
6 A Excuse me. Can you tell me the way to the hospital?
  B Sure. It's that way.

Unit 8 Our past

Page 60, Exercises 3a & b

8.1 🔊
1 I was a good student.
2 My parents weren't rich.
3 Were you clever?
4 Yes, I was.
5 Was she nice?
6 No, she wasn't.

Page 61, Exercises 10b & c

8.2)))

1 Australia Day is on the 26th of January.
2 New Year's Eve is on the 31st of 3 December.
3 International Workers Day is on the 1st of May.
4 Independence Day in the USA is on the 4th of July.
5 World Book Day is on the 23rd of April.
6 Nelson Mandela Day is on the 18th of July.

Page 62, Exercise 1b

8.3)))

1 Leonardo da Vinci was born in 1452 and he died in 1519.
2 Joan of Arc was born in 1412 and she died in 1431.
3 Mahatma Gandhi was born in 1869 and he died in 1948.
4 Helen Keller was born in 1880 and she died in 1968.
5 Genghis Khan was born in 1162 and he died in 1227.
6 Jane Austen was born in 1775 and she died in 1817.

Page 62, Exercise 3b

8.4)))

1 Dante Alighieri was born in 1265.
2 Agatha Christie died in 1976.
3 Christopher Columbus was born in1451.
4 Galileo Galilei died in 1642.
5 Alfred Hitchcock was born in 1899.
6 Catherine the Great died in 1796.
7 William Shakespeare was born in 1564.
8 Emmeline Pankhurst died in 1928.

Page 63, Exercises 6b & c

8.5)))

1 lived started studied used
2 hated loved opened travelled
3 helped liked visited walked
4 finished painted talked worked
5 died married showed wanted

Page 65, Exercises 4a, b & c

8.6)))

1 I like it.
2 She hates it.
3 He helped us.
4 We love it.
5 They waited for us.
6 You called us.

Page 65, Exercise 6b

8.7)))

My wife and I were in Croatia for a week last year with a group of twelve people. It was cold because we were there in February. We were in Dubrovnik on Wednesday and Thursday, and then we travelled to Plitvice. It was great! Last week, I received an email from a woman in the group called Fabiola. She invited us to lunch at her house, so that's where we were yesterday. We had a great time, and we arrived home very late last night. I called Fabiola this morning to say *thank you* for a lovely day.

Page 66, Exercise 1b

8.8)))

1 A I've got an exam tomorrow.
   B Good luck!
2 A I'm twenty-one today.
   B Happy birthday!
3 A My brother's got a new girlfriend.
   B Really?
4 A I've got a new job!
   B Congratulations!
5 A I can't go out tonight.
   B Never mind.
6 A My mother's in hospital.
   B I'm sorry to hear that.
7 A Here's to Keegan and Angie!
   B Cheers!
8 A My sister's got a place at university!
   B That's great!

Page 67, Review, Exercise 8

8.9)))

1 Can I take this chair?
2 I've got a job interview tomorrow.
3 Can you tell me the way to the bank?
4 I'm thirty today.
5 Can I have a pen?
6 We've got a new car.
7 Can you help me?
8 I haven't got any money.

Unit 9 Unusual stories

Page 69, Exercises 4b & c

9.1)))

1 an easy life
2 a happy time
3 a sad ending
4 a new friend
5 an interesting book
6 my old life

Page 71, Exercises 4b & c

9.2)))

1 go to the doctor
2 sleep badly
3 meet an old friend
4 miss my train
5 fall in the shower
6 have a headache
7 forget the time
8 feel sick

Page 71, Exercises 6a & b

9.3)))

1 Did you know the answer?
2 Did you buy any clothes?
3 Did you call your friend?
4 I didn't have a shower.
5 I didn't ride my bike.
6 I didn't go to work.

Page 72, Exercises 2b & c

9.4)))

1 Katia cooked dinner five minutes ago.
2 She used her new bike four hours ago.
3 She met her friends two days ago.
4 She saw her grandparents a week ago.
5 She went to a concert three months ago.
6 She bought a house a year ago.

Page 73, Exercises 5b & c

9.5)))

1 answer colour correct
2 about ago fashion
3 address meeting lucky
4 forget hotel story
5 arrive decide marry
6 listen return study
7 happy mistake present
8 excuse headache waiter

Page 74, Exercise 2b

9.6)))

1 A What's the weather like with you?
   B It's very stormy.
2 A What was the weather like yesterday?
   B It was cloudy, but warm.
3 A What's the weather like now?
   B It's very snowy.
4 A What was the weather like when you were on holiday?
   B It was nice and warm.
5 A What was the weather like last summer?
   B It was hot and sunny.

Page 75, Listening for pleasure, Exercise 1

9.7)))

Presenter Hello and welcome to the programme. Do you have a good memory? Can you remember where you were, what you did and what happened on every day of your life? Well, believe it or not, there are people who can. One man with an amazing memory was the American Kim Peek. He had a memory like a computer, and people called him Kim-puter, not Kim Peek! In his life, he read around 12,000 books, and he could remember each word of each book. Clara Fox is here to tell us all about him.

Page 75, Listening for pleasure, Exercise 2

9.8)))

Presenter Clara Fox is here to tell us all about him.

Clara That's right, Kim Peek remembered everything he read. If he read a phone book, he remembered the names, addresses and phone numbers of all the people in the book.

Presenter That's incredible! Was Kim a very clever child, Clara?

Clara Kim had a lot of problems when he was a child. He couldn't do the things that other children did. He couldn't walk, and he couldn't talk. The doctors wanted Kim to live in a kind of hospital.

Presenter So what did Kim's parents do?

Clara They didn't do what the doctors said. They knew Kim was clever because he read his first book before he was two years old.

Presenter Wow!

Clara So they didn't take him to the hospital.

Presenter So what happened then? Did Kim go to school?

Clara Yes, but only once, and he didn't have a good time. He couldn't sit in the chair and the teacher couldn't teach him. After only seven minutes of his first class, Kim went home. After that, he studied at home. A teacher went to his house two days a week for forty-five minutes. Kim studied the same as the other children at school, but he finished secondary school when he was fourteen.

Presenter That's very young. So when did Kim become famous, Clara?

Clara Do you remember the film *Rain Man*?

Presenter Yes, I do. It's about two brothers – Charlie and Raymond Babbitt, played by Tom Cruise and Dustin Hoffman.

Clara That's right. Well, one of the brothers – Dustin Hoffman – has an amazing memory. The director got the idea for the film when he met Kim Peek. He was very interested in Kim, so he wrote a story for a film. *Rain Man* isn't about Kim's life, but Raymond Babbitt has some of the problems that Kim had. The film won four Oscars, and after that, Kim Peek was famous.

Presenter Did his life change after the film?

Clara Yes, it did. Before the film, Kim didn't meet many people. He went to the library every day to read, but he only talked to his father. Kim only knew about twenty people, and when he spoke to them, he didn't look at their faces. After the film, he felt good about himself. He wanted to meet people and talk to them.

Presenter So what did he do?

Clara Kim travelled around the world to meet people. They tried to ask him difficult questions, like: What day was 3rd March 1916? Who was King of England in 1509? Kim always knew the answer. But Kim didn't travel to show people his memory. He wanted to show them that it was OK to be different. A lot of people were very sad when he died in 2009. He was fifty-eight years old.

Presenter Yes, that was very sad, Clara. But what an amazing man! Thank you so much for telling us his story.

Clara You're welcome.

Unit 10 New places, new projects

Page 77, Exercises 5a & b

10.1)))

1 I'm going to check my emails.
2 He's going to buy a present.
3 We aren't going to see friends.
4 They're going to get married.
5 She isn't going to have a party.
6 I'm not going to meet him for lunch.

Page 79, Exercise 4b

10.2)))

A Sam, what are you going to do when you finish university?

B I'm not really sure.

A Well, are you going to get a job?

B Yes, of course, but first I want to go travelling.

A Really? Where are you going to go?

B I want to go to India.

A How interesting! What are you going to see in India?

B I don't really know. I want to travel around and see all the country.

A Great! Who are you going to travel with?

B That's the problem. My friends aren't interested.

A Oh. So, what are you going to do?

B I think I'm probably going to go on my own.

A Oh! Well, good luck and have fun!

Page 79, Exercise 4c

10.3)))

1 What are you going to do when you finish university?
2 Are you going to get a job?
3 Where are you going to go?
4 What are you going to see in India?
5 Who are you going to travel with?
6 What are you going to do?

Page 81, Exercise 6

10.4)))

1 Would you like a coffee?
2 Would you like a sandwich?
3 Would you like a biscuit?
4 Would you like an orange juice?
5 Would you like a doughnut?

Page 82, Exercise 1b

10.5)))

The Queen's Pearl

Waiter Would you like to order?

Customer Yes, can I have a salad, please?

Waiter Would you like anything else?

Customer Yes, please. I'd like an orange juice.

Customer Can I have the bill, please?

Waiter Of course. Just a moment.

Ben's Burger Bar

Shop assistant What can I get you?

Customer A burger, please.

Shop assistant Anything else?

Customer No, thanks. Just the burger.

Customer How much is that?

Shop assistant £4.50.

Answer key

Unit 1 First meetings

1.1 On business or on holiday?
page 4

Vocabulary introductions

1 1 *on holiday*
    2 to study
    3 on business
    4 on holiday

2 1 e 2 f 3 h 4 b 5 g 6 c
    7 a 8 d

3 1 *Hello*   6 No
    2 Hi   7 study
    3 Nice   8 holiday
    4 And   9 Yes
    5 you

Grammar verb *be* (I/you)

4 1 *I*   4 I
    2 you   5 you
    3 I   6 I

5 1 *I'm, I'm*
    2 I'm, I'm
    3 Are you, I'm not
    4 I'm, I'm
    5 Are you, I am
    6 Are you, I'm

6a 1 *I'm*   5 I'm here
    2 I'm not   6 Are you
    3 Are you   7 I'm not
    4 Are you   8 You're

1.2 Where are you from? page 6

Vocabulary numbers 1–10; countries

1 Across ▶
    2 *eight*   7 five
    5 seven   8 two

    Down ▼
    1 ten   6 nine
    3 three   7 four
    4 one

2 1 *three*   5 seven
    2 six   6 ten
    3 nine   7 one
    4 five   8 eight

3 1 *Russia*   6 the USA
    2 Australia   7 Japan
    3 China   8 Inonesia
    4 Brazil   9 Spain
    5 Turkey

Pronunciation saying names of countries

4a Stress on syllable one:
    China, Russia, Turkey
    Stress on syllable two:
    Australia, Brazil, Japan

Grammar verb *be* (we/you)

5a 1 *I'm*   4 We're
    2 We're   5 I'm
    3 I'm   6 We're

6 1 *We aren't from the USA.*
    2 'm not from China.
    3 aren't here on business.
    4 'm not Amy.
    5 aren't here on holiday.
    6 aren't from New York.
    7 You aren't from Spain.

7 1 *I'm*   6 I'm
    2 I'm   7 Are you
    3 I'm   8 we aren't
    4 are you   9 We're
    5 I'm

8 *My name is Marisol.*
    I'm from Seville in Spain.
    Javier and I are on holiday in Turkey.
    We are in a hotel in Istanbul.

1.3 How do you spell that? page 8

Vocabulary the alphabet

1a 1 *G* 2 C 3 I 4 O 5 Y 6 R
    7 K 8 E

2a 1 *USA*   5 USB
    2 DVD   6 VIP
    3 UHT   7 LCD
    4 ATM   8 GMT

2b A 5 B 2 C 4 D 7 E 1 F 8
    G 6 H 3

Pronunciation the alphabet

3a /eɪ/ day name
    /iː/ meet see
    /e/ address spell
    /aɪ/ bye hi
    /əʊ/ home phone
    /juː/ you
    /ɑː/ are

Grammar question words

4a 1 What   4 Where
    2 How   5 What
    3 Where

4b a 3 b 4 c 1 d 5 e 2

5a 1 *What's your name?*
    2 What's your last name?
    3 How do you spell that?
    4 Where are you from?
    5 What's your phone number?

6a a 1 b 3 c 5 d 9 e 2 f 8
    g 6 h 4 i 7

1.4 Speaking and writing page 10

Speaking *hello* and *goodbye*

1 Hello: *Good morning*, Hello, Hi,
    How are you?, Morning
    Goodbye: Bye, Goodbye, Have a nice
    day, See you later

2 1 *Hi*   4 day, too
    2 Bye   5 Good, Morning
    3 How, Fine, 6 See
    thanks

Writing filling in a form

3 1 e 2 f 3 b 4 a 5 c 6 d

4 1 *Faruk*
    2 Akkaya
    3 39 Beykoz Sokak
    4 Turkey
    5 0090 508 99200437

1.5 Listening for pleasure page 11

Murder in Kingston

1 C 1 A 2 D 3 B 4

Unit 2 Questions

2.1 What's this in English? page 12

Vocabulary objects; numbers 11–100

1
1 *a tablet*
2 – books
3 phones
4 a notepad
5 pens
6 a laptop
7 keys
8 apples
9 an umbrella
10 a wallet

2
1 *eleven*
2 sixteen
3 thirty-four
4 a hundred
5 twelve
6 twenty
7 forty-nine
8 eighty

Pronunciation word stress: *-teen* and *-ty*

3a
1 *30*
2 16
3 70
4 40
5 18
6 15
7 90
8 14
9 60
10 13

Grammar *this/that/these/those*; verb *be* (it/they)

4
1 *this*
2 that
3 these
4 those
5 that
6 these
7 this
8 those

5a
a *They're*
b It's
c It's
d They're
e It's
f They're
g It's
h They're

5b
1 *g* 2 c 3 a 4 f 5 e 6 h
7 b 8 d

6
1 *'s, 's*
2 Are, are
3 Is, is
4 are, 're
5 Are, are
6 's, 's

2.2 What's your job? page 14

Vocabulary jobs

1
1 *shop assistant*
2 doctor
3 nurse
4 taxi driver
5 teacher
6 engineer
7 waiter
Mystery word: student

2
1 *a shop assistant*
2 a taxi driver
3 a teacher
4 a waiter
5 an engineer
6 a doctor
7 a nurse

Pronunciation word stress: jobs

3
Two syllables: stress on syllable one:
doctor, student, teacher, waiter
Four syllables: stress on syllable one:
shop assistant, taxi driver

Grammar verb *be* (he/she/it/they)

4a
1 *It's*
2 She's
3 They're
4 It's
5 They're
6 She's
7 She's
8 He's

5a
1 *'s*
2 Is
3 's
4 Are
5 's
6 Is
7 are
8 Is

5b
a *3*
b 6
c 8
d 1
e 5
f 7
g 2
h 4

6
1 *'m*
2 's
3 'm
4 Are
5 am
6 's
7 's
8 's
9 Is
10 is
11 are
12 're
13 Are
14 aren't
15 're

2.3 Where are they? page 16

Grammar subject pronouns

1
1 *a*
2 b
3 b
4 a
5 a
6 b
7 b
8 b

2
1 *I*
2 it
3 they
4 he
5 they
6 she
7 we
8 I

3
1 *you*
2 I
3 you
4 you
5 I
6 We
7 she
8 She
9 they
10 They
11 It
12 he
13 He

Vocabulary prepositions of place

4
1 *d* 2 f 3 a 4 e 5 b 6 c

5
1 *in*
2 near
3 on
4 on
5 next to
6 on

2.4 Speaking and writing page 18

Speaking telling the time

1
1 *It's three ten.*
2 It's eight fifty-five.
3 It's ten fifteen.
4 It's two o'clock.
5 It's nine twenty.
6 It's four forty-five.
7 It's eleven oh five.
8 It's five thirty.

2a
1 *It's*
2 your bus
3 from
4 it
5 It's at
6 the party
7 It's at
8 the next class

Writing a blog

3
1 *My name's Fabiana.*
2 I'm not a student.
3 He's from Indonesia.
4 We're here to study.
5 He isn't on business.
6 She's a friend.
7 We aren't at home.
8 It's a company in Berlin.
9 She isn't a doctor.
10 In this photo I'm with Paola.

4
1 *name's*
2 from
3 in
4 I'm
5 We're
6 a
7 it's
8 he's

Review: Units 1 and 2 page 19

Grammar

1
1 *'s*
2 Are
3 isn't
4 'm
5 Is
6 aren't

2
1 *What's*
2 Where
3 How
4 Who
5 What

3
1 *these*
2 that
3 They're
4 this
5 those

4 1 *He's a waiter.*
2 They're friends.
3 It's in Indonesia.
4 She's from Australia.
5 You're late.

Vocabulary

5 1 *twelve*   4 fifty-eight
2 thirty-six   5 forty
3 nineteen   6 a hundred

6 1 *doctor*   4 shop assistant
2 engineer   5 taxi driver
3 nurse   6 teacher

7 1 *an apple*   3 a pen
2 a key   4 a wallet

8 1 *in*   4 near
2 near   5 in
3 on   6 in

Functional language

9 1 *one forty-five.*
2 from nine-thirty to eleven o'clock.
3 at three thirty.
4 from six fifteen to seven forty-five.
5 four twenty-five.
6 at twelve oh five.

Unit 3 People and possessions

3.1 My neighbours page 20

Vocabulary adjective + noun phrases (1); irregular plurals

1 1 *great*   4 dog
2 waiter   5 hard
3 funny   6 book

2 1 *That's a nice phone.*
2 Ireland is a friendly country.
3 Judith Polgár is a clever woman.
4 Noma's a great restaurant.
5 Prague is a lovely city.
6 Jonah Hill is a funny man.

3 1 *They're good friends.*
2 They're clever children.
3 They're old men.
4 They're friendly neighbours.
5 They're funny women.
6 They're interesting houses.
7 They're lovely people.
8 They're great books.

Grammar *have got, has got*

4 1 *'ve got*   5 've got
2 've got   6 's got
3 's got   7 've got
4 's got

5a 1 *He's got a laptop.*
2 They've got a car.
3 We've got a dog and a cat.
4 She's got a phone and a tablet.
5 It's got a gym.
6 I've got a bike.

6 1 *'ve got*   4 've got
2 's got   5 's got
3 've got   6 've got

7 1 *'ve got*   4 's got
2 's got   5 's got
3 've got   6 've got

3.2 Possessions page 22

Grammar *have got* negatives and questions

1 1 *I haven't got a bank account.*
2 Kim hasn't got an interesting job.
3 We haven't got nice neighbours.
4 Ali hasn't got a mobile phone.
5 Yola and Paul haven't got a new TV.
6 My village hasn't got a hospital.

2a 1 *Have you got children?*
2 Have your friends got cars?
3 Has your house got a garden?
4 Have you got my number?
5 Has your neighbour got a dog?
6 Has Kate got a job?

2b a *has*   d have, 've
b has   e haven't, 've
c hasn't, 's   f haven't

2c 1 *d* 2 e 3 b 4 f 5 c 6 a

Pronunciation stress in *yes/no* questions and answers

3a A Have you got a **car**?
B No, I **haven't**. And **you**?
A Yes, I **have**. I've got a **Mini**.

Vocabulary opposite adjectives

4 1 *b* 2 c 3 g 4 a 5 f 6 d
7 h 8 e

5a 1 *happy*   5 new
2 cold   6 expensive
3 old   7 good
4 big   8 rich

6 1 *a hot country.*
2 an old building
3 an expensive car
4 a rich man
5 a big city
6 a young woman
7 a good person
8 a sad story

3.3 Family page 24

Vocabulary family

1a 1 *grandfather*, grandmother, grandparents
2 brother, sister
3 father, mother, parents
4 husband, wife
5 son, daughter, children

2 1 *husband*   6 brother
2 children   7 sister
3 daughter   8 grandfathers
4 son   9 grandmothers
5 parents

Grammar possession

3 1 *Our*   4 Her
2 His   5 Your
3 Their   6 My

4 1 *your*   4 her
2 his   5 my
3 their   6 our

5 1 *Tony's*
2 Emily's
3 Marco's
4 Miriam and Cathy's (or Cathy and Miriam's)
5 Susie's
6 Helena and Nico's (or Nico and Helena's)
7 Miriam and Rick's (or Rick and Miriam's)
8 Tony's
9 Susie and Tony's (or Tony and Susie's)
10 Susie's

6a 1 *That laptop's expensive.*
2 Susie's got three children.
3 My mother's car is new.
4 Rick's children are on holiday.
5 Our son's an engineer.
6 His wife's got a good job.

6b is: 1 and 5
has: 2 and 6
possession: 3 and 4

3.4 Speaking and writing page 26

Speaking everyday expressions

1a 1 *c* 2 b 3 a 4 c 5 a 6 b
7 c 8 b

Writing a social media message

2 1 *and it's got a big garden.*
2 and they've got an expensive car
3 but I haven't got a dog
4 but they aren't our friends
5 and she's got two daughters
6 but he's very happy

3 1 *b*   4 f
2 c   5 e
3 d   6 a

3.5 Listening for pleasure page 27

Unusual collections

1 1 collection
2 collector
3 collect

2 A 2
B 3
C 1

Unit 4 My life

4.1 About me page 28

Grammar present simple positive

1 1 *goes*   6 studies
2 has   7 teach
3 like   8 watches
4 lives   9 work
5 play

2a 1 *live*   5 plays
2 works   6 teaches
3 study   7 watch
4 go   8 reads

3 1 *live*   6 likes
2 teach   7 plays
3 love   8 watches
4 read   9 studies
5 works   10 go

Pronunciation present simple with *he/she/it*

4a 1 ✓ 2 ✗ 3 ✓ 4 ✗ 5 ✓

Vocabulary common verbs

5 1 *d* 2 h 3 f 4 a 5 g 6 c
7 i 8 e 9 b

6 1 *job*   6 school
2 to the beach   7 Australia
3 North Street   8 restaurant
4 phone   9 a book
5 films

7 1 *like*   6 work
2 watch   7 study
3 read   8 go
4 live   9 play
5 teach

8 1 *likes*   6 goes
2 plays   7 love
3 have   8 go
4 works   9 play
5 live

4.2 Journeys page 30

Vocabulary transport

1 Nouns: *bus*, ferry, motorbike, train
Verbs: cycle, drive, go, walk

2 1 *go, by train*
2 walk
3 go, by ferry
4 drive
5 cycle
6 go, by bus

3 1 *bus*   4 cycle
2 train   5 motorbike
3 drive   6 walk

Grammar present simple negative

4a 1 *doesn't play*
2 doesn't teach
3 don't live
4 don't study
5 doesn't work
6 don't like
7 don't watch
8 doesn't go

5 1 *studies*
2 plays
3 play
4 don't play
5 doesn't like
6 like
7 watch
8 doesn't watch
9 watches
10 drives
11 don't drive
12 cycle

6a 1 *I don't play golf.*
2 That phone isn't cheap.
3 We haven't got a car.
4 My parents aren't old.
5 He doesn't live here.
6 My husband hasn't got a job.

6c *be*: That phone isn't cheap.,
My parents aren't old.
have got: We haven't got a car.,
My husband hasn't got a job.
Other verbs: *I don't play golf.*,
He doesn't live here.

4.3 My day page 32

Vocabulary days of the week; daily activities

1a 1 *get up*
2 get dressed
3 check emails
4 have breakfast
5 start work
6 get home
7 have dinner
8 go to bed

2 1 *get up*
2 start work
3 get dressed
4 have breakfast
5 check emails
6 get home
7 have dinner
8 go to bed

3 1 *Thursday* 5 Tuesday
2 Saturday 6 Wednesday
3 Friday   7 Sunday
4 Monday

Grammar present simple *yes/no* questions

4 1 *d* 2 f 3 c 4 b 5 a 6 e

5a 1 *Does Tim Armstrong live in London?*
2 Does he get up early?
3 Does he have a coffee in the morning?
4 Does he go to work by train?
5 Does he read a book to his children in the evening?
6 Does he go to bed at 10 p.m.?
7 Do he and his wife go out on Friday nights?
8 Do he and his children like sport?

5b 1 *No, he doesn't.*
2 Yes, he does.
3 Yes, he does.
4 No, he doesn't.
5 Yes, he does.
6 No, he doesn't.
7 No, they don't.
8 Yes, they do.

Pronunciation stress in present simple *yes/no* questions and answers

6a **A** Do you have **coffee** for **breakfast**?
B Yes, I **do**. And **you**?
A No, I **don't**. I have **tea**.

4.4 Speaking and writing page 34

Speaking in a shop

1 1 d 2 e 3 f 4 c 5 a 6 b

2a 1 *Can I help you?*
2 Yes, do you have any comics?
3 Yes, they're over there.
4 How much is the *Spider-Man* comic?
5 It's €2.75.
6 OK. I'll take it.
7 Is that everything?
8 No, I need a car magazine, too.
9 The magazines are here.
10 *Great. Thank you.*

Writing an informal email

3 Hello, Atena
How are you? I'm in Poland now. I like it, but it's very cold. I get to Kraków on Wednesday, but I get there very late. Can I see you on Thursday? My phone number is 69 220 81 834.
Can't wait to see you!
Detelina

4 1 d 2 f 3 a 4 b 5 c 6 e

Review: Units 3 and 4 page 35

Grammar

1 1 *have got*   4 Has, got
2 *hasn't got*   5 haven't got
3 've got   6 hasn't got

2 1 *My wife's brother is an engineer.*
2 I don't like my neighbour's cat.
3 Alex hasn't got his sister's tablet.
4 Tina drives her mother's car.
5 Maya and Yusef's friends are very nice.

3 1 *I don't go to work by bus.*
2 My friends and I watch films at the weekend.
3 Anisa doesn't work in a hospital.
4 Sonny and Monica live in a village.
5 We don't go abroad on holiday.
6 My partner teaches maths at a school.

4 1 *Do, do*
2 Does, doesn't
3 Do, do
4 Does, does
5 Do, don't

Vocabulary

5 1 *expensive*   4 cold
2 happy   5 poor
3 new

6 1 *mother*
2 father
3 grandparents
4 brothers
5 sisters
6 parents
7 son
8 grandfather
9 children

7 1 *bus*   4 train
2 drive   5 motorbike
3 cycle

Functional language

8 1 *help*   4 much
2 any   5 take
3 there   6 need

Unit 5 Style and design
5.1 Clothes style page 36

Grammar adverbs of frequency

1a 1 *Krzysztof usually wears a jacket to work.*
2 We always play tennis on Saturdays.
3 My wife doesn't often go clothes shopping.
4 I sometimes have a bath in the evening.
5 It is never cold in my house.
6 I don't usually buy shoes online.

2 1 *always wears*
2 usually wears
3 never wears
4 sometimes wears
5 often buys
6 is/'s always
7 usually wear
8 often wear
9 sometimes wear
10 always wear
11 never buy
12 are/'re always

Vocabulary colours and clothes

3 Across ▶
2 red   6 black
4 green   7 white
Down ▼
1 *brown*   4 grey
3 yellow   5 blue

4 singular: *a dress*, a hat, a jacket, a jumper, a shirt, a skirt, a top, a T-shirt
plural: jeans, shoes, trousers, trainers

Pronunciation word stress: clothes

5a 1 *top* (one syllable)
2 jeans (one syllable)
3 fashion (two syllables)
4 T-shirt (two syllables)
5 casual (two syllables)

6 1 *trainers*, trousers, a T-shirt
2 a jacket, a shirt
3 a dress, a hat, shoes
4 jeans, a jumper

7 1 *because*   4 and
2 and   5 because
3 but

5.2 Amazing architecture page 38

Vocabulary adjectives

1a 1 *big*, beautiful
2 modern, unusual
3 different, exciting
4 old, interesting

2 1 *unusual*   5 beautiful
2 modern   6 big
3 different   7 old
4 exciting   8 interesting

Grammar *Wh-* questions

3a 1 *What*   5 Where
2 Where   6 What
3 When   7 Why
4 Why   8 When

3b a 1   e 6
b 4   f 8
c 3   g 7
d 2   h 5

4a 1 *are*   5 do
2 do   6 are
3 does   7 does
4 is   8 is

5a 1 *What is*
2 Where is
3 Where does
4 Why does
5 What do
6 Where do
7 When is
8 Why is

5.3 Styles around the world page 40

Grammar *present simple (all forms)*

1a 1 *wear*   5 wears
2 have   6 usually doesn't
3 don't go   7 doesn't know
4 don't wear   8 teaches

2a 1 *What do Scottish men wear?*
2 When do they wear kilts?
3 Do Scottish women wear kilts?
4 What does an Indian woman wear?
5 Does a young woman wear a sari every day?
6 When does a mother help her daughter with a sari?

2b a *1* b 5 c 2 d 6 e 3 f 4

3 1 *Do*   6 does
2 don't   7 Does
3 do   8 doesn't
4 Do   9 Does
5 do   10 does

Vocabulary parts of the body

4 1 *face*   5 legs
2 hair   6 arm
3 feet   7 hands
4 head   8 body

Pronunication plural forms

5a 1 *white arms*
2 small heads
3 beautiful bodies
4 happy faces
5 brown legs
6 big hands

5b faces

Vocabulary adjective modifiers

6 1 *really expensive*
2 very
3 really beautiful
4 very nice
5 really rich
6 very beautiful
7 really nice
8 very expensive

5.4 Speaking and writing page 42

Speaking travel information

1a 1 *How much is it to the airport?*
2 Where do I buy a ticket?
3 Does this train go to the airport?
4 What time is the next train?
5 What time does it arrive?
6 Where does it go from?

1b 1 *from*   4 It's
2 buy   5 at
3 It   6 goes

1c 1 *d* 2 b 3 f 4 c 5 e 6 a

Writing making arrangements by text

2 1 *Are you busy*
2 I'm not busy
3 Do you want
4 Where do you
5 Do you like
6 Can we meet
7 What time
8 See you there

3 1 *not busy* 4 In Bamboo
2 Where   5 What time
3 a lot   6 7.30

5.5 Reading for pleasure page 43

The Girl with Red Hair

1 c

2 Students' own answers

3 Students' own answers

Unit 6 Places and facilities

6.1 Two towns page 44

Vocabulary places in a town

1 Across ▶
1 *café*   6 bank
3 museum 7 supermarket
5 shop   9 hotel
Down ▼
1 cinema 4 theatre
2 restaurant 8 park

2a 1 *shop*   6 supermarket
2 cinema   7 park
3 restaurant 8 bank
4 hotel   9 theatre
5 museum 10 café

3 1 supermarket
2 park
3 bank
4 shop
5 cinema
6 café
7 theatre
8 museum
9 hotel
10 restaurant

Grammar *there is/there are*

4 1 *There's a car park.*
2 *There are two cafés.*
3 There's a museum.
4 There are four restaurants.
5 There's a river.
6 There's a bus stop.
7 There's a school.
8 There are five shops.

5a 1 *There aren't any cars.*
2 There aren't any cheap flats.
3 There isn't a supermarket.
4 There aren't any trainers.
5 There isn't an airport.
6 There isn't a hospital.

6 1 *there are* 6 there are
2 there's   7 There's
3 There's   8 there isn't
4 there aren't 9 there isn't
5 There are 10 There's

6.2 Is there Wi-fi? page 46

Vocabulary hotel facilities

1a 1 *air conditioning*
2 lift
3 refreshments
4 gym
5 Wi-fi
6 car park
7 iron
8 safe
9 towels
10 bath

2 1 *towels*
2 air conditioning
3 Wi-fi
4 safe
5 refreshments
6 car park
7 iron
8 gym
9 bath
10 lift

3
1 *lifts*
2 bath
3 towels
4 safe
5 refreshments
6 Wi-fi
7 air conditioning
8 iron
9 gym
10 car park

Grammar *Is there …?/Are there …?*

4
1 *any*   4 an
2 a   5 a
3 any   6 any

5a *a restraunt*, refreshments, free Wi-fi

5b
1 *Is there a restaurant in the hotel?*
2 Are there any meeting areas in the hotel?
3 Is there any air conditioning in the rooms?
4 Are there any refreshments in the rooms?
5 Is there free Wi-fi in the hotel?
6 Is there a swimming pool in the hotel?

5c
1 *Yes, there is.*
2 Yes, there are.
3 No, there isn't.
4 Yes, there are.
5 Yes, there is.
6 No, there isn't.

Pronunciation *Is there …?/Are there …?*

6a
1 A Is there a *lift*?
   B Yes, there **is**.
2 A Is there a **safe**?
   B No, there **isn't**.
3 A Are there any **toilets**?
   B Yes, there **are**.
4 A Are there any **parks**?
   B No, there **aren't**.

6.3 Has each flat got a kitchen?
page 48

Vocabulary rooms and furniture

1a
1 *kitchen*   5 dining area
2 living room   6 balcony
3 bathroom   7 garden
4 bedroom

2
1 *microwave*   5 fridge
2 TV   6 bed
3 shower   7 chair
4 sofa   8 table

Grammar *all the* and *each*

3
1 *All the*   4 Each
2 Each   5 Each
3 All the   6 All the

4
1 *All the*   5 Each
2 Each   6 all the
3 All the   7 Each
4 each   8 all the

Pronunciation linking (1)

5a
1 *There isn't a bath.*
2 Is there a fridge in the kitchen?
3 There's an old sofa in the living room.
4 Have all the rooms got air conditioning?
5 The room has got a phone and free Wi-fi.
6 Has each flat got a microwave?

6
1 *There aren't any towels.*
2 There's an iron on the table.
3 Has each room got a safe?
4 Is there a shop in the hotel?
5 Are all the chairs in the kitchen?
6 Are there any refreshments in the room?

7
1 *from*   6 red
2 four   7 two
3 sea   8 How
4 bad   9 bed
5 their   10 read

6.4 Speaking and writing page 50

Speaking explaining problems

1a
1 *Our room is very noisy.*
2 The heater is broken.
3 My room is very hot.
4 There aren't any refreshments.
5 I don't know the code for the safe.

1b
a *It's*
b The switch is
c I'll send someone
d You can have
e Try in the fridge

1c 1 *d*   2 c   3 b   4 e   5 a

Writing a hotel review

2 1 *c*   2 a   3 e   4 f   5 b   6 d

3
1 *This hotel*
2 the lift
3 The rooms
4 a heater
5 The bathroom
6 the TV
7 the food
8 Buses

Review: Units 5 and 6 page 51

Grammar

1
1 *My partner never goes to the gym at the weekend.*
2 Andy sometimes wears jeans to work.
3 I don't usually get dressed in the bathroom.
4 Do you always buy your clothes from the same shop?
5 Amara doesn't often have baths; she prefers showers.

2
1 *do, live*   6 does, live
2 live   7 works
3 Do, like   8 Does, go
4 don't   9 doesn't
5 don't see

3
1 *There's*
2 Are there
3 There isn't
4 Is there
5 There aren't

4
1 *All the*   4 Each
2 Each   5 All the
3 All the

Vocabulary

5
1 *dress*   5 red
2 jacket   6 hotel
3 interesting   7 gym
4 park   8 lift

6
1 *leg*   4 head
2 hand   5 hair
3 face   6 feet

Functional language

7
1 *What time*   4 is broken
2 go from   5 very cold
3 How much   6 don't know

Unit 7 Skills and interests

7.1 She can paint page 52

Vocabulary skills

1a 1 *drive* 5 understand
2 speak 6 paint
3 play 7 remember
4 use 8 ride

2a 1 *a bike* 5 a car
2 a book 6 maths
3 the internet 7 faces
4 television 8 a jacket

2b 1 *ride a bike*
2 read a book
3 use the internet
4 watch television
5 drive a car
6 study maths
7 remember faces
8 wear a jacket

3 1 *remember* 4 play
2 understand 5 use
3 paint 6 drive

Grammar *can/can't*

4 1 *can* 4 can
2 can 5 can't
3 can't 6 can't

5 1 *can fly* 4 can go
2 can swim 5 can see
3 can't run 6 can't sing

Pronunciation *can/can't*

6a 1 *I can swim.*
2 I can't ride a bike.
3 I can't drive a car.
4 I can sing.
5 I can't play the guitar.
6 I can speak English.

7.2 Can you help? page 54

Grammar *Can you …?*

1a 1 *Can you ride a bike?*
2 Can your daughter read?
3 Can Adam paint a picture?
4 Can your friends play the guitar?
5 Can your grandparents use a computer?
6 Can you and your sister sing?

1b 1 *I can* 4 they can't
2 she can 5 they can
3 he can't 6 we can't

2 ✓ *use a computer*, teach people about animals, speak Spanish

3 1 *can you speak*
2 I can
3 Can you speak
4 I can't
5 can learn
6 can you teach
7 I can
8 Can you use
9 I can

Pronunciation *can, can't* in questions and statements

4 1 *Can you drive?*
2 Yes, I can.
3 Can you swim?
4 No, I can't.
5 I can cook.
6 I can sing.

Vocabulary adverbs of manner

5 1 *well* 5 fast
2 fast 6 well
3 slowly 7 badly
4 badly 8 slowly

6 1 *I drive slowly.*
2 paints well
3 cook badly
4 swims fast
5 walk slowly
6 speaks well
7 run fast
8 play badly

7 1 *slow* 5 fast
2 fast 6 well
3 badly 7 slowly
4 good 8 bad

7.3 I like going out page 56

Vocabulary hobbies

1 1 *take photos*
2 go to the cinema
3 travel
4 cook
5 go out with friends
6 play sport
7 read

2 1 *work in the garden*
2 play video games
3 go on Facebook
4 watch TV
5 shop online
6 listen to music
7 take photos

Grammar *like + -ing*

3 listen + *-ing* = listening: *cooking*, eating, flying, singing
have + *-ing* = having: dancing, riding, using, writing
run + *-ing* = running: getting, shopping, swimming, travelling

4a 1 *like playing*
2 likes taking
3 like riding
4 likes listening
5 like going
6 likes watching
7 likes shopping
8 like using

5 1 *do you like running?*
2 like walking
3 doesn't like running
4 Does, like playing tennis
5 likes watching
6 Do, like playing
7 don't like running

Pronunciation linking vowels with /w/ or /j/

6a 1 *What do you like doing?*
2 Do you like being at home?
3 I don't like going out.
4 I like seeing my family.

6b /w/ doing, going
/j/ being, seeing

Vocabulary *like, love, hate + -ing*

7 1 *loves going out*
2 likes watching
3 doesn't like reading
4 hates cooking
5 love travelling
6 like working
7 don't like shopping
8 hate playing

7.4 Speaking and writing page 58

Speaking simple requests

1a 1 *Can I* 4 Can I
2 Can I 5 Can you
3 Can you 6 Can you

1b a *no problem* d I'm
b you are e that way
c It's f of course

1c 1 *c* 2 b 3 f 4 a 5 d 6 e

Writing a post on a social media website

2 a *My friend Fern is a great photographer.*
  b I can speak English well.
  c She helps me take amazing photos.
  d I often paint the flowers in my garden.
  e We always have a lot of guests from abroad.
  f I paint badly.

3 1 *b* 2 e 3 a 4 c 5 f 6 d

7.5 Reading and listening for pleasure page 59

Last Chance

1a 1 He's a cameraman.
   2 No, he isn't.
   3 To film a volcano.

1b camera, fire, rock, smoke

2 Because there's a woman with a broken leg.

Unit 8 Our past

8.1 When we were seven page 60

Grammar verb *be* past simple

1 1 *was*   4 were
   2 were   5 were
   3 wasn't   6 weren't

2 1 *Was*, was 4 Was, wasn't
   2 were, was 5 were, were
   3 Were, were 6 Were, weren't

Pronunciation *was* and *were*

3a 1 *I was a **good student**.*
   2 My **parents weren't rich**.
   3 Were you **clever**?
   4 Yes, I **was**.
   5 Was she **nice**?
   6 No, she **wasn't**.

4 1 *was*   5 was
   2 was   6 weren't
   3 was   7 were
   4 were   8 wasn't

Vocabulary dates

5 1 *sixth*   5 fifteenth
   2 third   6 twenty-first
   3 eleventh 7 twenty-eighth
   4 twelfth   8 thirtieth

6 1 *January*   7 July
   2 February 8 August
   3 March   9 September
   4 April   10 October
   5 May   11 November
   6 June   12 December

7 1 *d* 2 h 3 f 4 b 5 a 6 g
   7 c 8 e

8 1 *1914*   4 1996
   2 2015   5 2002
   3 2008   6 2020

9 1 eighteen seventy-six
   2 twenty forty
   3 nineteen fifty-seven
   4 two thousand and four
   5 eleven sixty-four
   6 twenty eighteen

10a 1 *26th January*
    2 31st December
    3 1st May
    4 4th July
    5 23rd April
    6 18th July

8.2 Lives from the past page 62

Vocabulary *was born/died*

1a 1 *Leonardo da Vinci*
   2 Joan of Arc
   3 Mahatma Gandhi
   4 Helen Keller
   5 Genghis Khan
   6 Jane Austen

2 1 *Bob Marley was born in 1945 and he died in 1981.*
   2 Pocahontas was born in 1595 and she died in 1617.
   3 Marco Polo was born in 1254 and he died in 1325.
   4 Anne Frank was born in 1929 and she died in 1945.
   5 Albert Einstein was born in 1879 and he died in 1955.
   6 Edith Piaf was born in 1915 and she died in 1963.
   7 Charles Darwin was born in 1809 and he died in 1882.
   8 Rosa Parks was born in 1913 and she died in 2005.

3 1 *was born in 1265*
   2 died in 1976
   3 was born in 1451
   4 died in 1642
   5 was born in 1899
   6 died in 1796
   7 was born in 1564
   8 died in 1928

Grammar past simple regular verbs

4 1 *painted*   5 finished
   2 walked   6 worked
   3 played   7 travelled
   4 watched   8 studied

5 1 *lived*   5 showed
   2 studied   6 helped
   3 loved   7 talked
   4 visited   8 died

Pronunciation regular past simple endings

6a 1 *started*   4 painted
   2 hated   5 wanted
   3 visited

8.3 Special moments page 64

Grammar object pronouns

1 1 *them*   4 it
   2 him   5 her
   3 them   6 them

2 1 *her*   5 us
   2 you   6 me
   3 them   7 him
   4 it

3 1 *you*   5 us
   2 it   6 her
   3 him   7 me
   4 them

Pronunciation linking (2)

4a 1 I like it.
   2 She hates it.
   3 He helped us.
   4 We love it.
   5 They waited for us.
   6 You called us.

4b 1 *I like it.*
   2 She hates it.
   3 He helped us.
   4 We love it.
   5 They waited for us.
   6 You called us.

Vocabulary past time phrases

5   1 *yesterday*   4 on Saturday
    2 last year   5 this morning
    3 last night   6 in June

6a 1 *last*   5 yesterday
    2 in   6 last
    3 on   7 this
    4 Last

8.4 Speaking and writing page 66

Speaking special occasions

1   1 *b*   5 a
    2 c   6 c
    3 c   7 a
    4 b   8 b

Writing a biography

2   1 *after*   3 Then
    2 then   4 After

3   1 *d*   3 a
    2 b   4 c

Review: Units 7 and 8 page 67

Grammar

1   1 *I can't remember*
    2 She can speak
    3 Can your brothers cook
    4 we can't swim
    5 Can you sing

2   1 *reading*   4 dancing
    2 shopping   5 painting
    3 taking

3   1 *We lived in a village.*
    2 Catrin studied languages at
      university.
    3 Was it a good hotel?
    4 Were those trousers expensive?
    5 My partner started work early.

4   1 *you*   4 him
    2 me   5 them
    3 us

Vocabulary

5   1 *drive a car*
    2 remember dates
    3 speak French
    4 play the piano
    5 paint a picture

6   1 *Erik is a good painter.*
    2 Helena and Leo are fast typists.
    3 Tommy can write slowly.
    4 I can't run fast.
    5 Birgit and I speak English badly.

7   1 *yesterday*
    2 in   4 on
    3 last   5 this

Functional language

8   1 *g*   2 h   3 e   4 a   5 d   6 f
    7 b   8 c

Unit 9 Unusual stories

9.1 Happy memories page 68

Grammar past simple irregular verbs

1   1 *was/were*   9 wrote
    2 met   10 left
    3 fell   11 knew
    4 got   12 sold
    5 lost   13 went
    6 said   14 came
    7 could   15 saw
    8 had

2   1 *had lunch*
    2 saw my parents
    3 could play golf
    4 came home
    5 sold cheap clothes
    6 lost my keys
    7 said hello
    8 wrote an email

3   1 *knew*   6 saw
    2 was   7 met
    3 left   8 fell
    4 went   9 got
    5 were

Vocabulary adjective + noun
phrases (2)

4a 1 *an easy life*
    2 a happy time
    3 a sad ending
    4 a new friend
    5 an interesting book
    6 my old life

5   1 *unusual*   4 happy
    2 an old   5 good
    3 a difficult   6 a new

6   1 *an interesting story*
    2 a difficult life
    3 an easy time
    4 a new friend
    5 a happy ending
    6 his new life

9.2 A good excuse page 70

Grammar past simple negatives and
questions

1   1 *didn't lose my phone.*
    2 didn't study science.
    3 didn't get home late.
    4 didn't watch the football.
    5 didn't meet his girlfriend.
    6 didn't visit friends.
    7 didn't have dinner at home.
    8 didn't paint the bedroom.

2a 1 *Did you like the book?*
    2 Did Galuh work yesterday?
    3 Did your friends walk to the
      theatre?
    4 Did Coline come to your party?
    5 Did you fall in love at university?
    6 Did the film finish late?

2b 1 *did*   4 did
    2 didn't   5 didn't
    3 didn't   6 did

2c 1 *d*   2 c   3 e   4 b   5 f   6 a

3   1 *where did you go*
    2 Where did you stay?
    3 How did you get
    4 When did you go?
    5 Who did you go with?
    6 What did you think

Vocabulary verb phrases (1)

4a 1 *go*   5 fall
    2 sleep   6 have
    3 meet   7 forget
    4 miss   8 feel

5   1 *met an old friend*
    2 felt sick
    3 missed my train
    4 forgot the time
    5 went to the doctor
    6 slept badly
    7 had a headache
    8 fell in the shower

Pronunciation sentence stress

6a 1 *Did you **know** the **answer**?*
    2 Did you **buy** any **clothes**?
    3 Did you **call** your **friend**?
    4 I **didn't** have a **shower**.
    5 I **didn't** ride my **bike**.
    6 I **didn't** go to **work**.

9.3 News stories page 72

Grammar *ago*

1 1 *Pierre lost his wallet a week ago.*
2 We saw a film three days ago.
3 You got a text message five minutes ago.
4 I wrote an email two hours ago.
5 Susie sold her car six months ago.
6 They went on holiday a year ago.

2a 1 *five minutes ago*
2 four hours ago
3 two days ago
4 a week ago
5 three months ago
6 a year ago

3 1 *When did you last leave a tip?;*
How much did you leave?
2 When did you last get; Who did you get
3 When did you last read; What book did you read?
4 When did you last eat; Where did you eat

4a 1 She's a student.
2 She helped a man with no home.

4b 1 *was Dominique Harrison-Bentzen*
2 lost her bank card
3 met Robbie
4 had £3
5 wrote about him on Facebook
6 said he was an amazing person
7 slept on the street
8 gave it to a local charity

Pronunication word stress in two-syllable words

5a 1 *correct*   5 marry
2 fashion   6 return
3 address   7 mistake
4 story   8 excuse

9.4 Speaking and writing page 74

Speaking the weather

1 Across▶
1 *sunny*   5 cloudy
3 rainy   6 warm
Down▼
1 stormy   4 hot
2 snowy   5 cold

2a 1 A *What's the weather like with you?*
B *It's very stormy.*
2 A What was the weather like yesterday?
B It was cloudy, but warm.
3 A What's the weather like now?
B It's very snowy.
4 A What was the weather like when you were on holiday?
B It was nice and warm.
5 A What was the weather like last summer?
B It was hot and sunny.

Writing a review of an event

3 boring, terrible

4 1 f a big festival
2 c a beautiful walk
3 h terrible weather
4 e amazing bands
5 a good songs
6 g friendly people
7 b a boring time
8 d a great atmosphere

9.5 Listening for pleasure page 75

1 He could remember each word of the 12,000 books he read.

2 1 c   2 c

3 Students' own answers

Unit 10 New places, new projects

10.1 We're going to raise £5,000 page 76

Grammar *going to* positive and negative

1 1 *He's going to*
2 She isn't going to
3 They aren't going to
4 He's going to
5 She's going to
6 They aren't going to

2 1 *I'm going to get up late.*
2 My husband isn't going to watch the football.
3 That shop's going to close.
4 I'm not going to play tennis.
5 Marta and Dino are going to travel to Brazil.
6 We aren't going to go out.

3

Josh	The volunteers
1 be a volunteer in the Philippines	6 paint the classrooms
3 stay there for two months	8 play games with the children

4 1 *Josh is going to be a volunteer in the Philippines.*
2 He isn't going to work in a hospital.
3 He's going to stay there for two months.
4 He isn't going to live abroad for a year.
5 The volunteers aren't going to be teachers.
6 They're going to paint the classrooms.
7 They aren't going to cook for the children.
8 They're going to play games with the children.

Pronunciation *going to*

5a 1 *I'm going to check my emails.*
2 He's going to buy a present.
3 We aren't going to see friends.
4 They're going to get married.
5 She isn't going to have a party.
6 I'm not going to meet him for lunch.

Vocabulary future time phrases

6 1 *today*
2 this evening
3 tomorrow
4 the day after tomorrow
5 in three days
6 next week
7 next month
8 next year

7 1 *Today*
2 this evening
3 tomorrow
4 the day after tomorrow
5 in three days
6 Next week
7 next month
8 next year

10.2 A new life page 78

Vocabulary verb phrases (2)

1a 1 *jobs*   4 university
2 abroad   5 a car
3 a baby   6 English

1b 1 *change jobs*
2 move abroad
3 have a baby
4 finish university
5 buy a car
6 learn English

2 1 *I'm probably not going to learn Chinese.*
2 going to finish school.
3 I'm probably not going to move abroad.
4 I'm probably going to buy a house.
5 I'm not going to change jobs.
6 I'm probably going to have a baby.

Grammar *going to* questions and short answers

3a 1 *Are Lou and Vicky going to have a baby?*
2 Is Alec going to move abroad?
3 Are you going to buy a flat?
4 Is your sister going to change jobs?
5 Are you going to learn a new language?
6 Is Matt going to finish school next week?

3b a *isn't*   d isn't
b am   e aren't
c are   f is

3c 1 *c*   2 a   3 e   4 d   5 b   6 f

4a 1 *are you going to do*
2 are you going to get
3 are you going to go
4 are you going to see
5 are you going to travel
6 are you going to do

Vocabulary prepositions of time

5 *in*: 2010, autumn, February, the afternoon
on: 15th August, 2nd March, Saturday, Wednesday
at: 10.30, night, 9 o'clock, the weekend

6 1 *in*   5 in
2 in   6 at
3 on   7 on
4 at   8 in

10.3 Café cities page 80

Vocabulary café food

1 1 *coffee*   7 apple juice
2 croissant   8 biscuit
3 salad   9 milk
4 sandwich   10 cake
5 doughnut   11 water
6 tea
The mystery word is: orange juice

2 1 *sandwich*   5 salad
2 water   6 tea
3 croissant   7 coffee
4 milk   8 cake

Grammar *would like*

3 1 *I'd like*
2 Would you like to
3 I'd like to
4 He'd like
5 Would she like
6 We'd like to
7 Would they like to
8 Would you like

4 1 *Would you like*
2 *I'd like*
3 Would you like
4 I'd like
5 I'd like
6 Would you like
7 I'd like
8 Would you like

5 1 *'d like*
2 Would you like to
3 'd like to
4 'd like
5 'd like
6 Would you like
7 Would you like to
8 'd like

10.4 Speaking and writing page 82

Speaking ordering food and drink

1a The Queen's Pearl: *a*, d, e, g, j, l
Ben's Burger Bar: *b*, c, f, h, i, k

Writing invitations and thank-you notes

2 1 *c*   2 e   3 a   4 b   5 f   6 d
7 g

Review: Units 9 and 10 page 83

Grammar

1 1 *had*   4 left
2 saw   5 went
3 met   6 got up

2 1 *Did you enjoy*
2 didn't want
3 did, do
4 worked
5 Did, see
6 didn't have

3 1 *My parents are going to call*
2 Is your brother going to sell
3 are you going to arrive
4 Kate isn't going to go
5 I'm going to visit

4 1 *Would you like a biscuit?*
2 What would you like to drink?
3 I'd like to try the cake.
4 I'd like a cup of tea.
5 Would you like anything else?

Vocabulary

5 1 *have a headache*
2 change jobs
3 go to the doctor
4 move abroad
5 miss my train

6 1 *In*   5 on
2 In   6 in
3 at   7 in
4 at

Functional language

7 1 *can I*
2 you
3 Can I have
4 Would you like
5 What was
6 Would you like to

OXFORD
UNIVERSITY PRESS

Great Clarendon Street, Oxford, OX2 6DP, United Kingdom

Oxford University Press is a department of the University of Oxford. It furthers the University's objective of excellence in research, scholarship, and education by publishing worldwide. Oxford is a registered trade mark of Oxford University Press in the UK and in certain other countries

© Oxford University Press 2016

The moral rights of the author have been asserted

First published in 2016

2020 2019 2018 2017 2016

10 9 8 7 6 5 4 3 2 1

No unauthorized photocopying

ISBN: 978 0 19 456504 2

Printed in China

This book is printed on paper from certified and well-managed sources

ACKNOWLEDGEMENTS

The publisher would like to thank the following for their permission to reproduce photographs: 123RF pp.5, 6 (Moscow, Beijing, Rio de Janeiro, Istanbul, Tokyo, Java, Madrid), 7 (1–5), 8 (DVD, alphabet), 9, 12 (1, 3, 5, 7), 14 (Gregor, Carmelo), 15 (selfie, Camembert, taxi driver), 16, 17 (UK map), 20 (singer, cinema, dog, book), 22 (car), 23 (Paris, woman with big bag, wallet, pen, private jet), 24 (couple with baby), 25, 27 (cars), 30 (train, car), 36 (man), 38 (Pisa, St Petersburg), 40 (woman in sari), 41 (sad face, feet, flamingoes, arm, body diagram), 46, 52 (car, Moscow, flowers, cycling), 53 (child, geese, wheelchair, phone, penguins, ostrich), 54 (both), 55 (classroom, car, cooking, cycling, sloth, octopus), 56 (basketball, cycling), 57 (cinema, TV, online shopping), 61 (Big Ben), 64 (girls hiking), 68 (family), 72 (bicycle, house), 76 (bus), 77 (pinned notes), 79, 80 (doughnut, juice, biscuit, cake), 81 (sandwich, croissant, salad, doughnuts, orange juice, apple juice), 82 (restaurant); Alamy pp.8 (UHT/Art Directors & TRIP), 15 (dancer/Michelle Chaplow), 21 (couple/ Adrian Weinbrecht), 24 (wedding/FEV Images), 27 (stamps/Flirt, couple shopping/Jim West, magnets/Tim Gainey, comics/Art Directors & TRIP), 30 (beach/Agencja Fotograficzna Caro, ferry/Angus McComiskey, cyclists/ Alan Auld), 38 (Hang Nga/imageBROKER, Upside Down House/Olga Gajewska), 40 (men in kilts/Ilene MacDonald), 45 (Torcross/Banana Pancake, Kingsbridge/ Jeff Gilbert), 47 (Hemis), 55 (woman on crutches/BSIP SA), 61 (Australia Day/ Manfred Gottschalk, Independence Day/Blend Images, World Book Day/Veryan Dale), 62 (Helen Keller/Everett Collection Historical, Leonardo da Vinci/North Wind Picture Archives, Joan of Arc/GL Archive, Genghis Khan/GL Archive, Jane Austen/GL Archive, Mahatma Gandhi/Everett Collection Historical), 63 (Ada Lovelace/Pictorial Press Ltd), 64 (Charlotte Dujardin/Steve Arkley), 66 (Everett Collection Historical), 74 (Simon Newbury), 76 (car/Orada Jusatayanond, theatre/The Photolibrary Wales, typhoon damage/imagegallery2), 78 (couple outside house, job-hunting/Roger Bamber), 82 (fast food counter/David R. Frazier Photolibrary, Inc.); Corbis p.8 (Sam Kahamba Kutesa/M. Stan Reaves), 29 (Leo Mason); Getty pp.33 (Melody Hahm/© NBCUniversal), 37 (Victor Virgile), 38 (Torre Galatea/Lipnitzki), 41 (big head puppet/Pablo Blazquez Dominguez), 49 (Koichi Kamoshida), 52 (Karishma/Carl Court), 64 (Lionel Messi/Ander Gillenea), 69 (Daniel Tammet/Lionel Bonaventure), 76 (couples/ Jupiterimages), 78 (language learners/Image Source, baby/JGI/Tom Grill); Oxford University Press pp.4 (Aneta, Sachi, Ryan), 6 (Sydney, New York), 8 (USB, LCD, USA), 10 (ex 2), 12 (2, 4, 6, 8, 9, 10), 14 (Jane, Hannah, Mike, Carmen), 15 (doctor, students, sushi, shop assistant), 20 (waiter, firefighters), 22 (ATM), 23 (toddler, man, friends), 24 (senior couple, Indian family), 31, 32, 36 (women), 38 (Taj Mahal), 39 (lion), 42, 52 (man looking at phone, woman painting), 53 (whale), 55 (girl writing, running, painting), 56 (photographer, listening to music), 57 (teens), 58, 64 (city, sushi, grandparents), 65 (both), 68 (Machu Picchu), 72 (curry, two girls, couple, concert), 76 (bookshop), 77 (Amy, corkboard), 80 (coffee, croissant, salad, sandwich, teacup, milk, water), 81 (cakes, coffee); Rex Features pp.35 (Moviestore), 39 (Lord Bath/David Hartley), 53 (Katherine Jenkins/Ken McKay/ITV), 60 (Everett), 64 (Il Divo/Ken

McKay/ITV), 75 (Kim Peek/ITV, Rain Man poster/U.A./Everett); Shutterstock pp.4 (Haluk/Zurijeta), 7 (6), 8 (ATM, GMT), 10 (Faruk/Antonio Guillem), 14 (Phei), 19 (all), 24 (brother and sister/Racorn), 27 (dolls/SNEHIT), 28, 30 (bus), 41 (man, hands), 52 (piano, flat-pack), 70 (holbox), 76 (swimmer), 78 (packed car, graduates); South West News Service p.73.

Illustrations by: Mark Duffin p.50; Dylan Gibson pp.11, 13, 43, 48, 59, 63, 71; Kerry Hyndman pp.32, 44; Joanna Kerr pp.21, 46, 57; Gavin Reece pp.37, 69; Fred van Deelen/The Organisation pp.17 (Manchester map), 45.

The authors and publisher are grateful to those who have given permission to reproduce the following extracts and adaptations of copyright material: p.43 Extract from Oxford Bookworms Library, Starter: *The Girl with Red Hair* by Christine Lindop, © Oxford University Press 2009. Reproduced by permission. p.59 Extract from Oxford Bookworms Library, Starter: *Last Chance* by Phillip Burrows and Mark Foster © Oxford University Press 2008. Reproduced by permission.

Sources: p.33 "What time do top CEOs wake up?" by Tim Dowling, Laura Barnett and Patrick Kingsley, www.theguardian.com, 1 April 2013.

Although every effort has been made to trace and contact copyright holders before publication, this has not been possible in some cases. We apologise for any apparent infringement of copyright and, if notified, the publisher will be pleased to rectify any errors or omissions at the earliest possible opportunity.